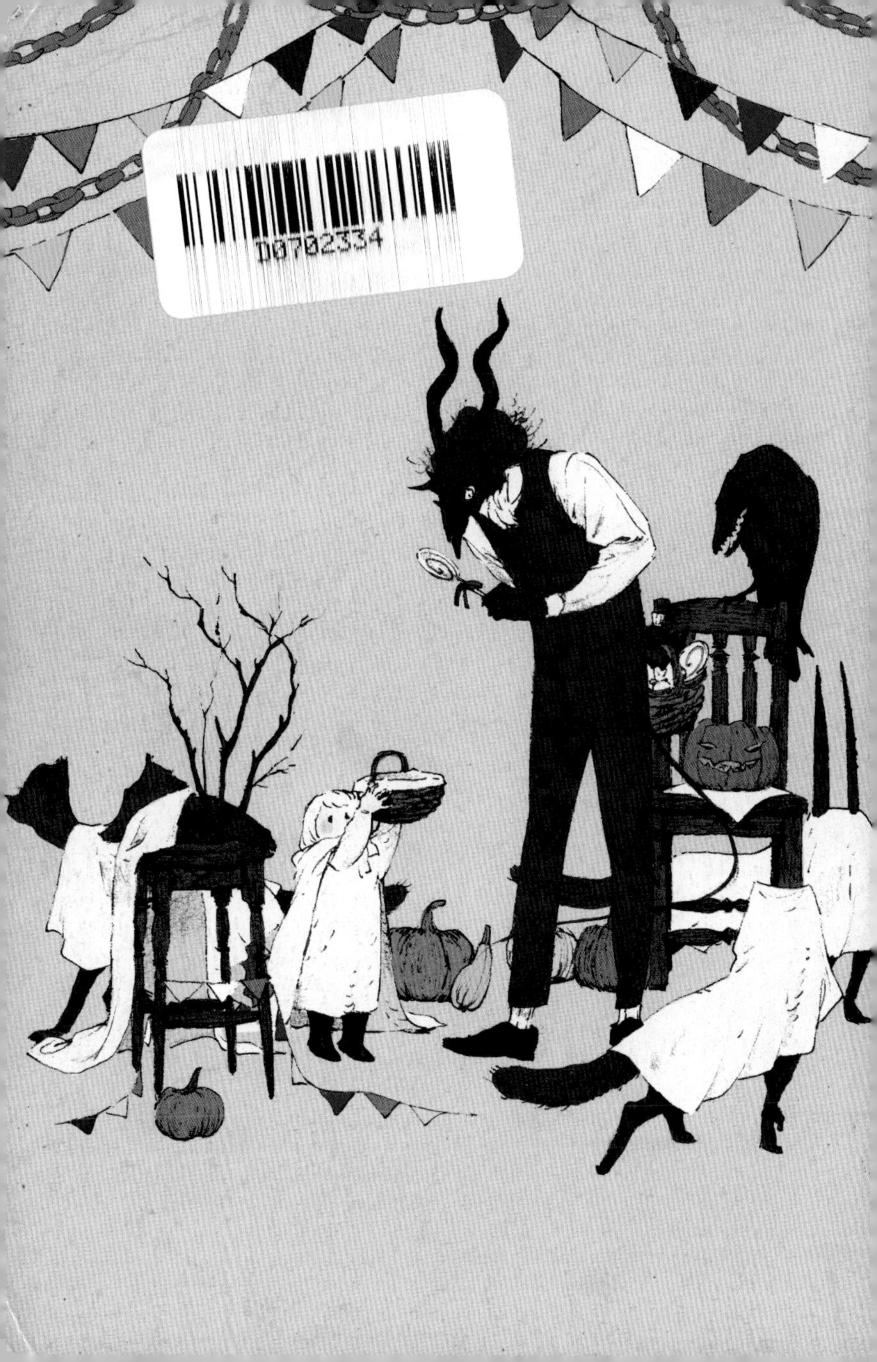

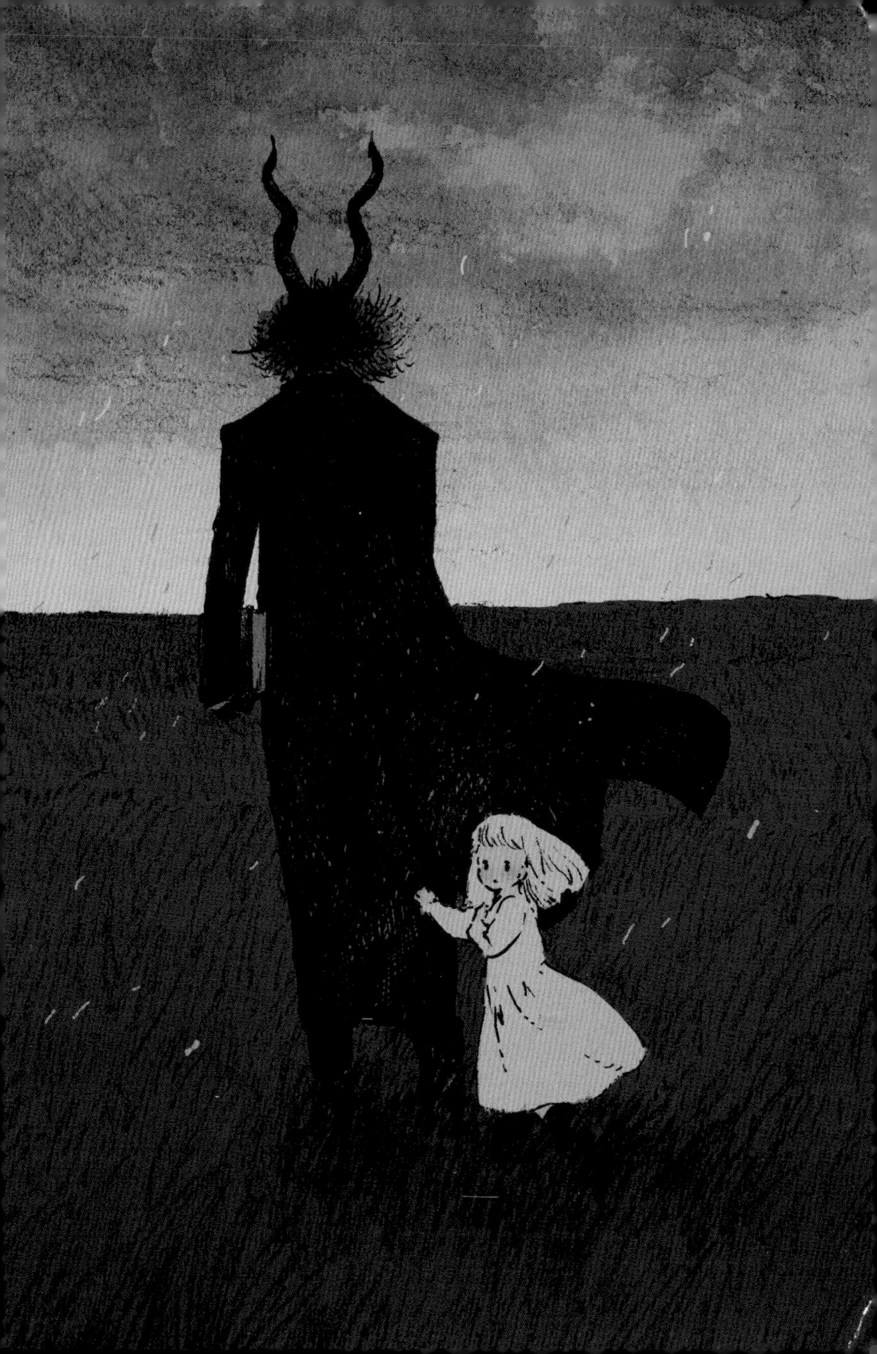

Chapter 11

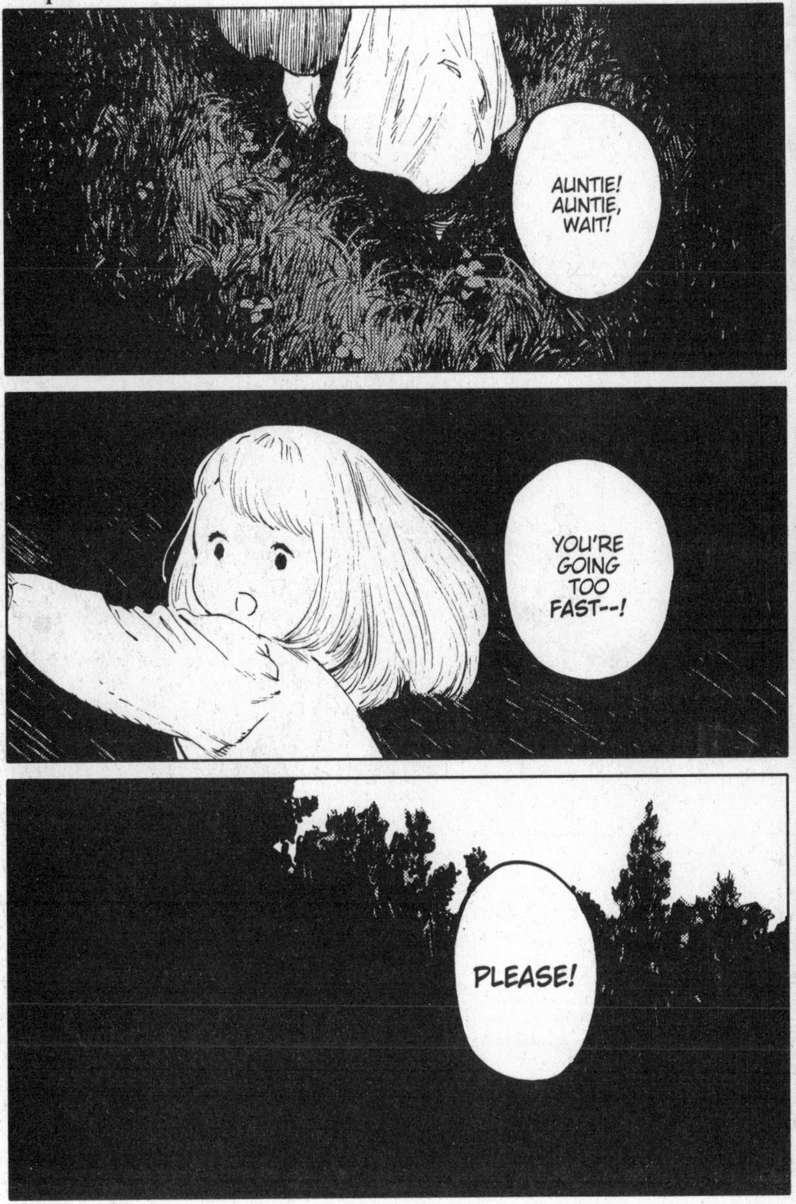
AUNTIE! AUNTIE, WAIT!
YOU'RE GOING TOO FAST--!
PLEASE!

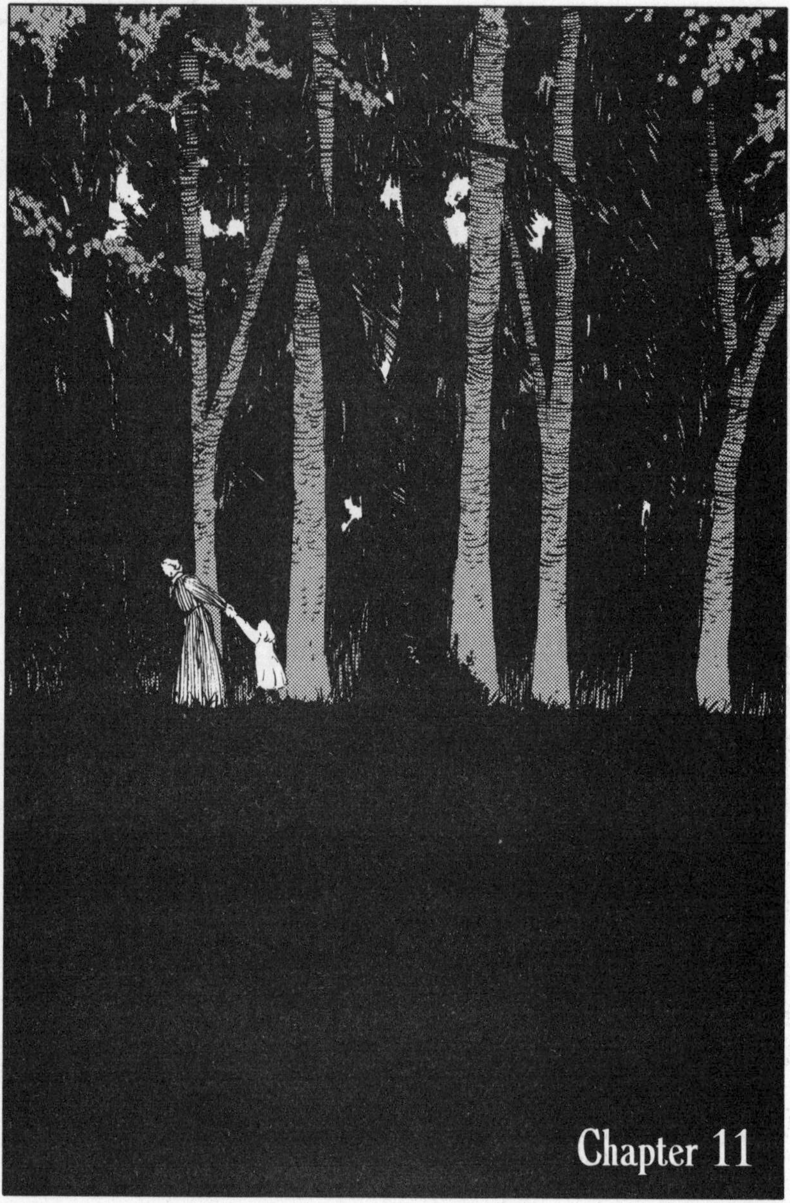

Chapter 11

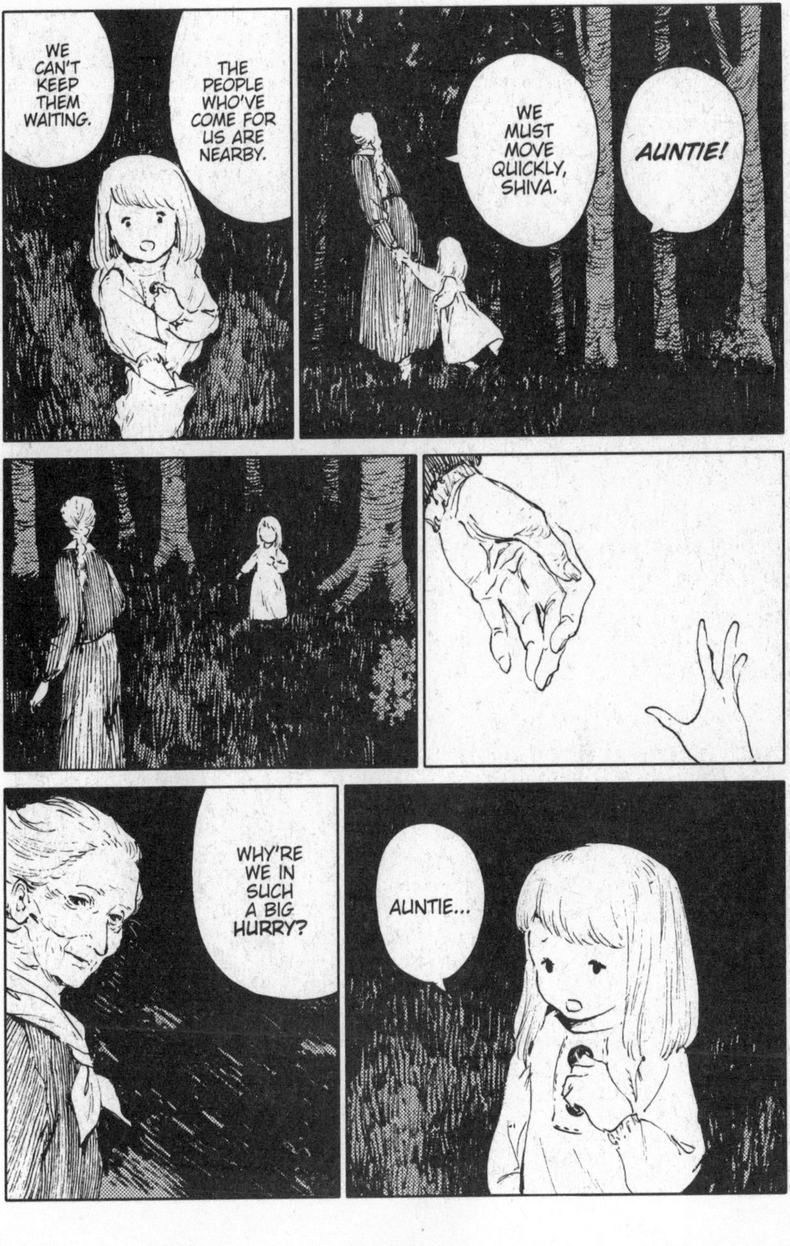
AUNTIE!
WE MUST MOVE QUICKLY, SHIVA.
THE PEOPLE WHO'VE COME FOR US ARE NEARBY.
WE CAN'T KEEP THEM WAITING.
AUNTIE...
WHY'RE WE IN SUCH A BIG HURRY?

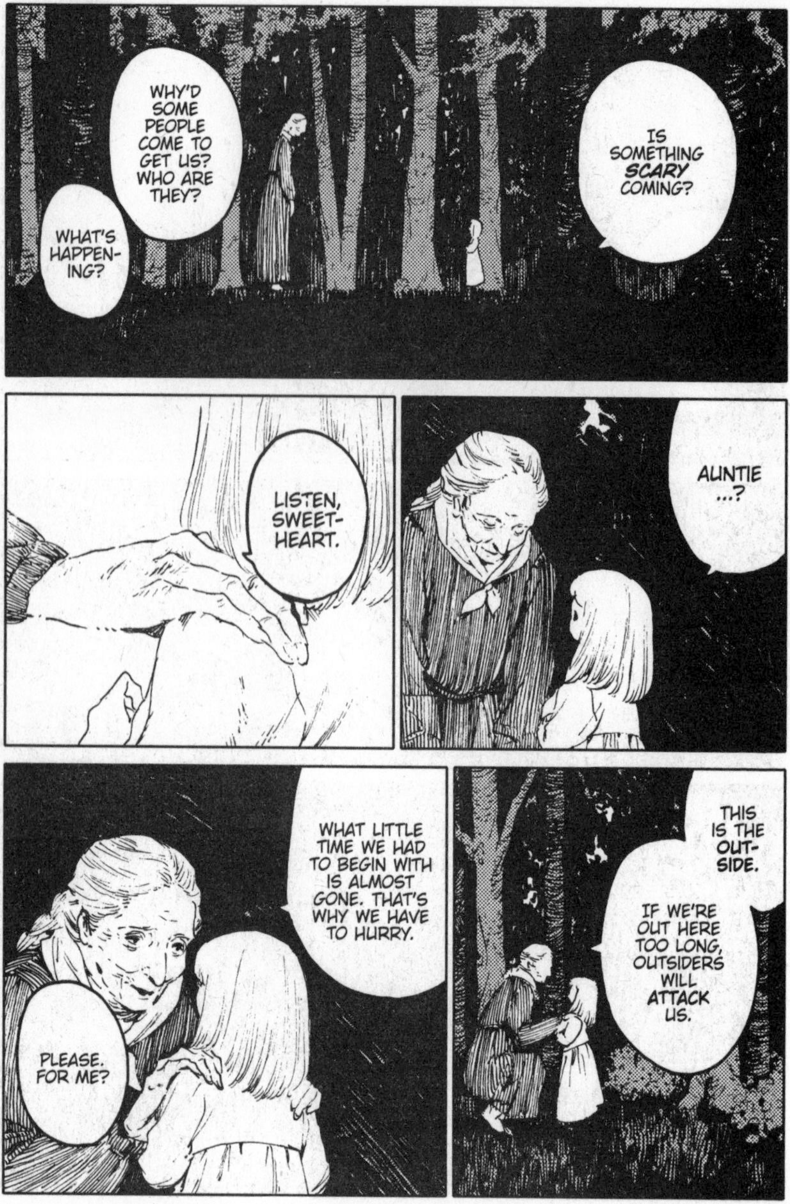
IS SOMETHING SCARY COMING?
WHY'D SOME PEOPLE COME TO GET US? WHO ARE THEY?
WHAT'S HAPPEN-ING?
AUNTIE ...?
LISTEN, SWEET-HEART.
THIS IS THE OUT-SIDE.
IF WE'RE OUT HERE TOO LONG, OUTSIDERS WILL ATTACK US.
WHAT LITTLE TIME WE HAD TO BEGIN WITH IS ALMOST GONE. THAT'S WHY WE HAVE TO HURRY.
PLEASE. FOR ME?

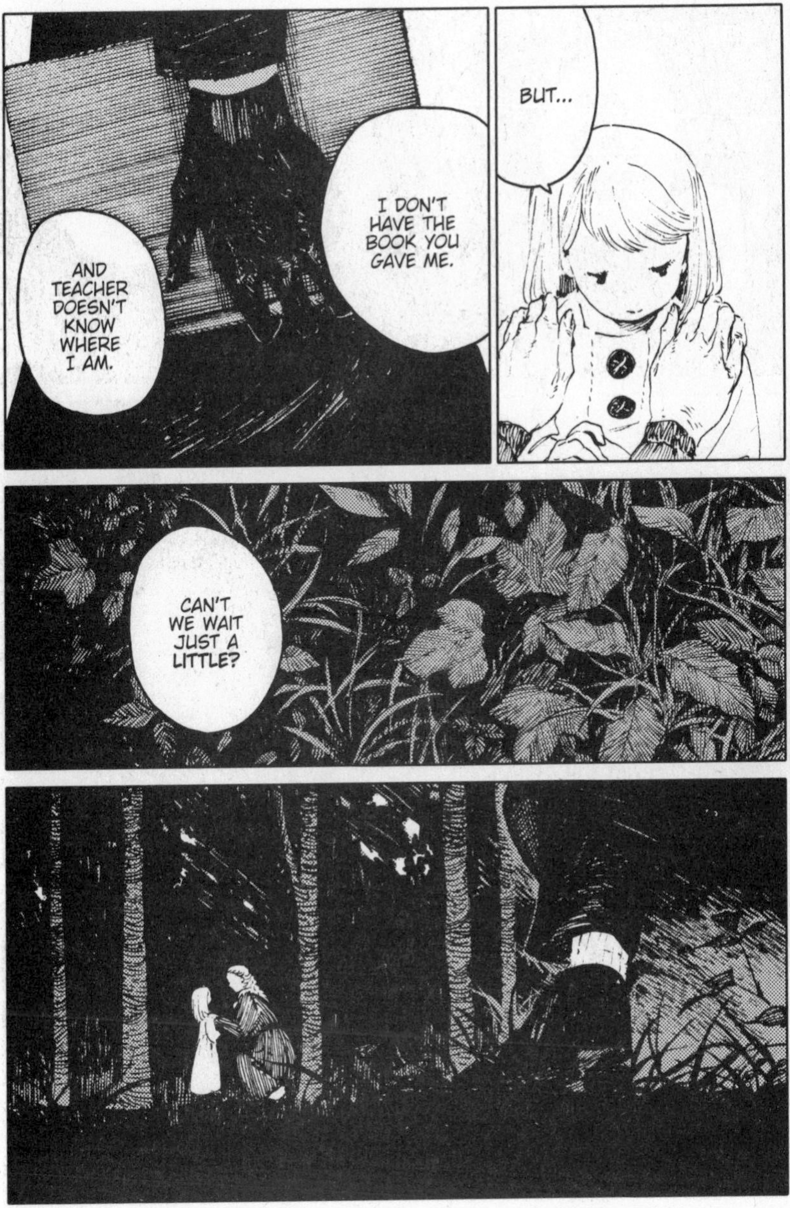
BUT...
I DON'T HAVE THE BOOK YOU GAVE ME.
AND TEACHER DOESN'T KNOW WHERE I AM.
CAN'T WE WAIT JUST A LITTLE?

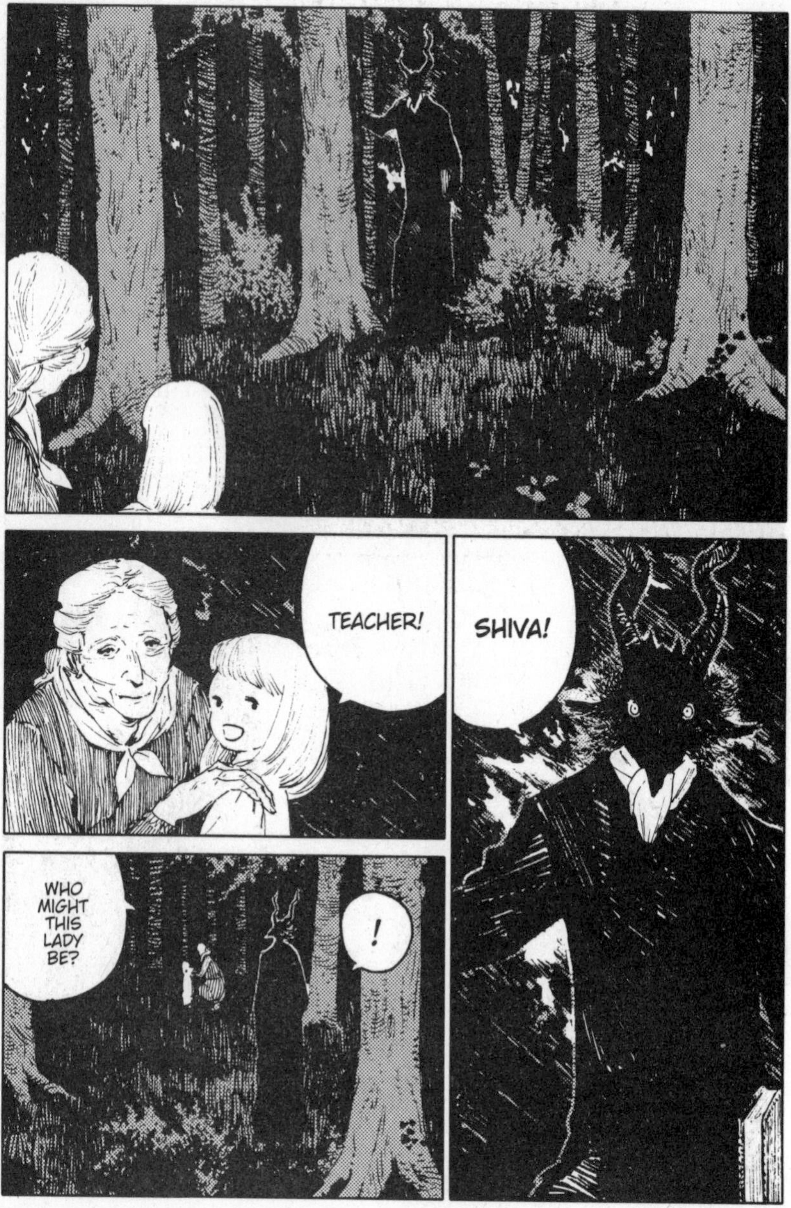
SHIVA!
TEACHER!
!
WHO MIGHT THIS LADY BE?

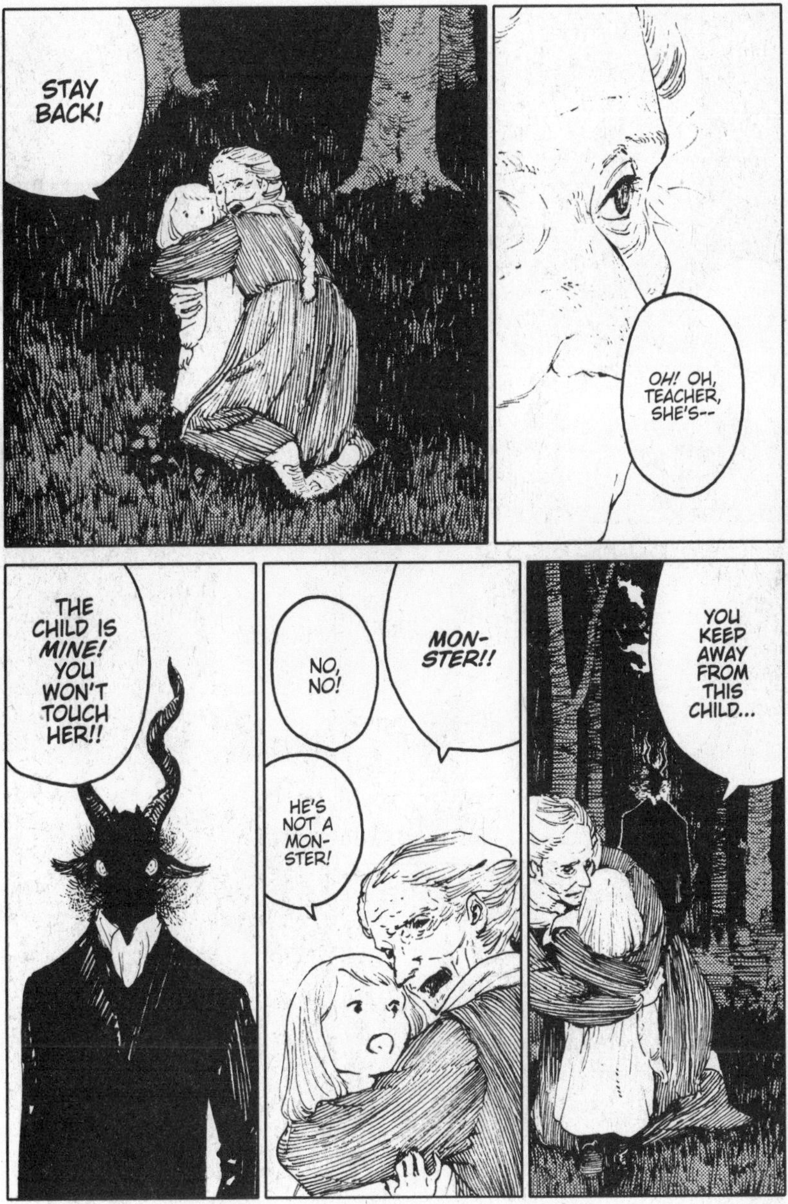
OH! OH, TEACHER, SHE'S--
STAY BACK!
YOU KEEP AWAY FROM THIS CHILD...
MON-STER!!
NO, NO!
HE'S NOT A MON-STER!
THE CHILD IS *MINE!* YOU WON'T TOUCH HER!!

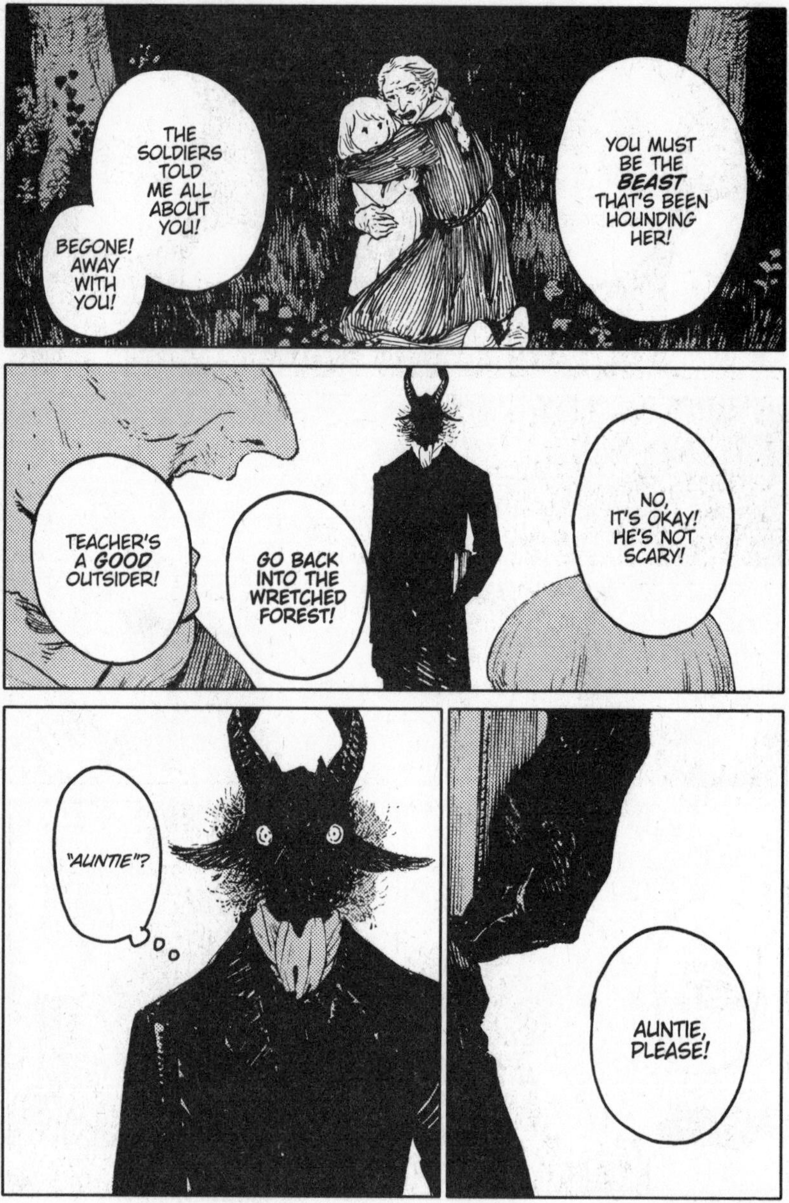
YOU MUST BE THE **BEAST** THAT'S BEEN HOUNDING HER!
THE SOLDIERS TOLD ME ALL ABOUT YOU!
BEGONE! AWAY WITH YOU!
NO, IT'S OKAY! HE'S NOT SCARY!
GO BACK INTO THE WRETCHED FOREST!
TEACHER'S A **GOOD** OUTSIDER!
AUNTIE, PLEASE!
"AUNTIE"?

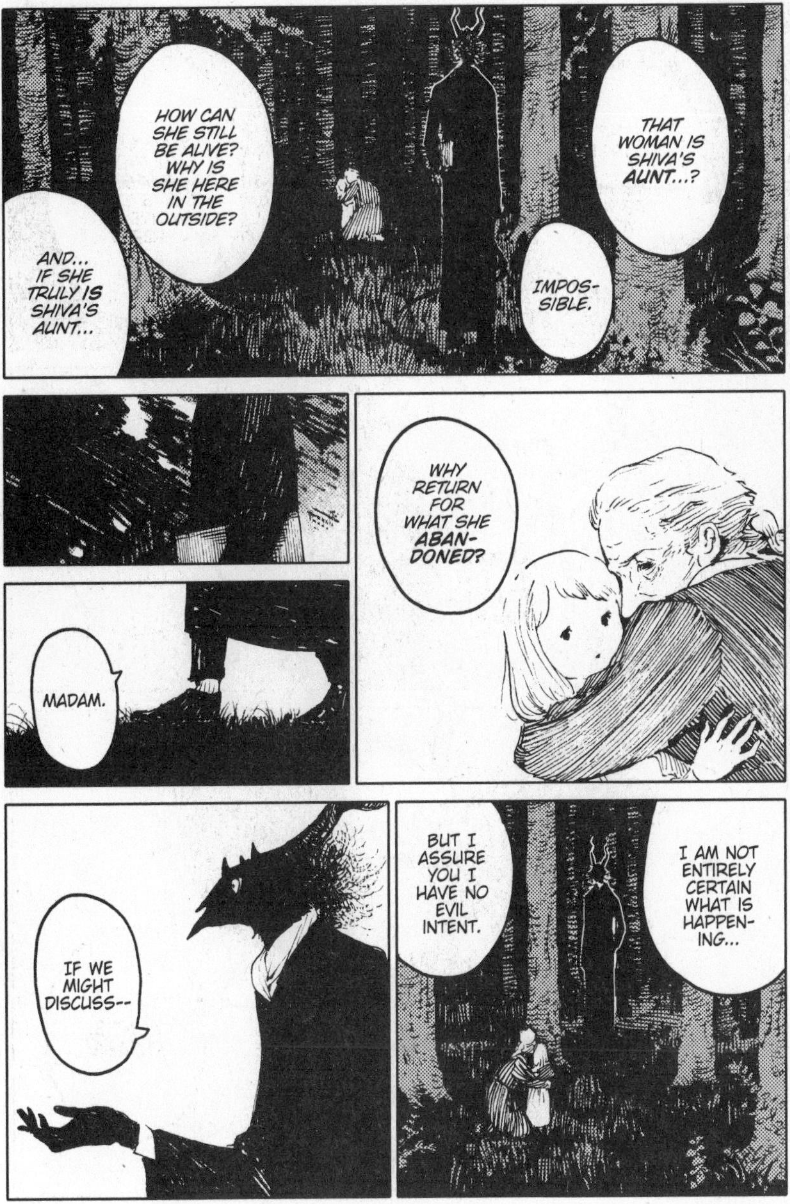
THAT WOMAN IS SHIVA'S AUNT...?
IMPOSSIBLE.
HOW CAN SHE STILL BE ALIVE? WHY IS SHE HERE IN THE OUTSIDE?
AND... IF SHE TRULY IS SHIVA'S AUNT...
WHY RETURN FOR WHAT SHE ABANDONED?
MADAM.
I AM NOT ENTIRELY CERTAIN WHAT IS HAPPENING...
BUT I ASSURE YOU I HAVE NO EVIL INTENT.
IF WE MIGHT DISCUSS--

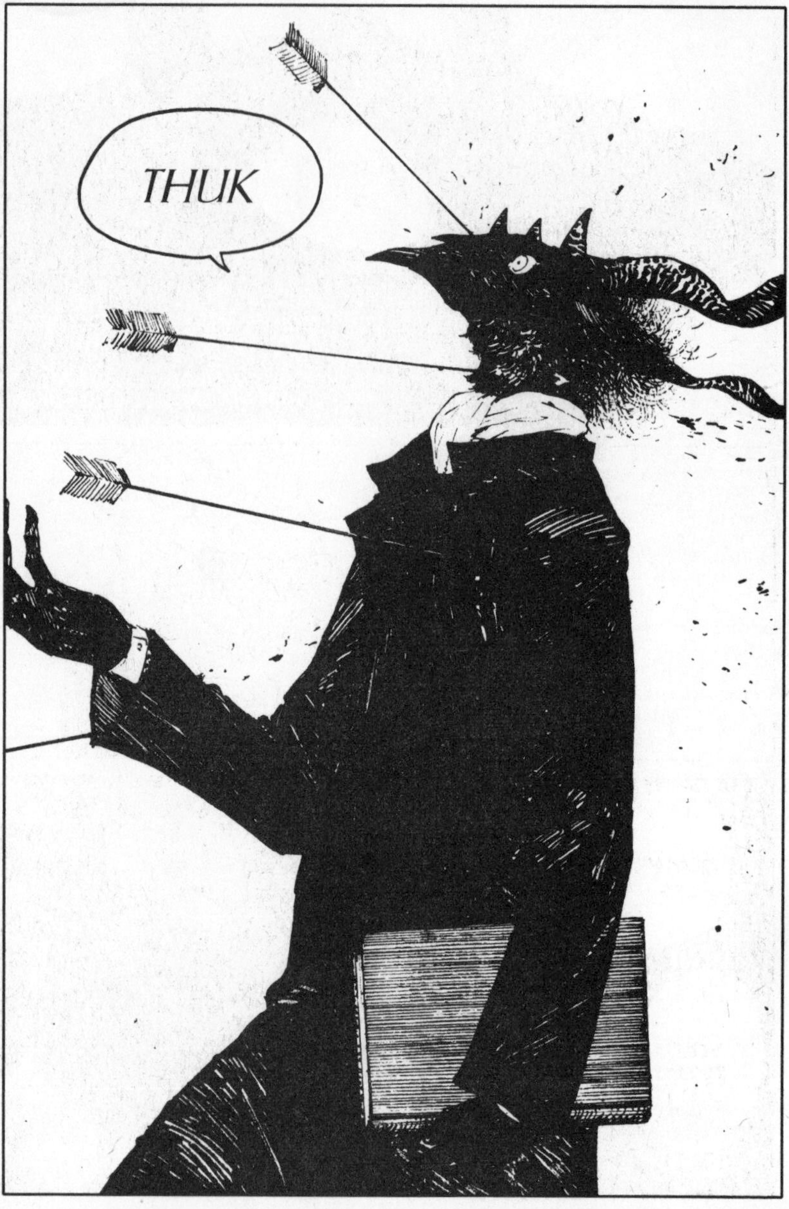
THUK

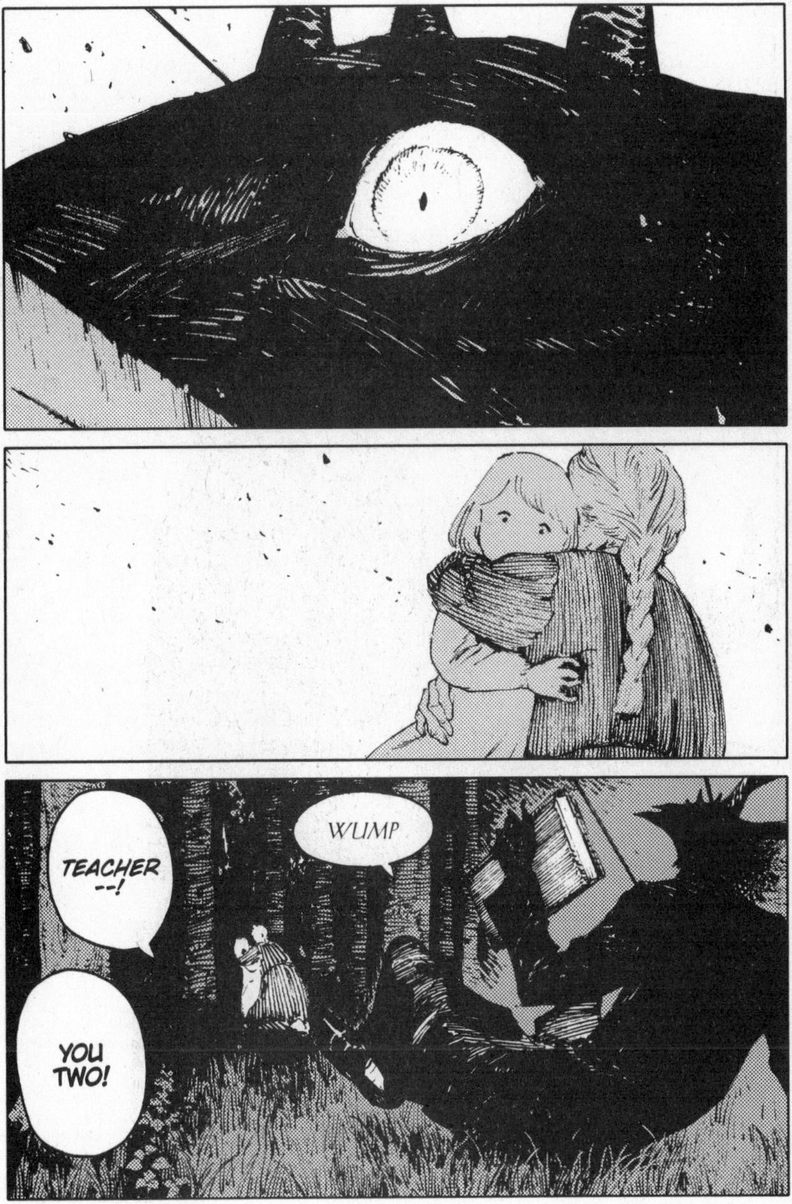
WUMP
TEACHER --!
YOU TWO!

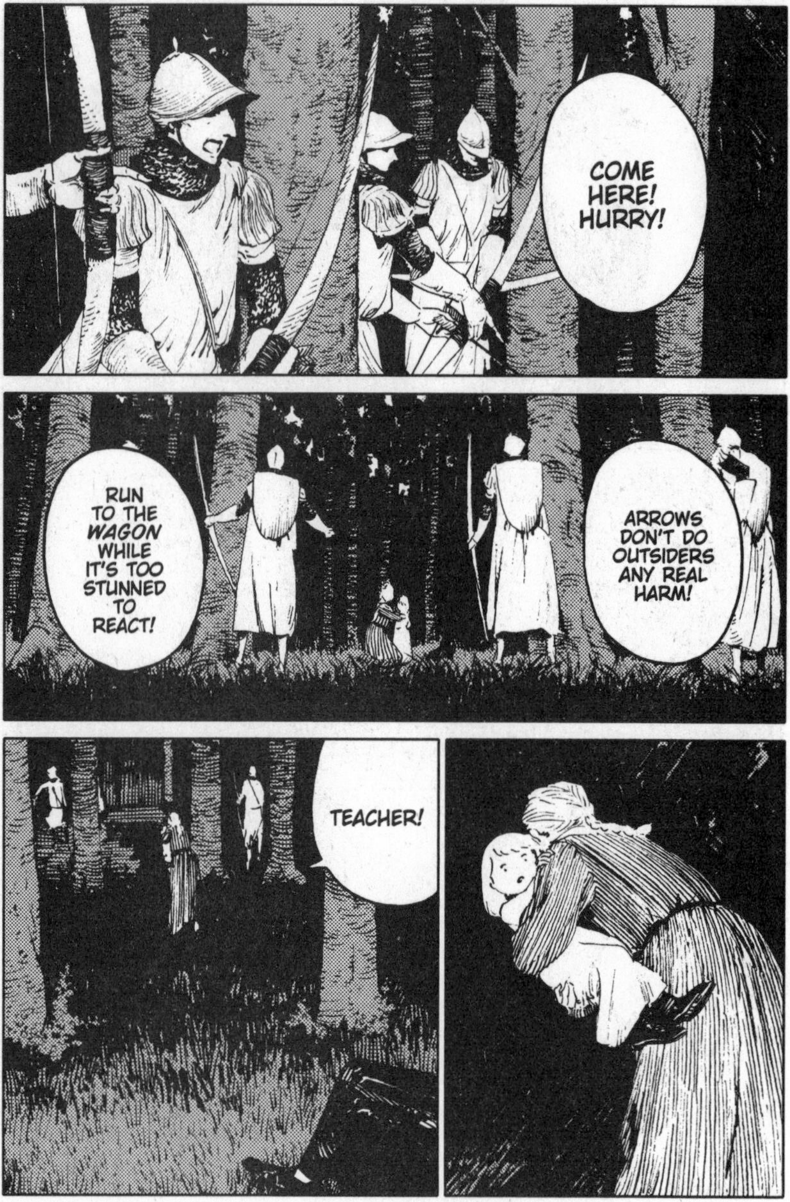
COME HERE! HURRY!
ARROWS DON'T DO OUTSIDERS ANY REAL HARM!
RUN TO THE *WAGON* WHILE IT'S TOO STUNNED TO REACT!
TEACHER!

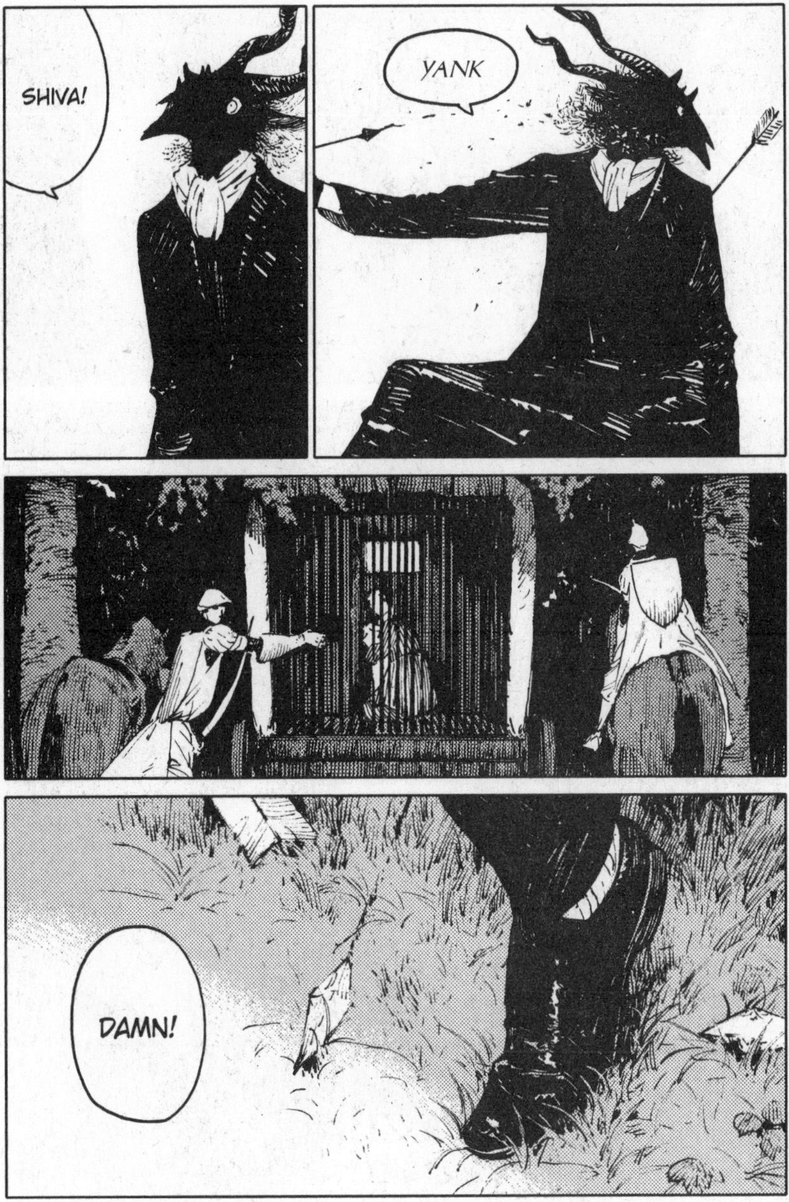
YANK
SHIVA!
DAMN!

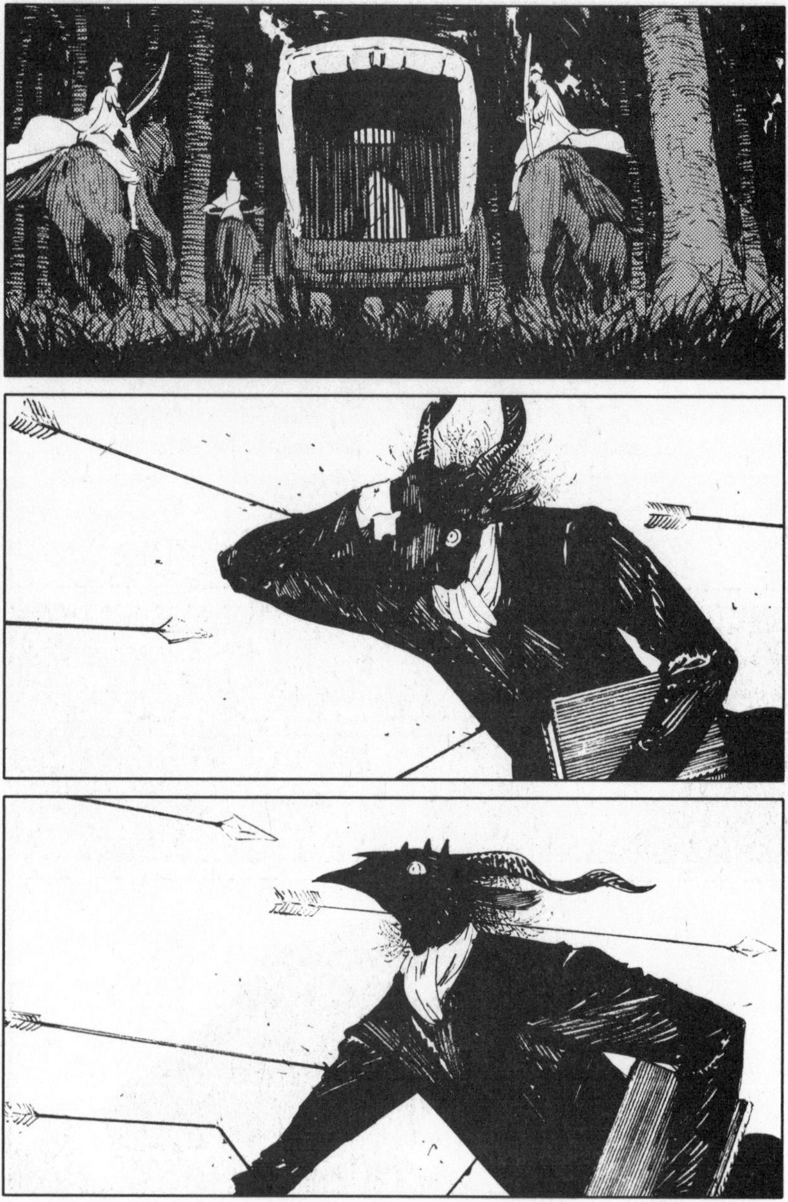

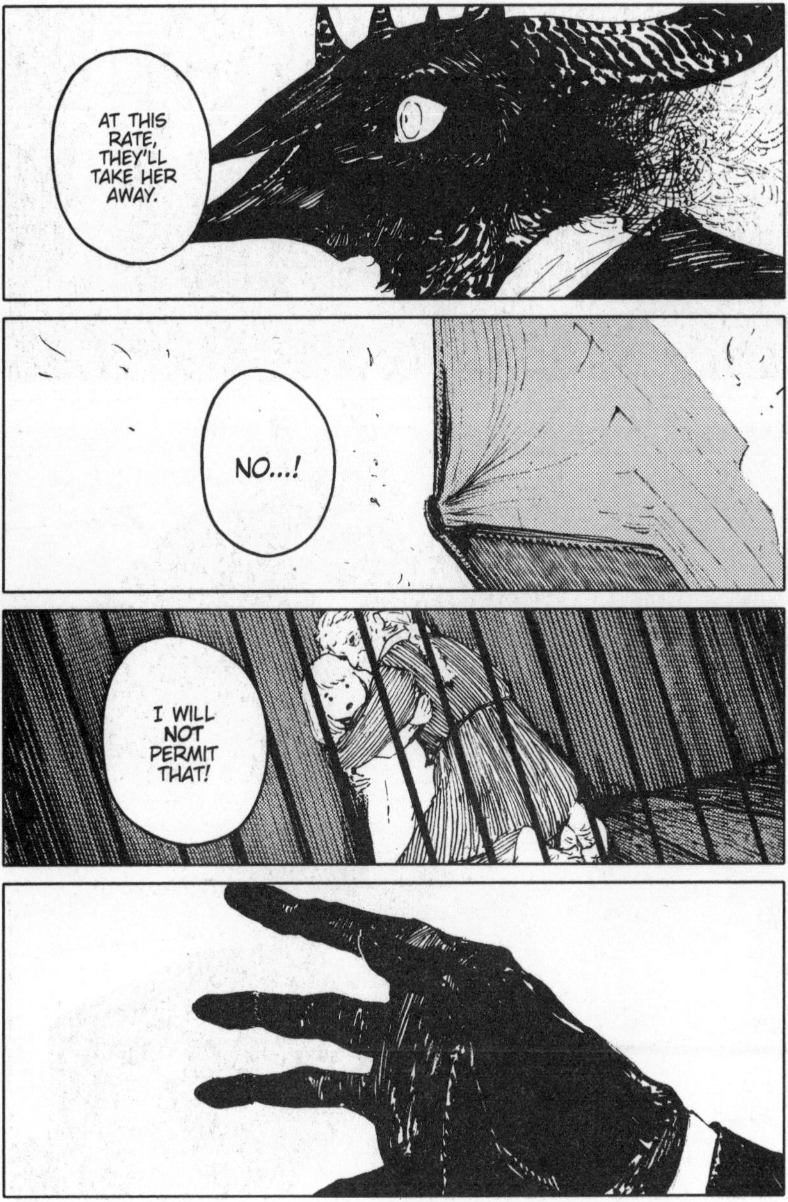
AT THIS RATE, THEY'LL TAKE HER AWAY.
NO...!
I WILL NOT PERMIT THAT!

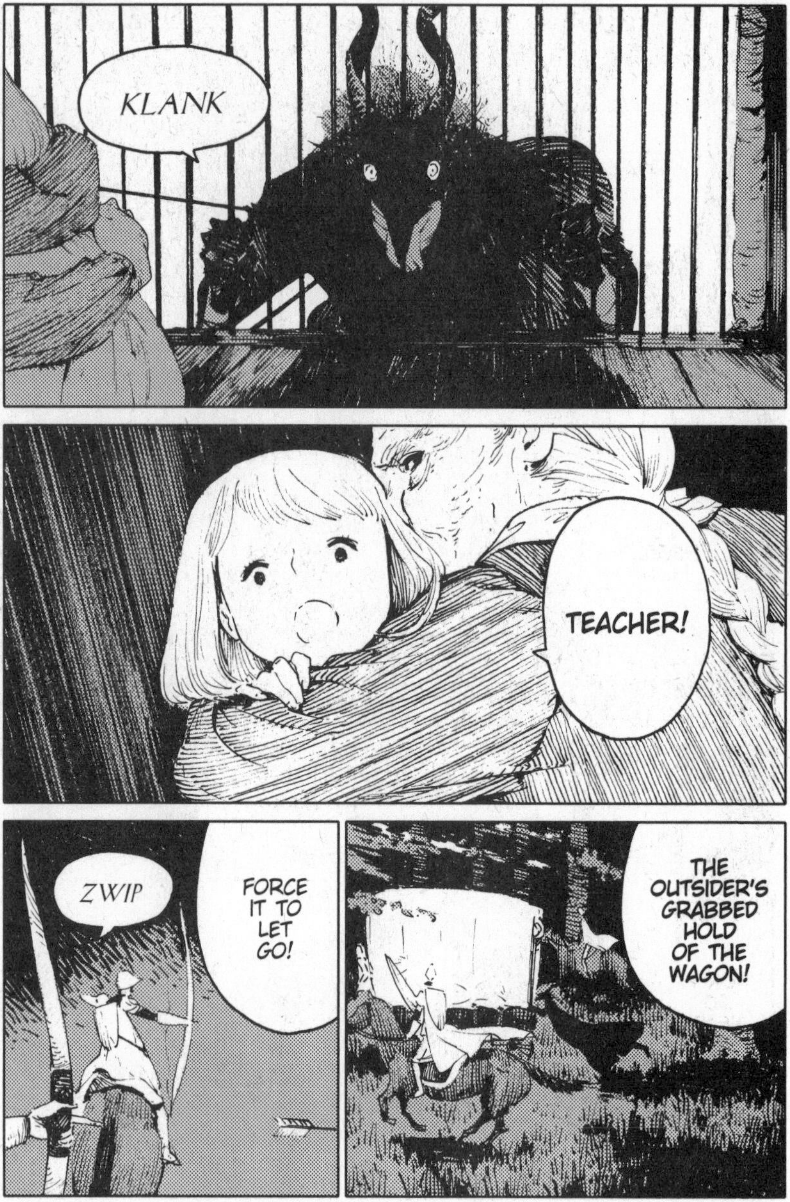
KLANK
TEACHER!
THE OUTSIDER'S GRABBED HOLD OF THE WAGON!
FORCE IT TO LET GO!
ZWIP

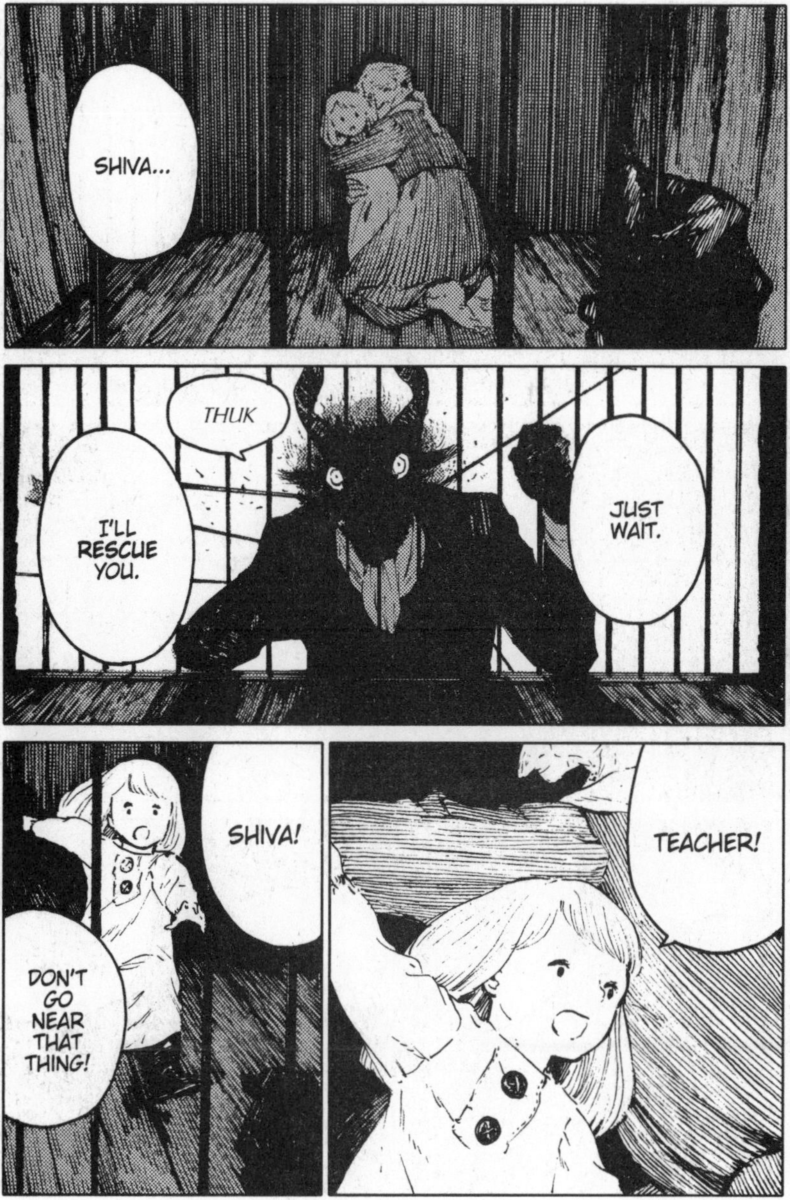
SHIVA...
THUK
JUST WAIT.
I'LL RESCUE YOU.
TEACHER!
SHIVA!
DON'T GO NEAR THAT THING!

SHIVA!

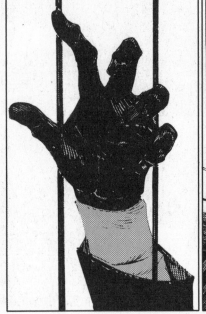

GA-WUNK

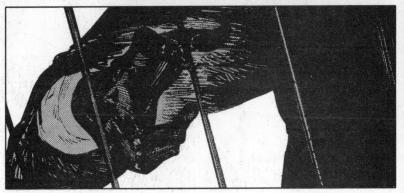

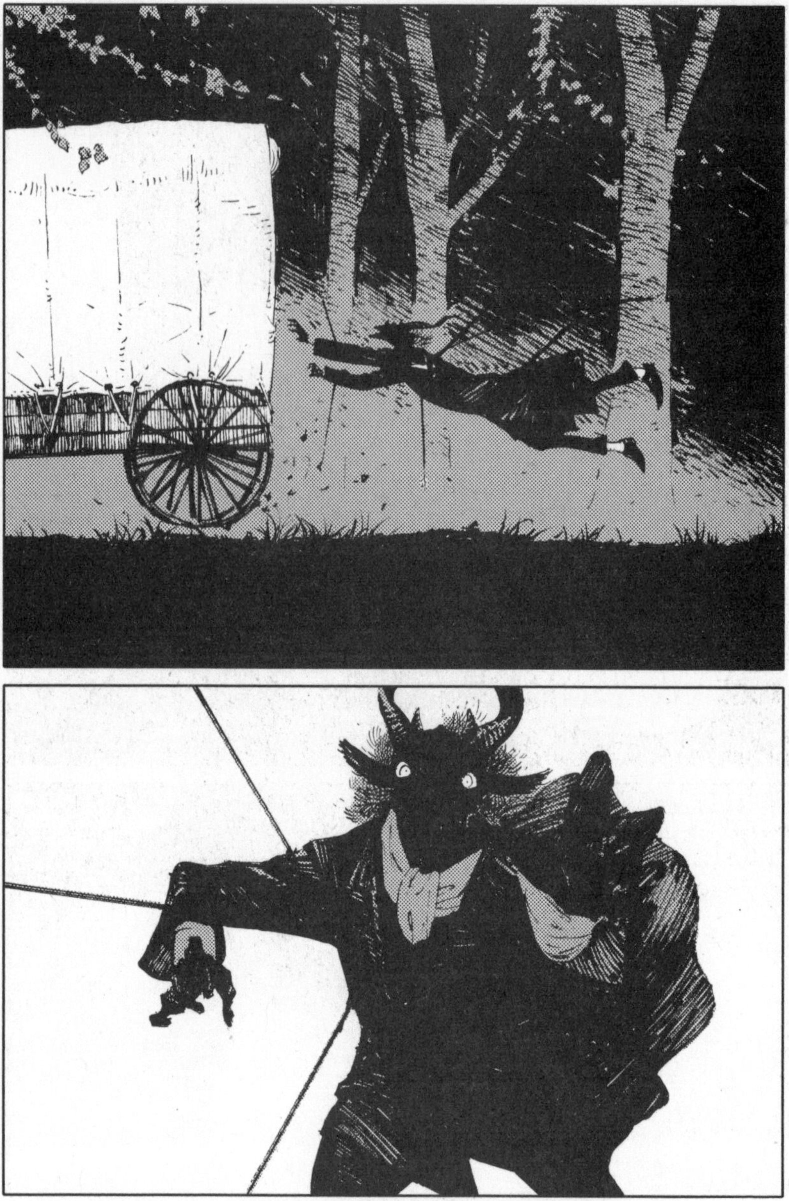

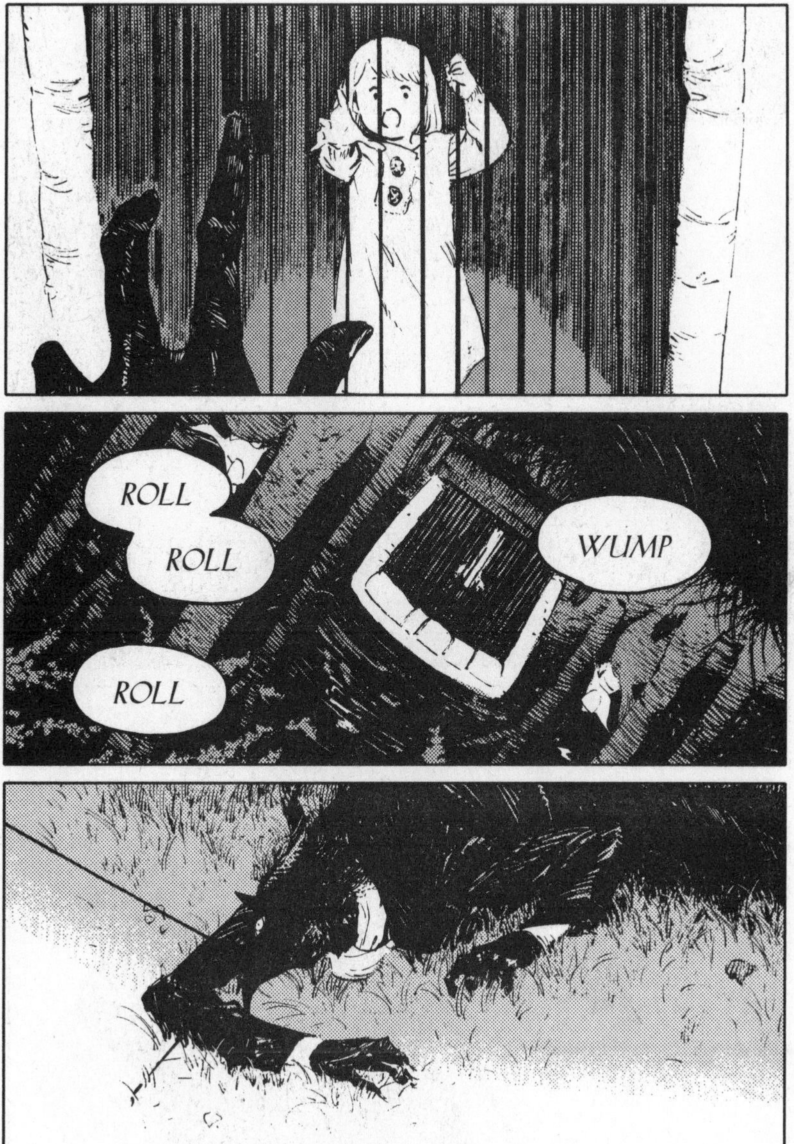
ROLL
ROLL
ROLL
WUMP

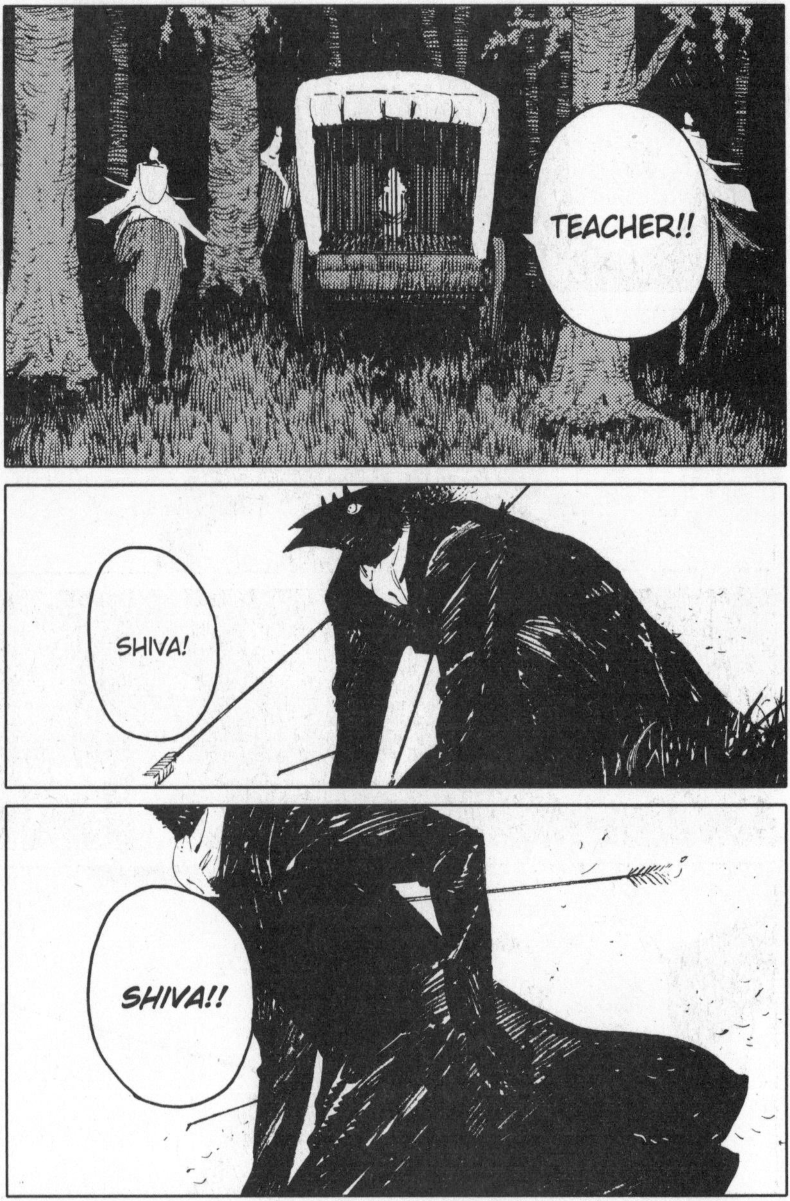
TEACHER!!
SHIVA!
SHIVA!!

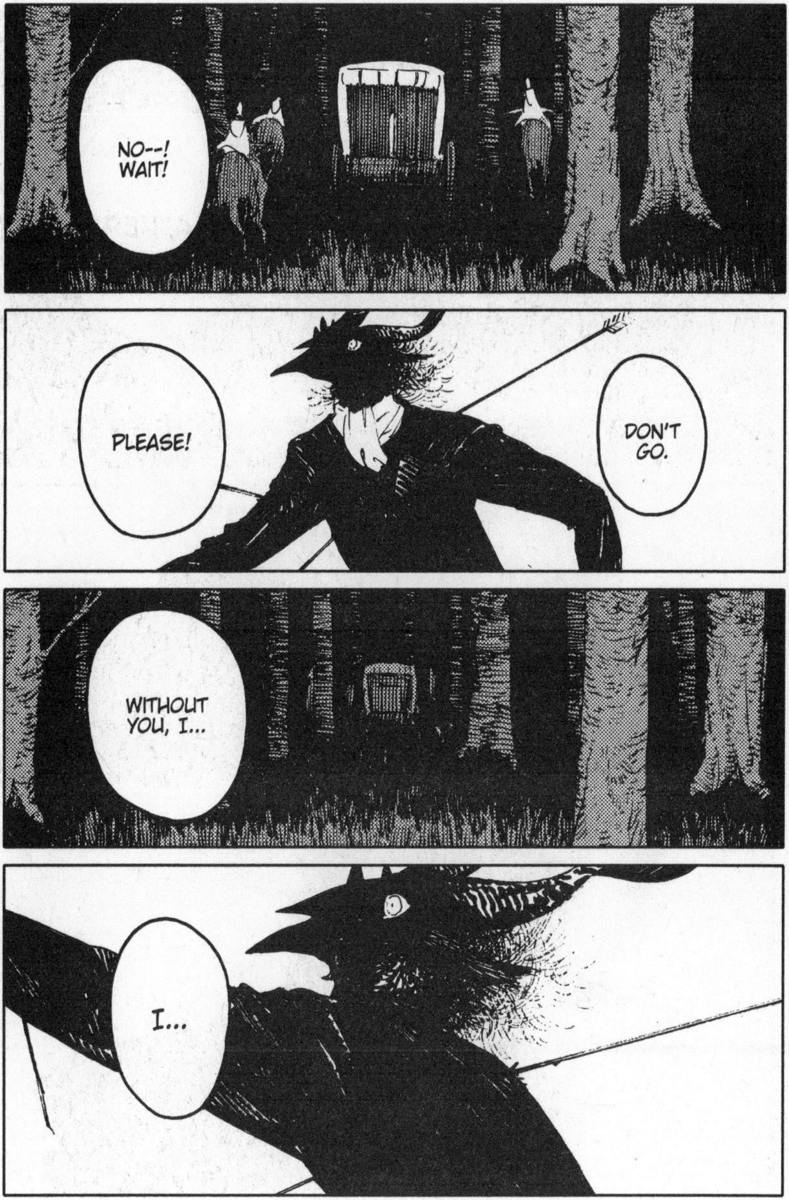
NO--! WAIT!
DON'T GO.
PLEASE!
WITHOUT YOU, I...
I...

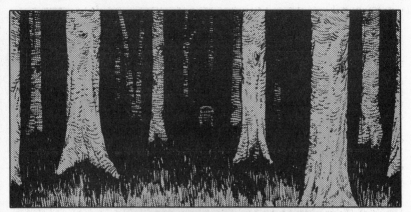

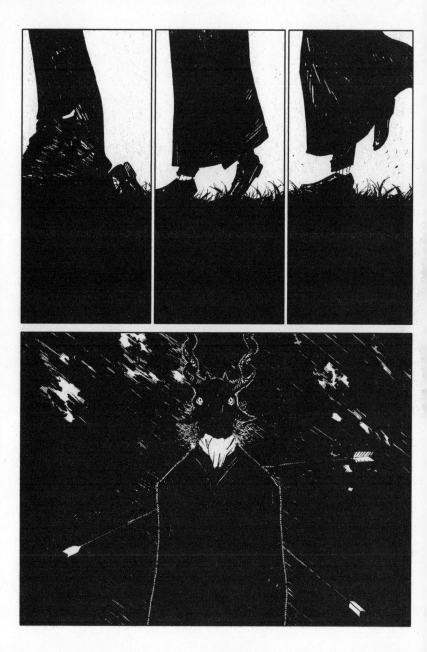

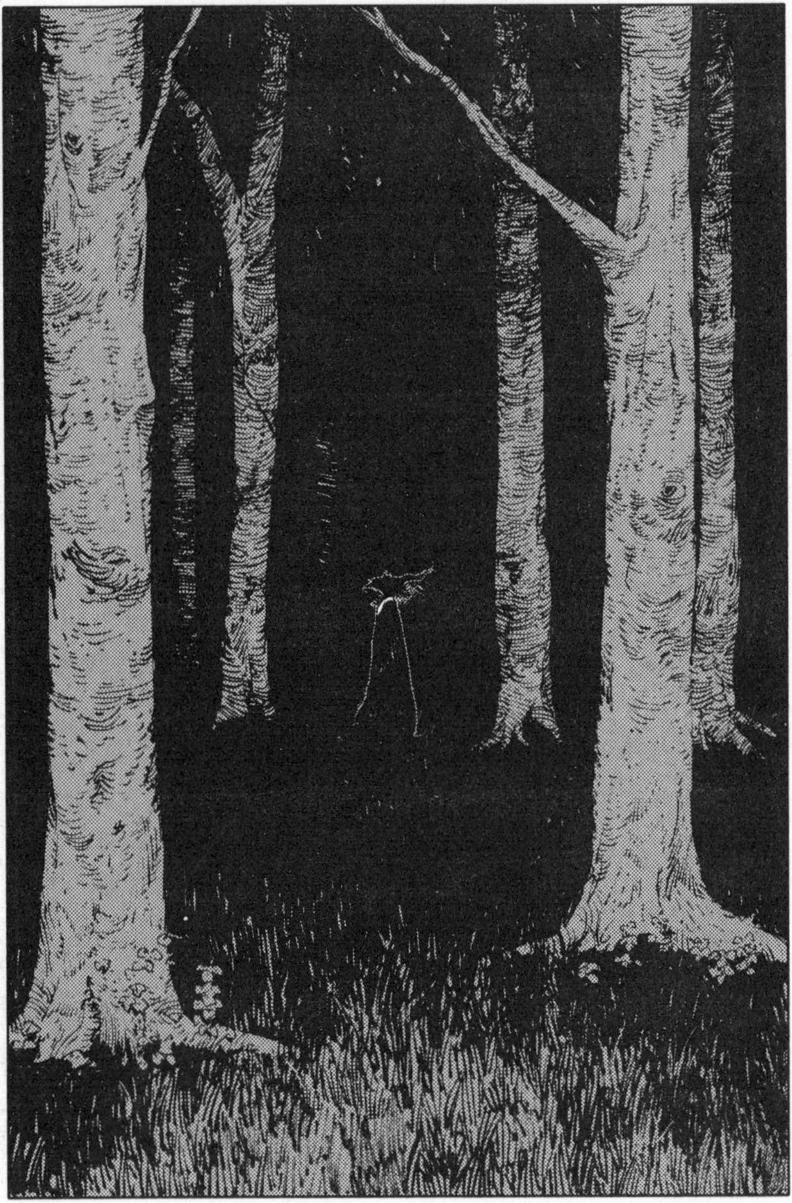

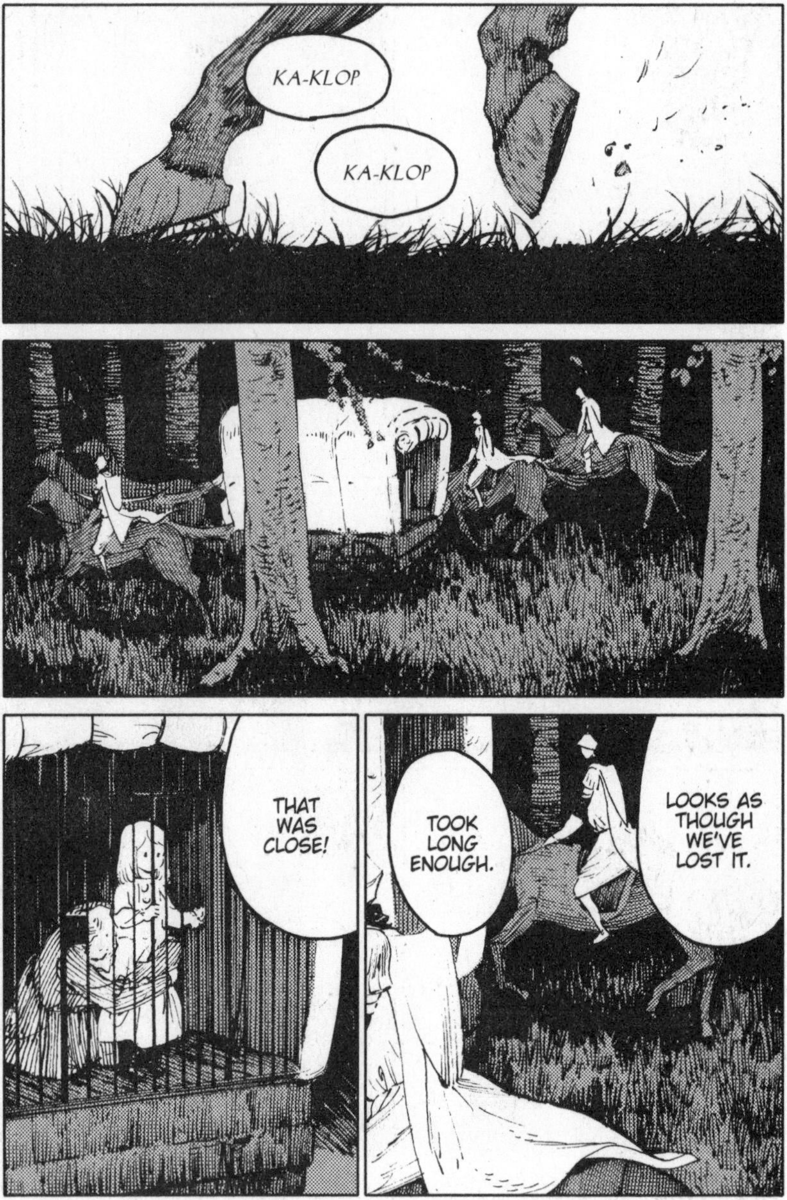
KA-KLOP
KA-KLOP
LOOKS AS THOUGH WE'VE LOST IT.
TOOK LONG ENOUGH.
THAT WAS CLOSE!

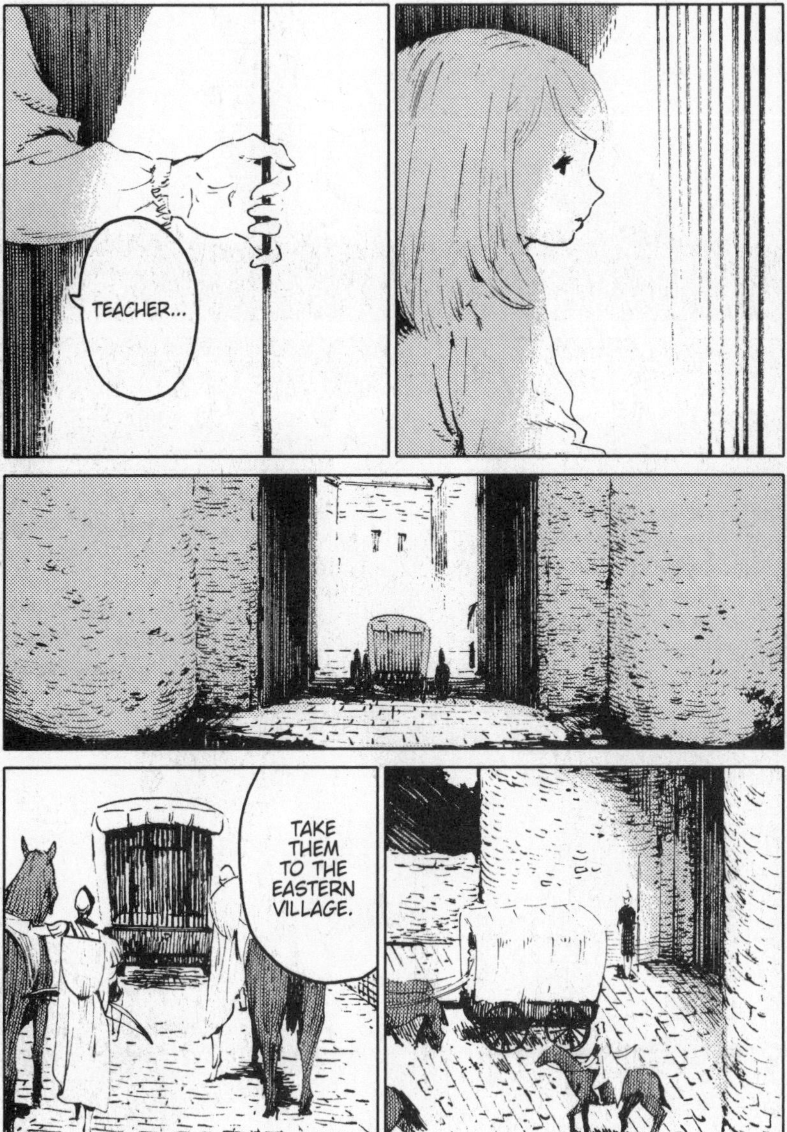
TEACHER...
TAKE THEM TO THE EASTERN VILLAGE.

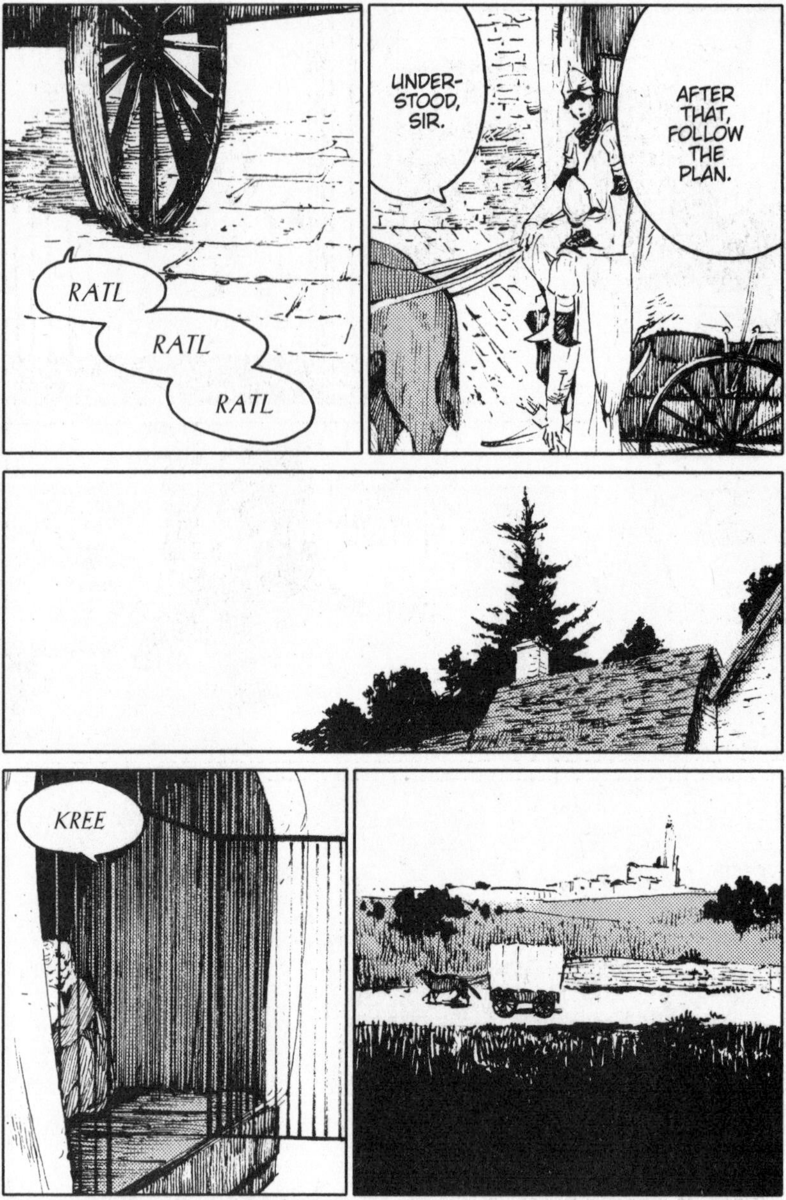
AFTER THAT, FOLLOW THE PLAN.
UNDERSTOOD, SIR.
RATL RATL RATL
KREE

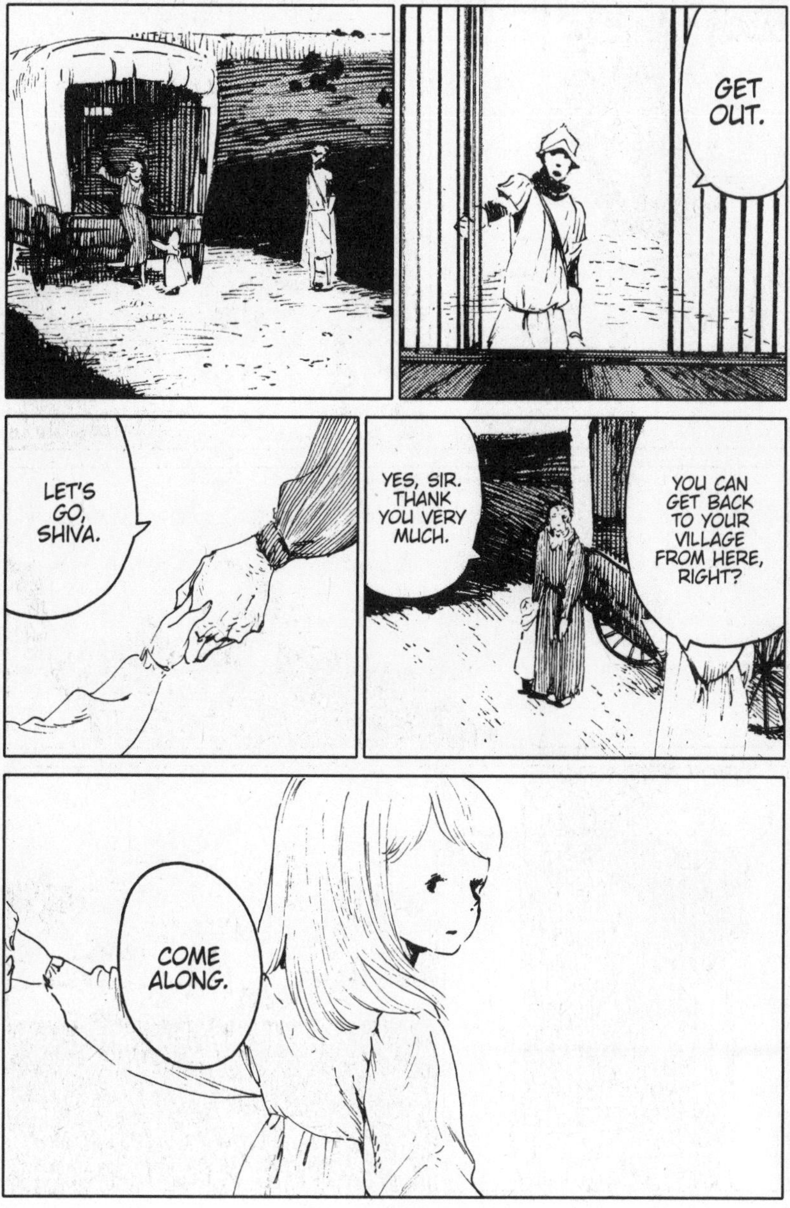
GET OUT.
YOU CAN GET BACK TO YOUR VILLAGE FROM HERE, RIGHT?
YES, SIR. THANK YOU VERY MUCH.
LET'S GO, SHIVA.
COME ALONG.

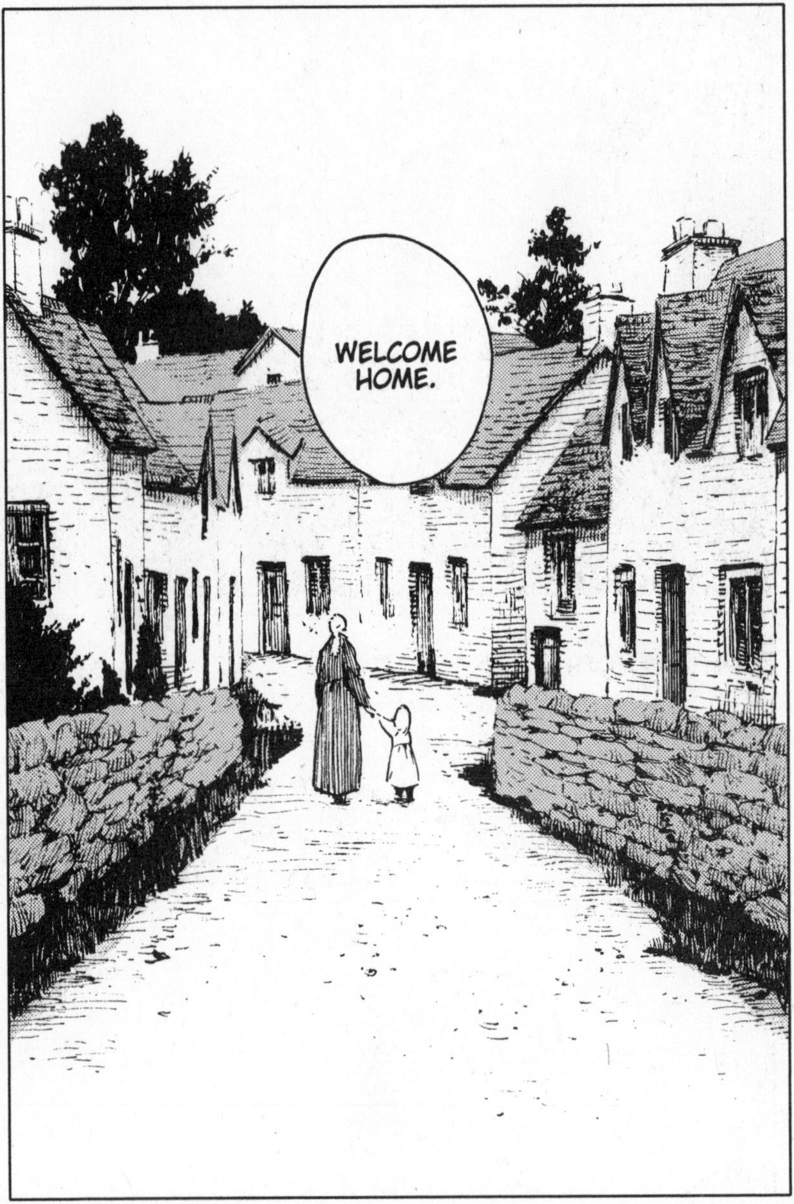
WELCOME HOME.

Chapter 12

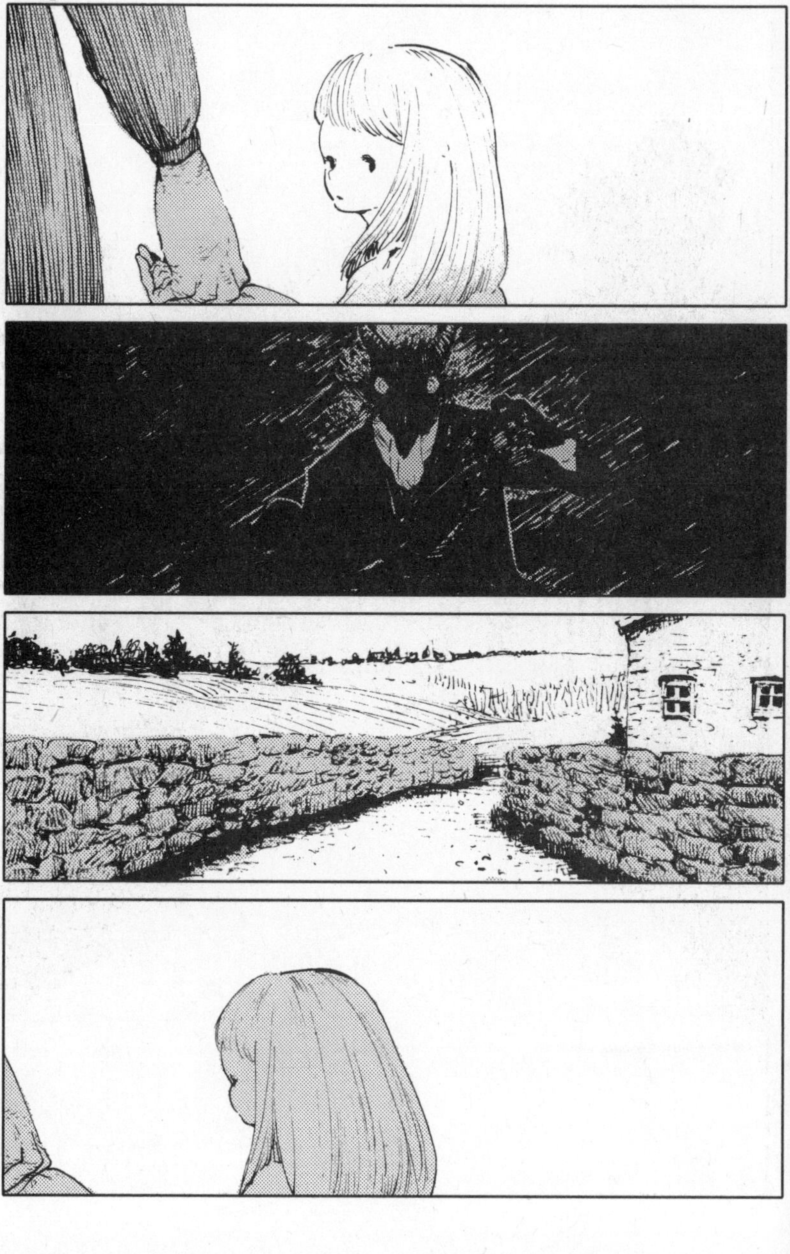

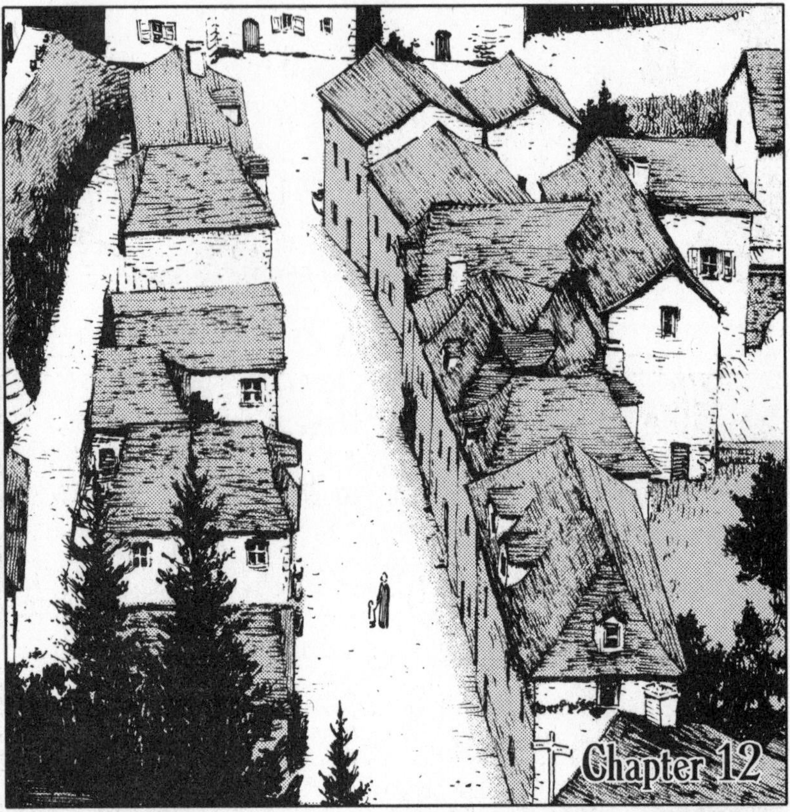
Chapter 12
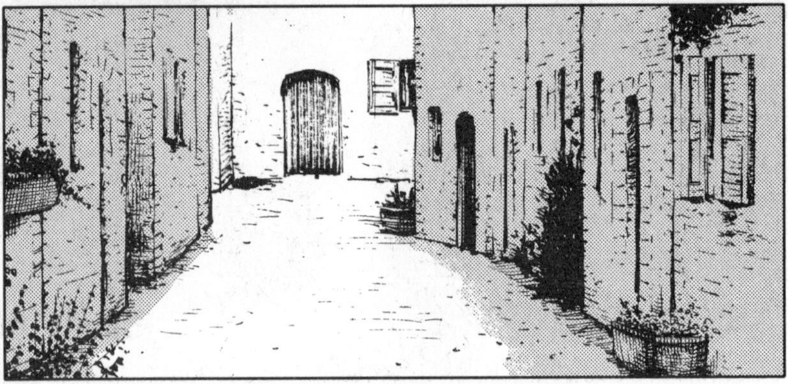

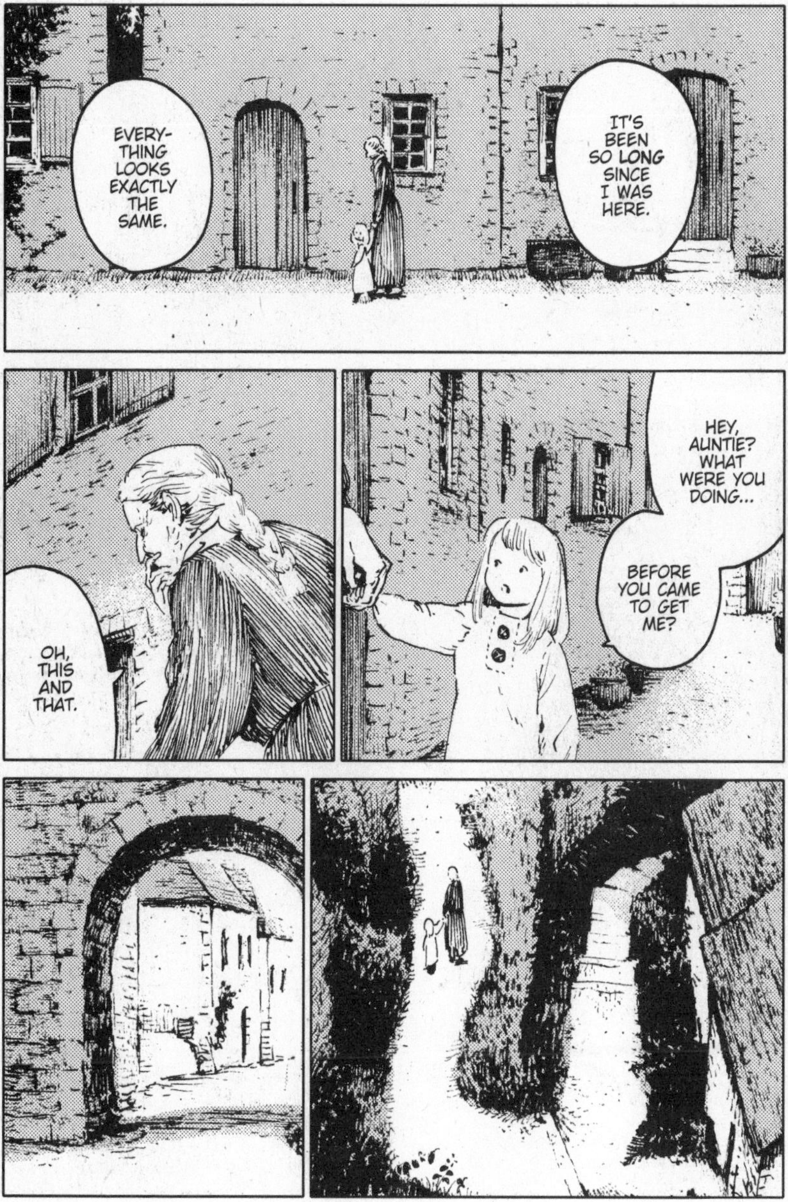
IT'S BEEN SO LONG SINCE I WAS HERE.
EVERYTHING LOOKS EXACTLY THE SAME.
HEY, AUNTIE? WHAT WERE YOU DOING...
BEFORE YOU CAME TO GET ME?
OH, THIS AND THAT.

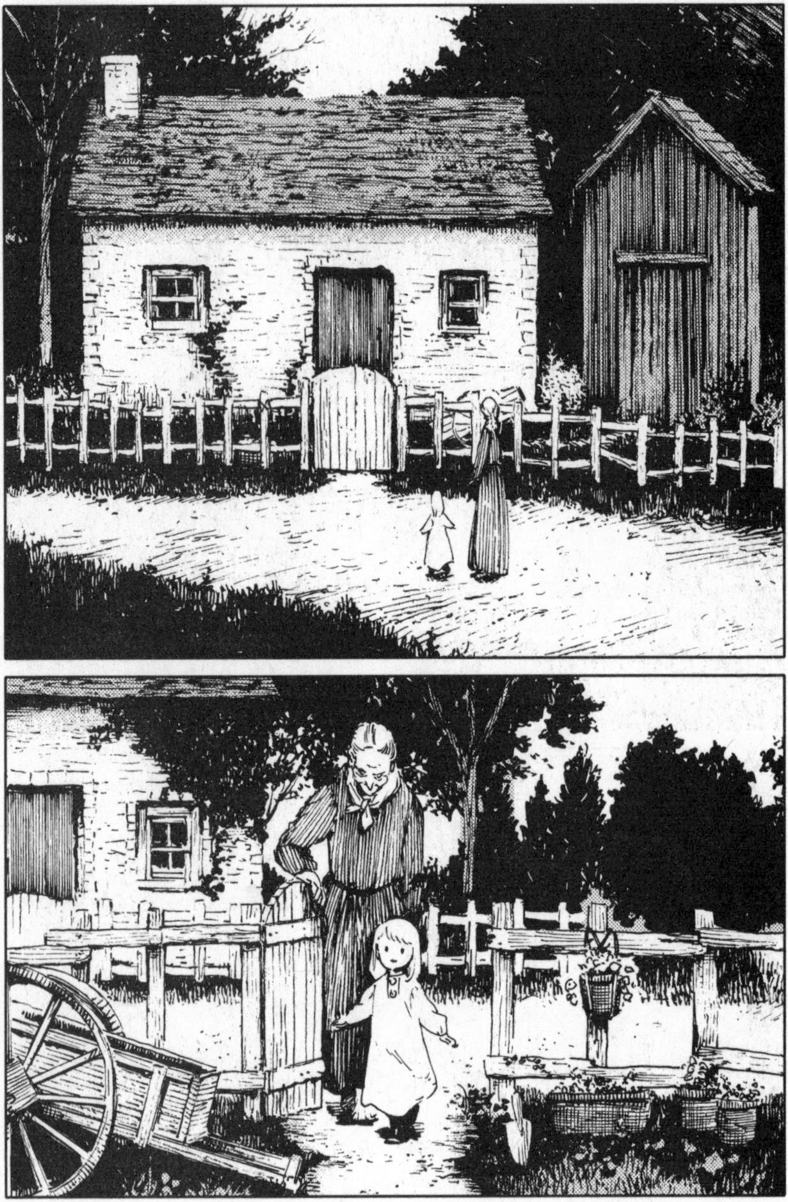

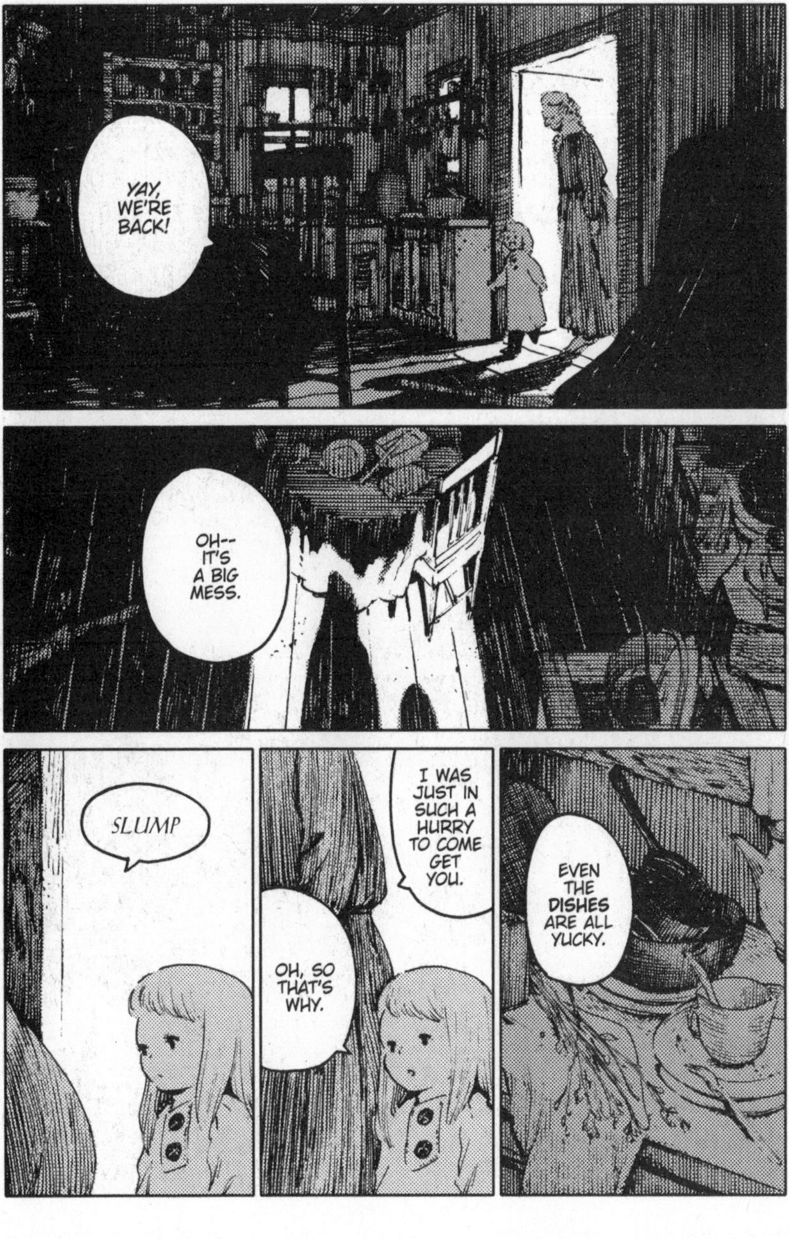
YAY, WE'RE BACK!
OH-- IT'S A BIG MESS.
EVEN THE DISHES ARE ALL YUCKY.
I WAS JUST IN SUCH A HURRY TO COME GET YOU.
OH, SO THAT'S WHY.
SLUMP

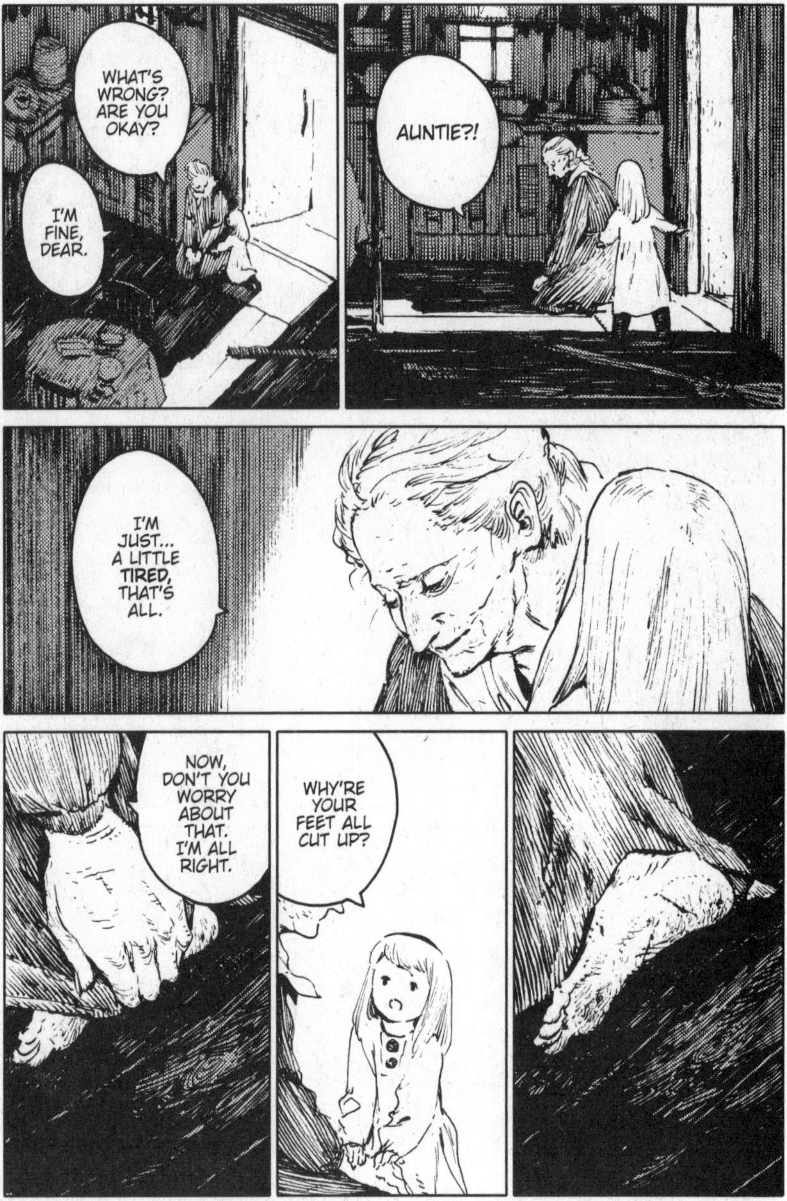
AUNTIE?!
WHAT'S WRONG? ARE YOU OKAY?
I'M FINE, DEAR.
I'M JUST... A LITTLE TIRED, THAT'S ALL.
WHY'RE YOUR FEET ALL CUT UP?
NOW, DON'T YOU WORRY ABOUT THAT. I'M ALL RIGHT.

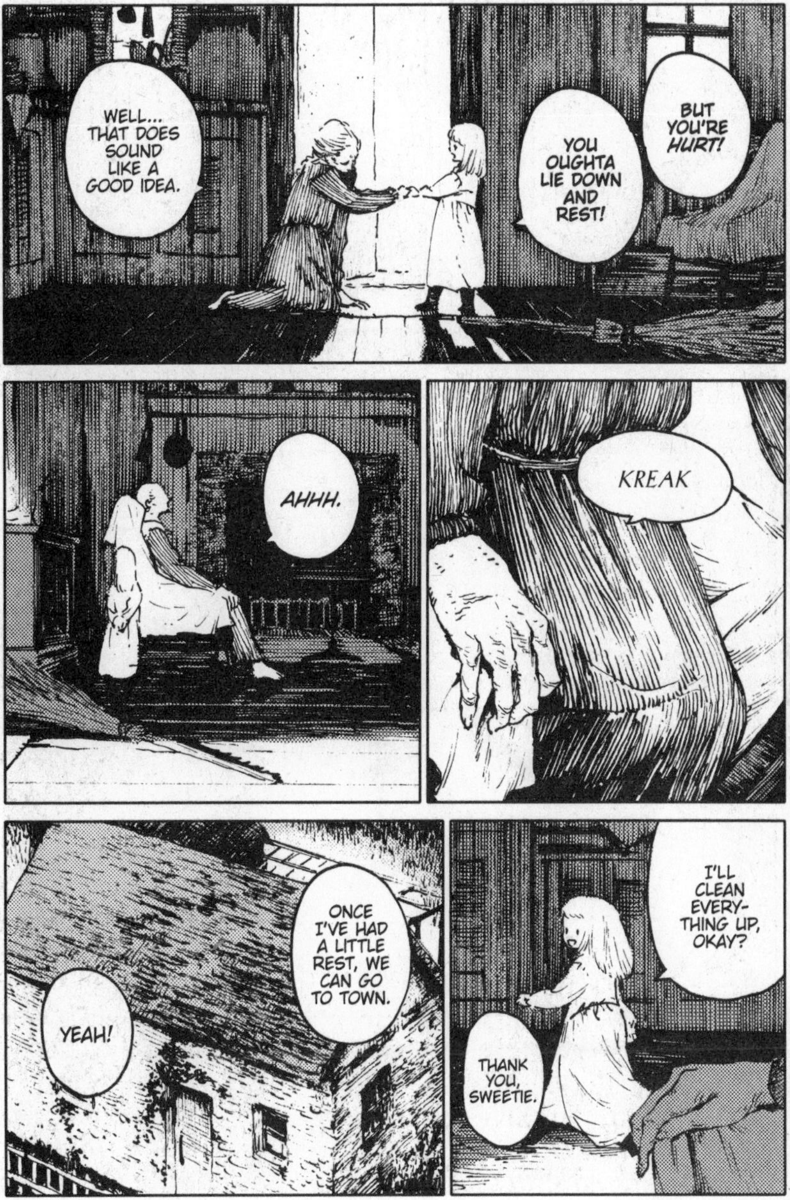
BUT YOU'RE *HURT!*
YOU OUGHTA LIE DOWN AND REST!
WELL... THAT DOES SOUND LIKE A GOOD IDEA.
KREAK
AHHH.
I'LL CLEAN EVERY-THING UP, OKAY?
THANK YOU, SWEETIE.
ONCE I'VE HAD A LITTLE REST, WE CAN GO TO TOWN.
YEAH!

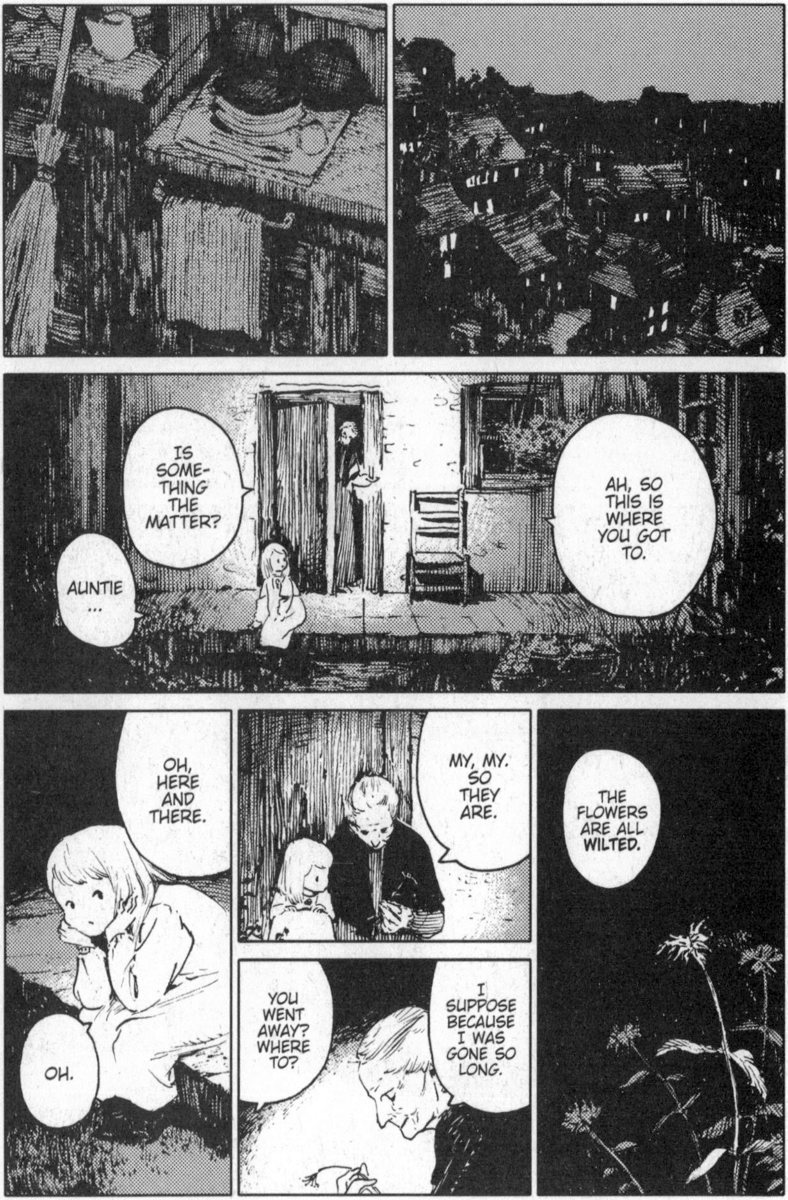
AH, SO THIS IS WHERE YOU GOT TO.
IS SOME-THING THE MATTER?
AUNTIE ...
THE FLOWERS ARE ALL WILTED.
MY, MY. SO THEY ARE.
I SUPPOSE BECAUSE I WAS GONE SO LONG.
YOU WENT AWAY? WHERE TO?
OH, HERE AND THERE.
OH.

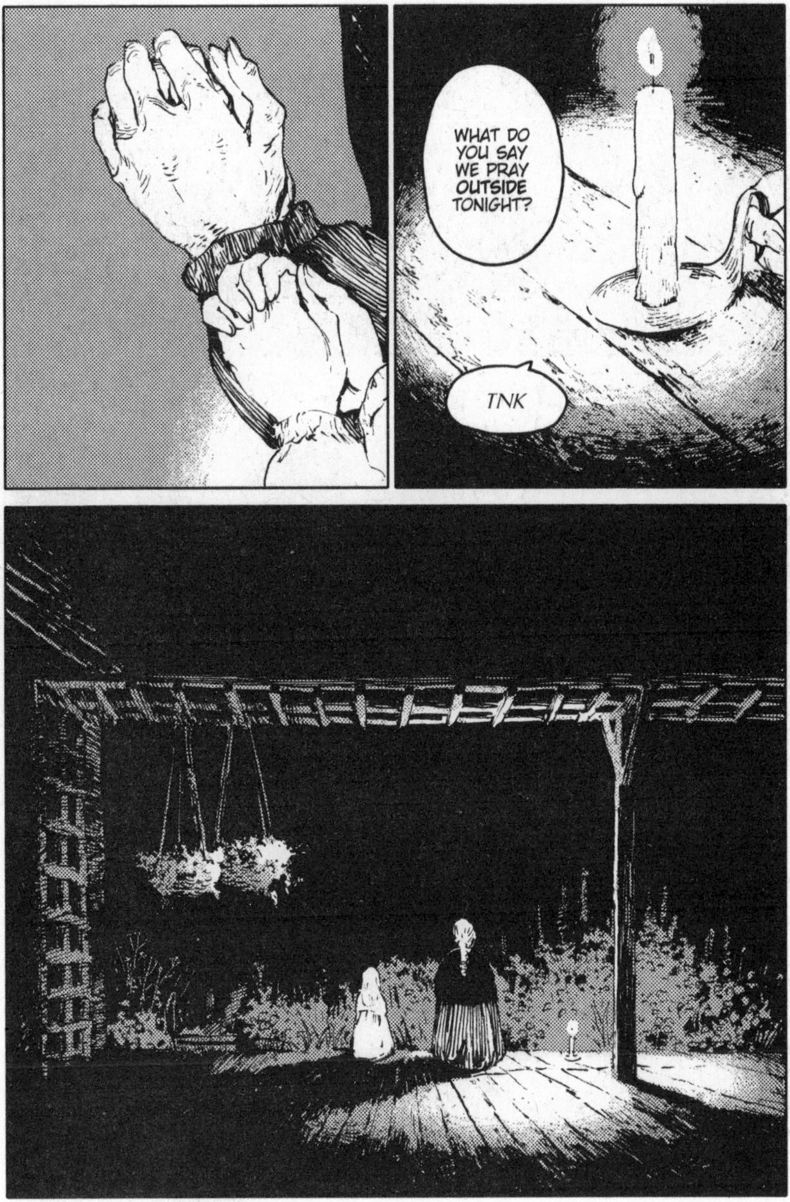
WHAT DO YOU SAY WE PRAY OUTSIDE TONIGHT?
TNK

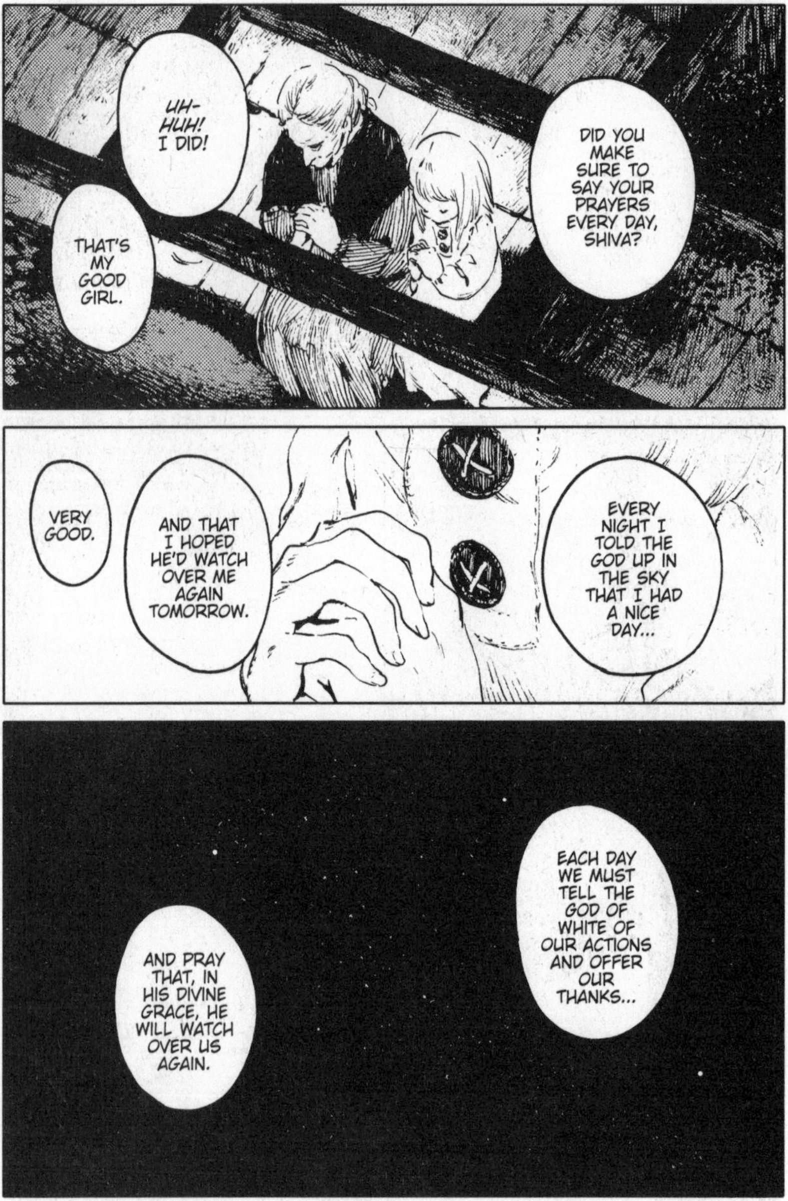
DID YOU MAKE SURE TO SAY YOUR PRAYERS EVERY DAY, SHIVA?
UH-HUH! I DID!
THAT'S MY GOOD GIRL.
EVERY NIGHT I TOLD THE GOD UP IN THE SKY THAT I HAD A NICE DAY...
AND THAT I HOPED HE'D WATCH OVER ME AGAIN TOMORROW.
VERY GOOD.
EACH DAY WE MUST TELL THE GOD OF WHITE OF OUR ACTIONS AND OFFER OUR THANKS...
AND PRAY THAT, IN HIS DIVINE GRACE, HE WILL WATCH OVER US AGAIN.

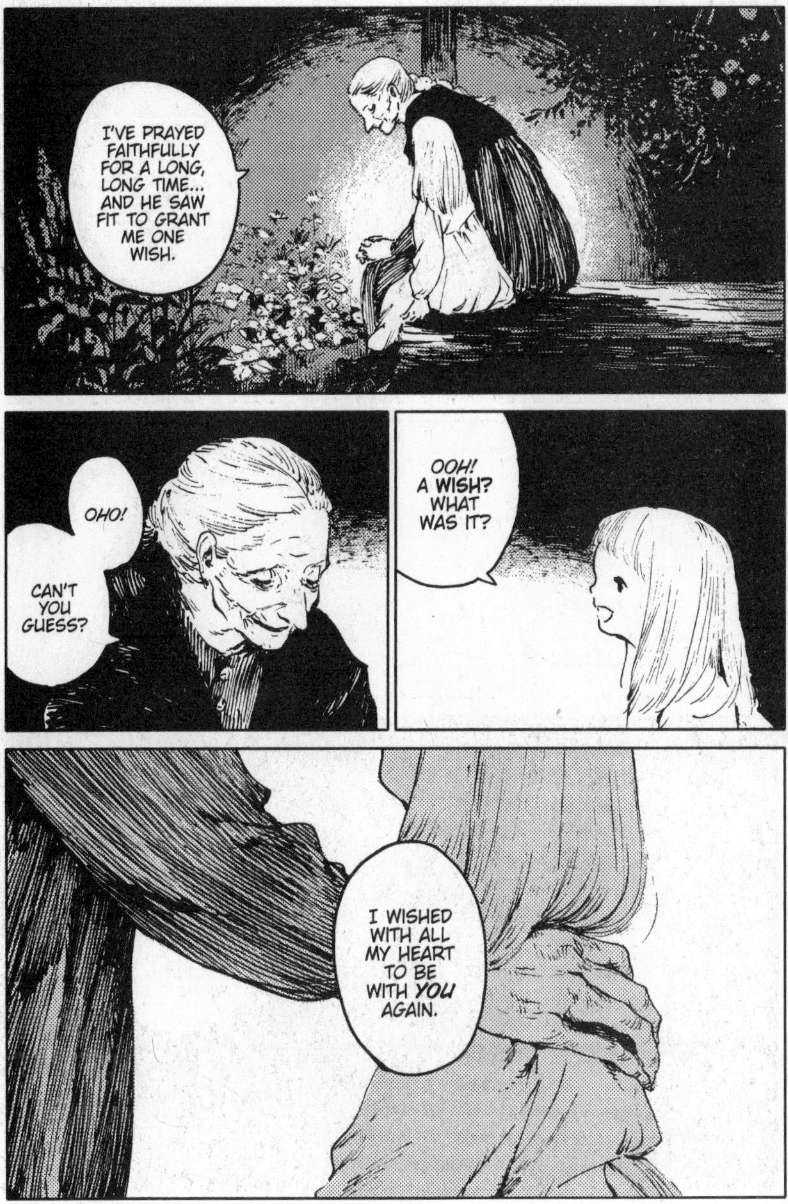
I'VE PRAYED FAITHFULLY FOR A LONG, LONG TIME... AND HE SAW FIT TO GRANT ME ONE WISH.
OOH! A *WISH*? WHAT WAS IT?
OHO!
CAN'T YOU GUESS?
I WISHED WITH ALL MY HEART TO BE WITH ***YOU*** AGAIN.

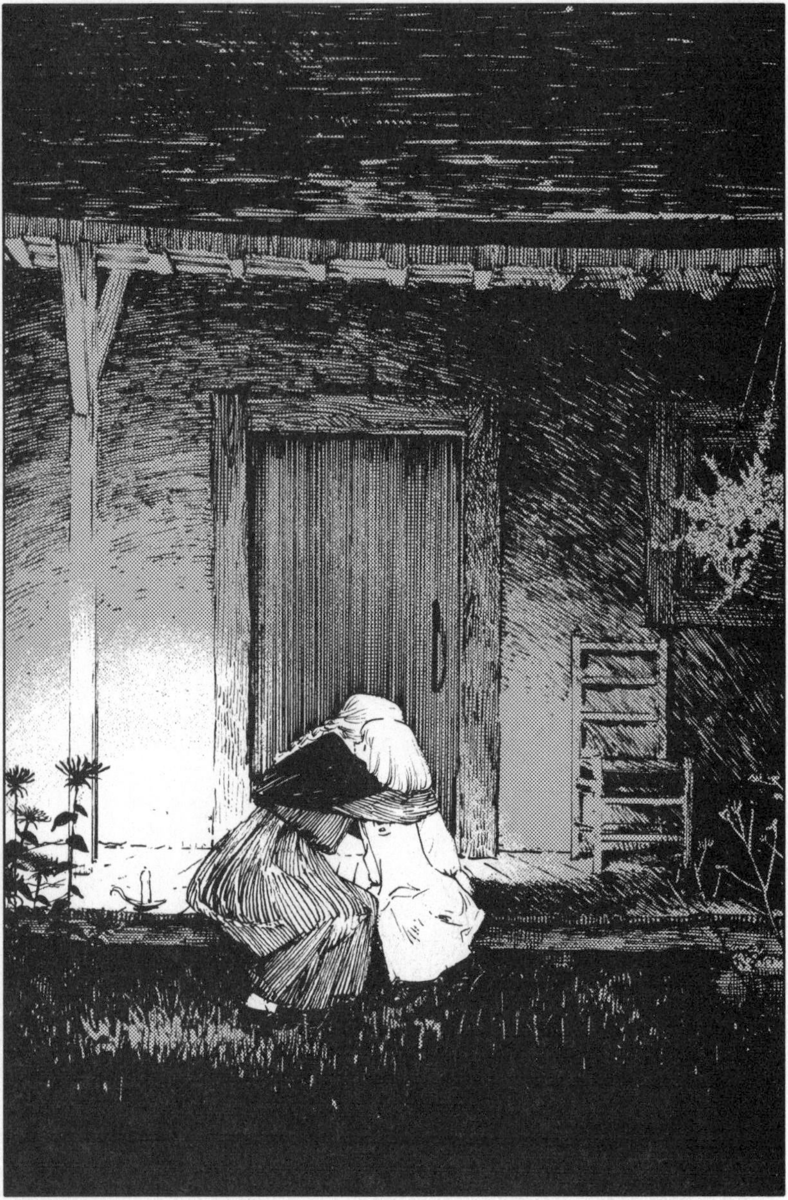

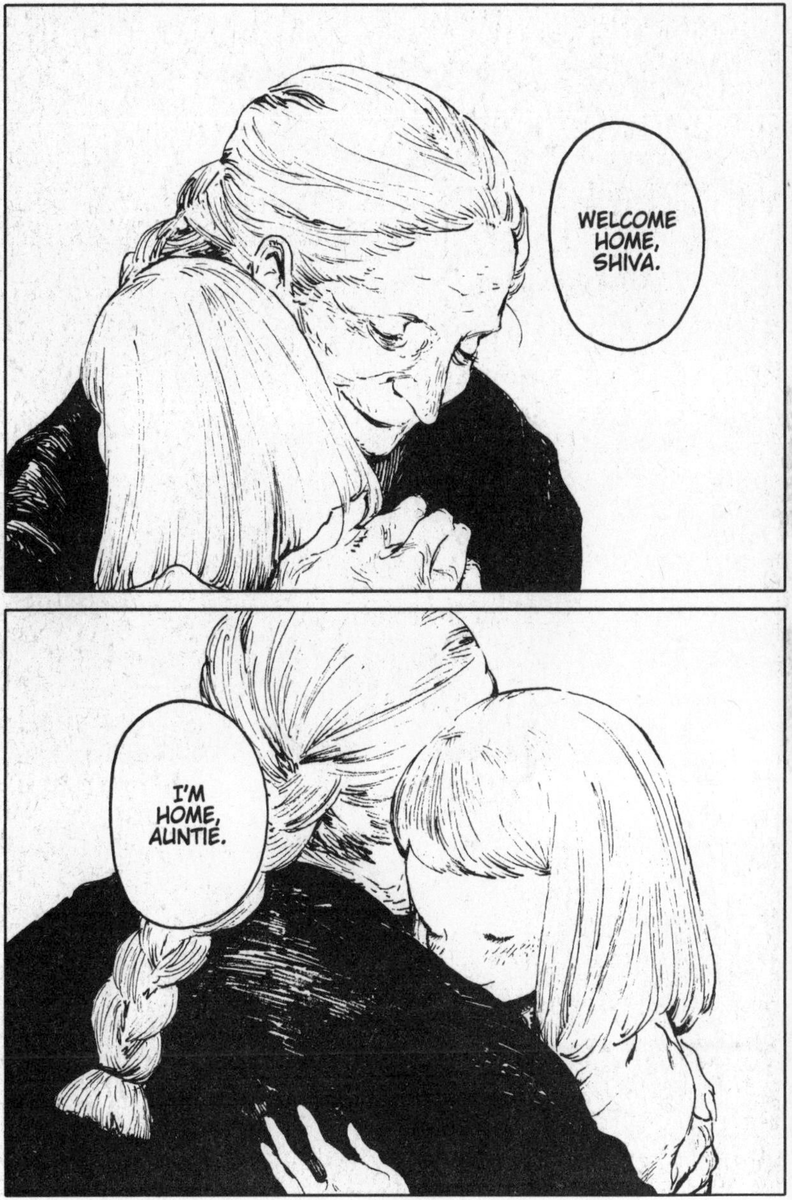
WELCOME HOME, SHIVA.
I'M HOME, AUNTIE.

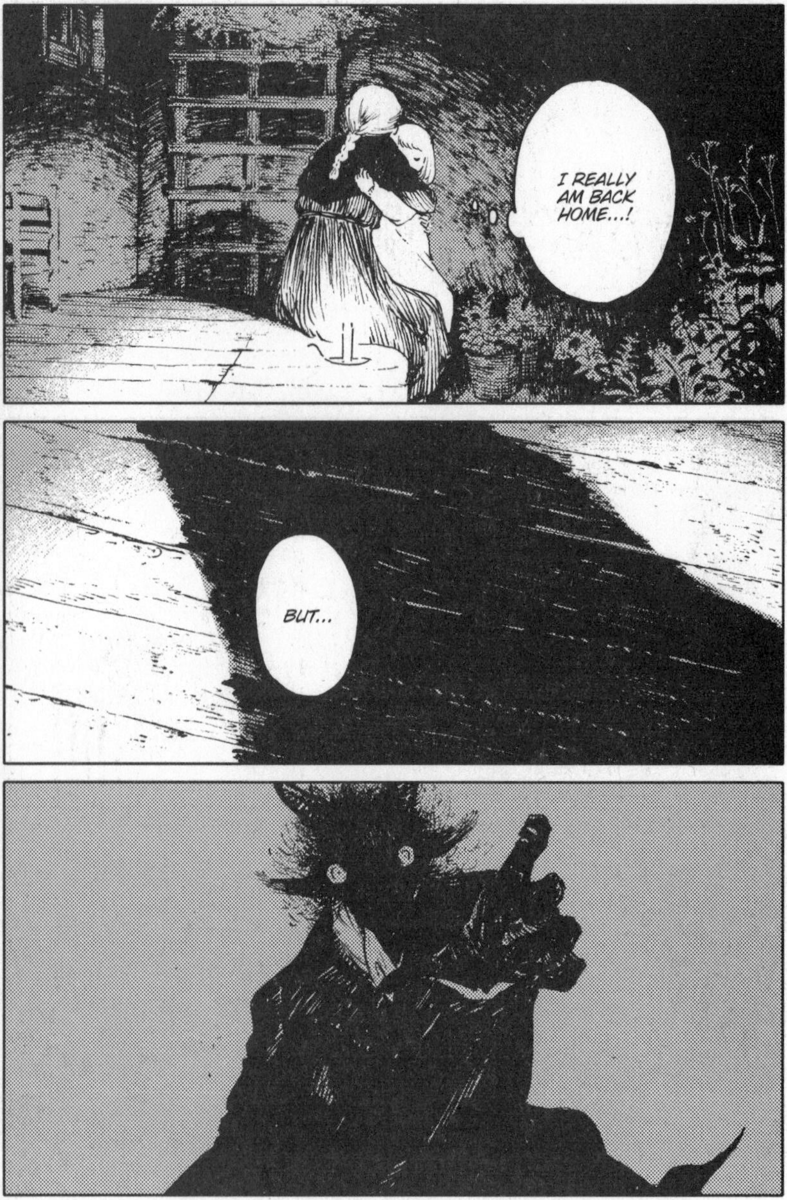
I REALLY AM BACK HOME...!
BUT...

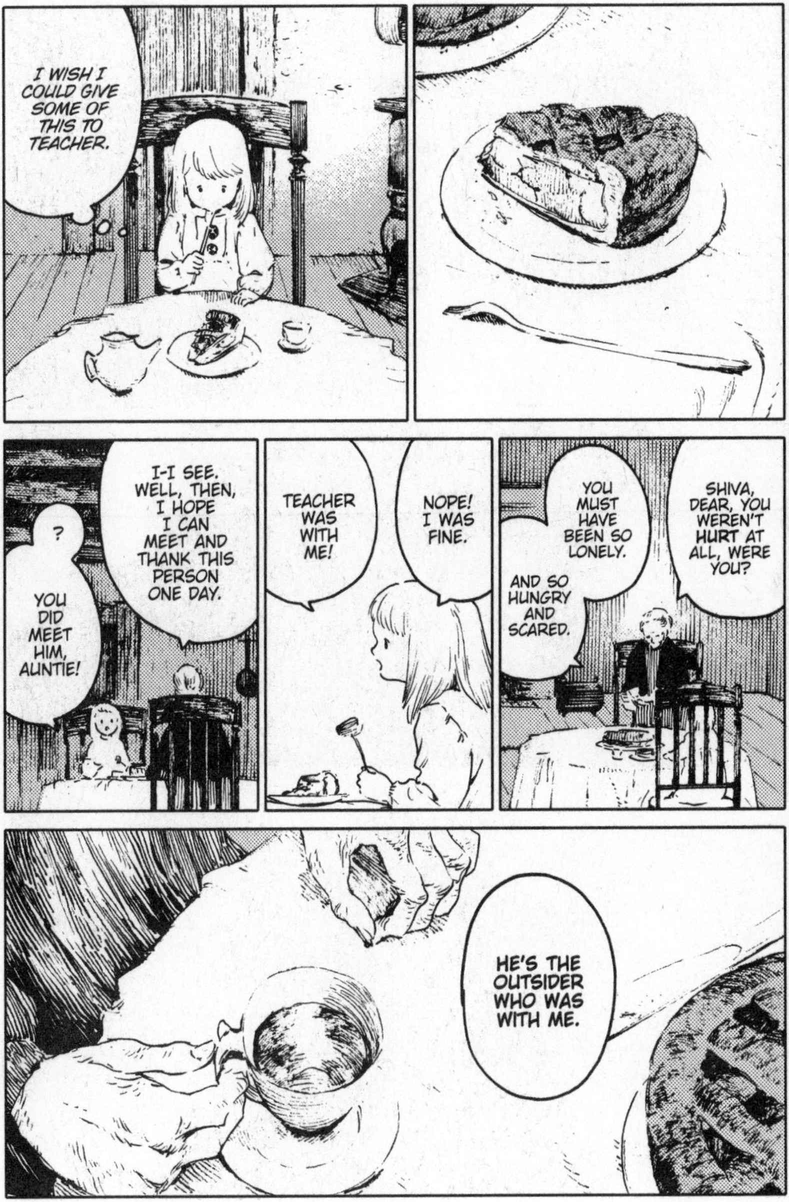
I WISH I COULD GIVE SOME OF THIS TO TEACHER.
SHIVA, DEAR, YOU WEREN'T HURT AT ALL, WERE YOU?
YOU MUST HAVE BEEN SO LONELY.
AND SO HUNGRY AND SCARED.
NOPE! I WAS FINE.
TEACHER WAS WITH ME!
I-I SEE. WELL, THEN, I HOPE I CAN MEET AND THANK THIS PERSON ONE DAY.
?
YOU DID MEET HIM, AUNTIE!
HE'S THE OUTSIDER WHO WAS WITH ME.

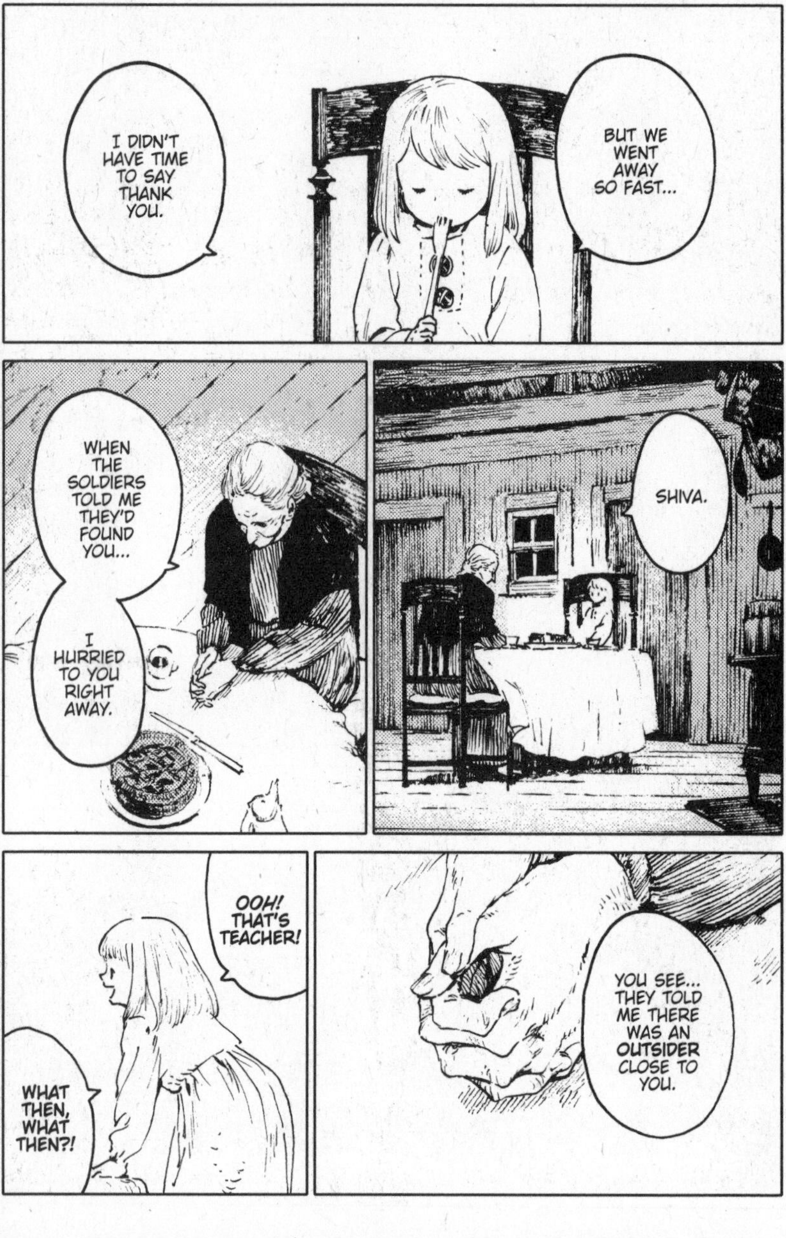
BUT WE WENT AWAY SO FAST...
I DIDN'T HAVE TIME TO SAY THANK YOU.
SHIVA.
WHEN THE SOLDIERS TOLD ME THEY'D FOUND YOU...
I HURRIED TO YOU RIGHT AWAY.
YOU SEE... THEY TOLD ME THERE WAS AN OUTSIDER CLOSE TO YOU.
OOH! THAT'S TEACHER!
WHAT THEN, WHAT THEN?!

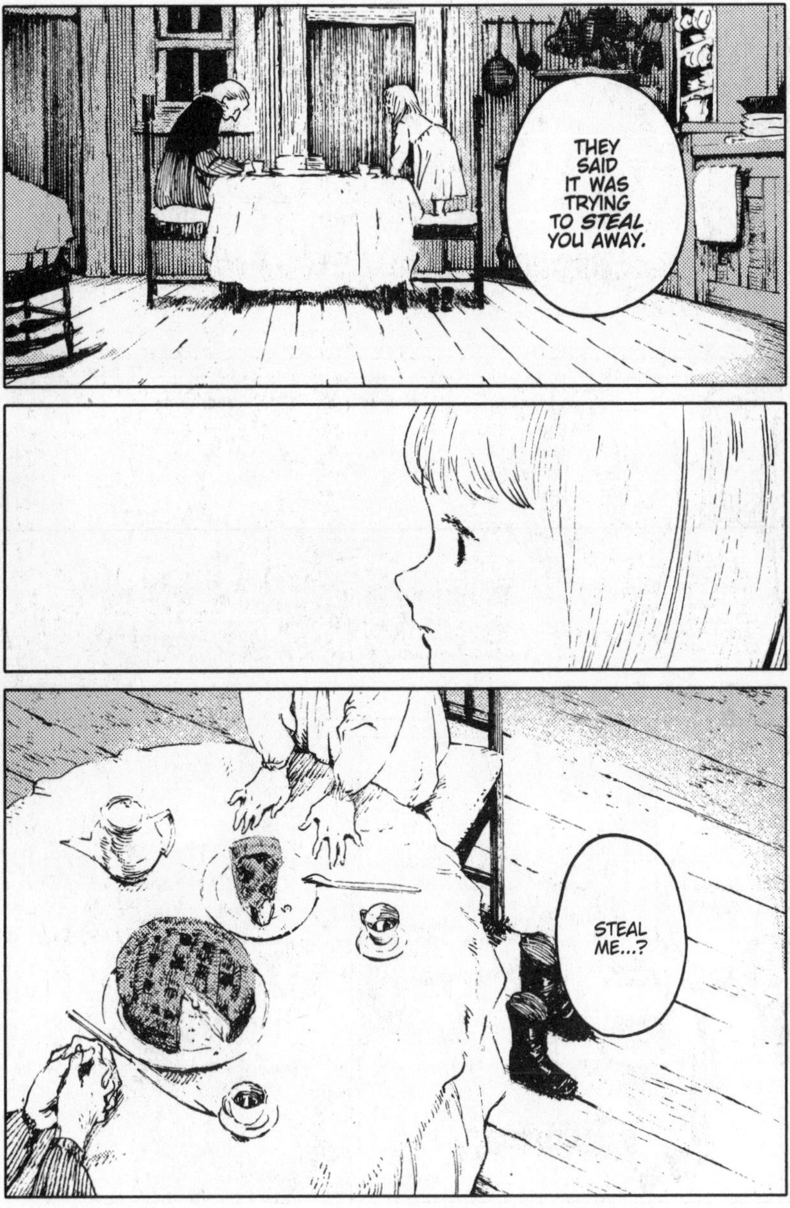
THEY SAID IT WAS TRYING TO *STEAL* YOU AWAY.
STEAL ME...?

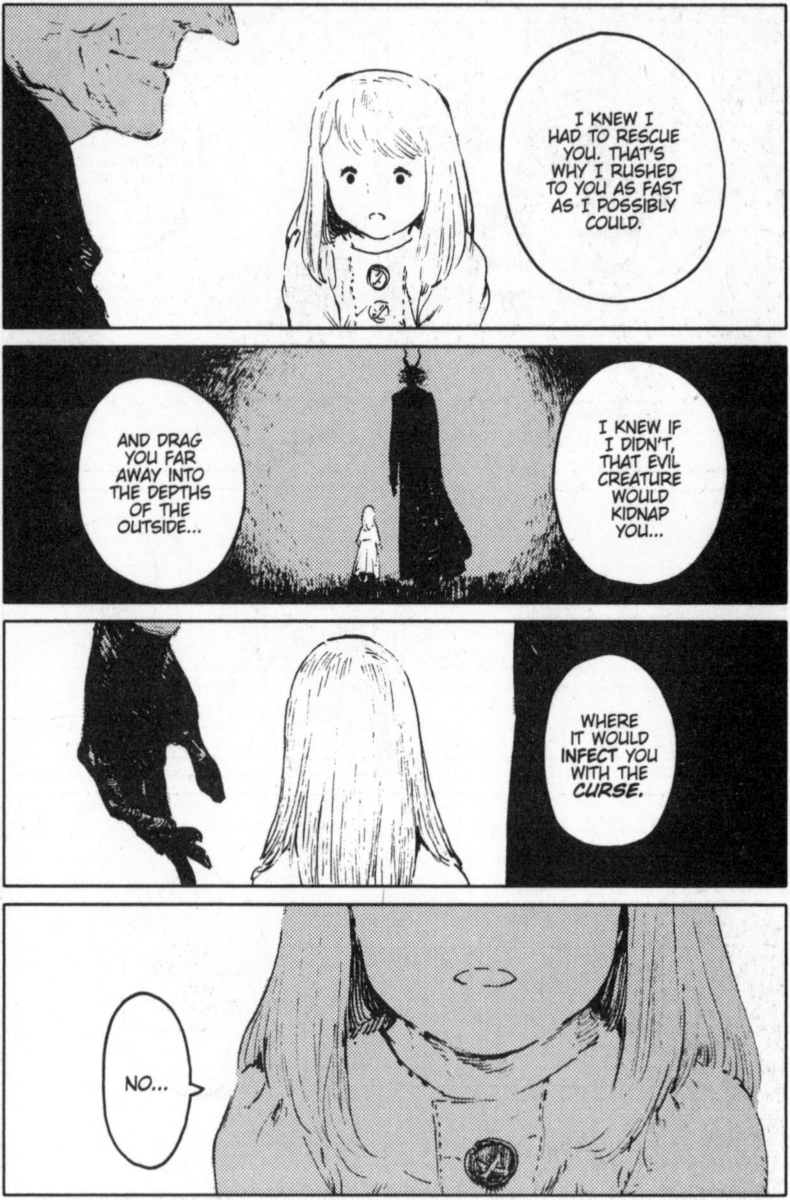
I KNEW I HAD TO RESCUE YOU. THAT'S WHY I RUSHED TO YOU AS FAST AS I POSSIBLY COULD.
I KNEW IF I DIDN'T, THAT EVIL CREATURE WOULD KIDNAP YOU...
AND DRAG YOU FAR AWAY INTO THE DEPTHS OF THE OUTSIDE...
WHERE IT WOULD INFECT YOU WITH THE *CURSE.*
NO...

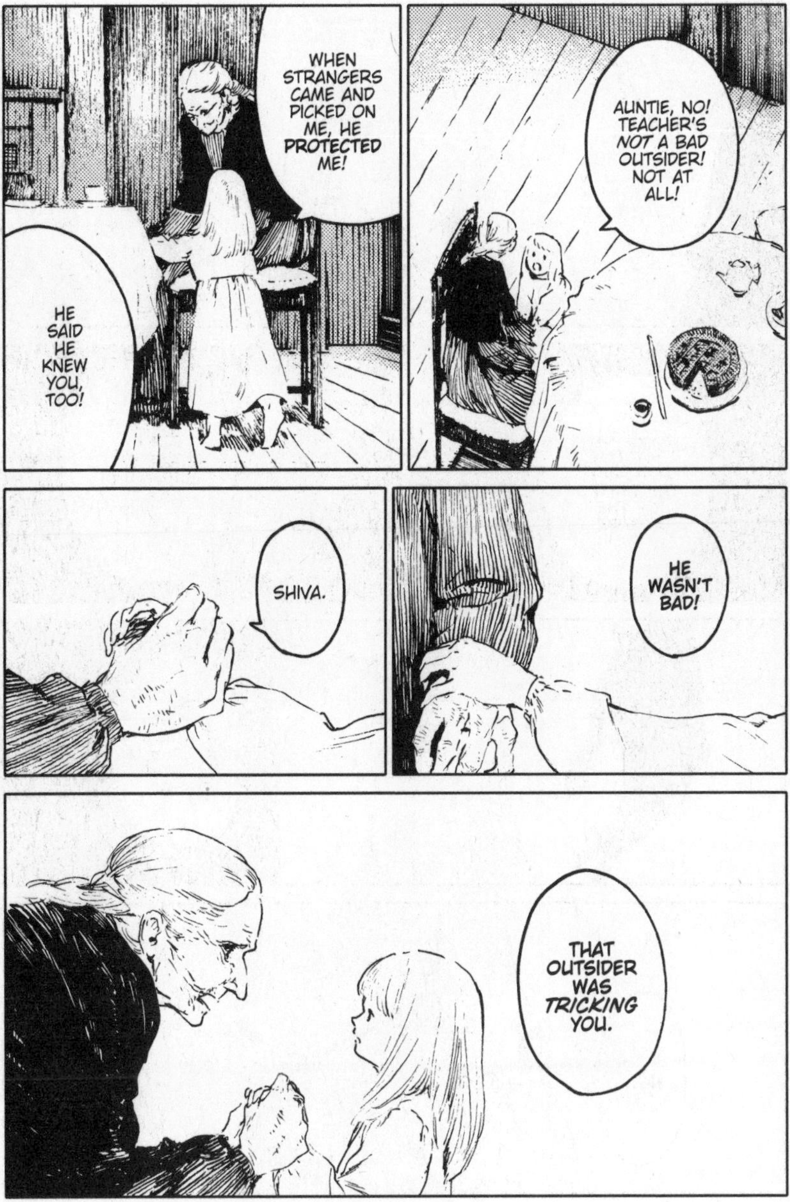
AUNTIE, NO! TEACHER'S *NOT* A BAD OUTSIDER! NOT AT ALL!
WHEN STRANGERS CAME AND PICKED ON ME, HE PROTECTED ME!
HE SAID HE KNEW YOU, TOO!
HE WASN'T BAD!
SHIVA.
THAT OUTSIDER WAS *TRICKING* YOU.

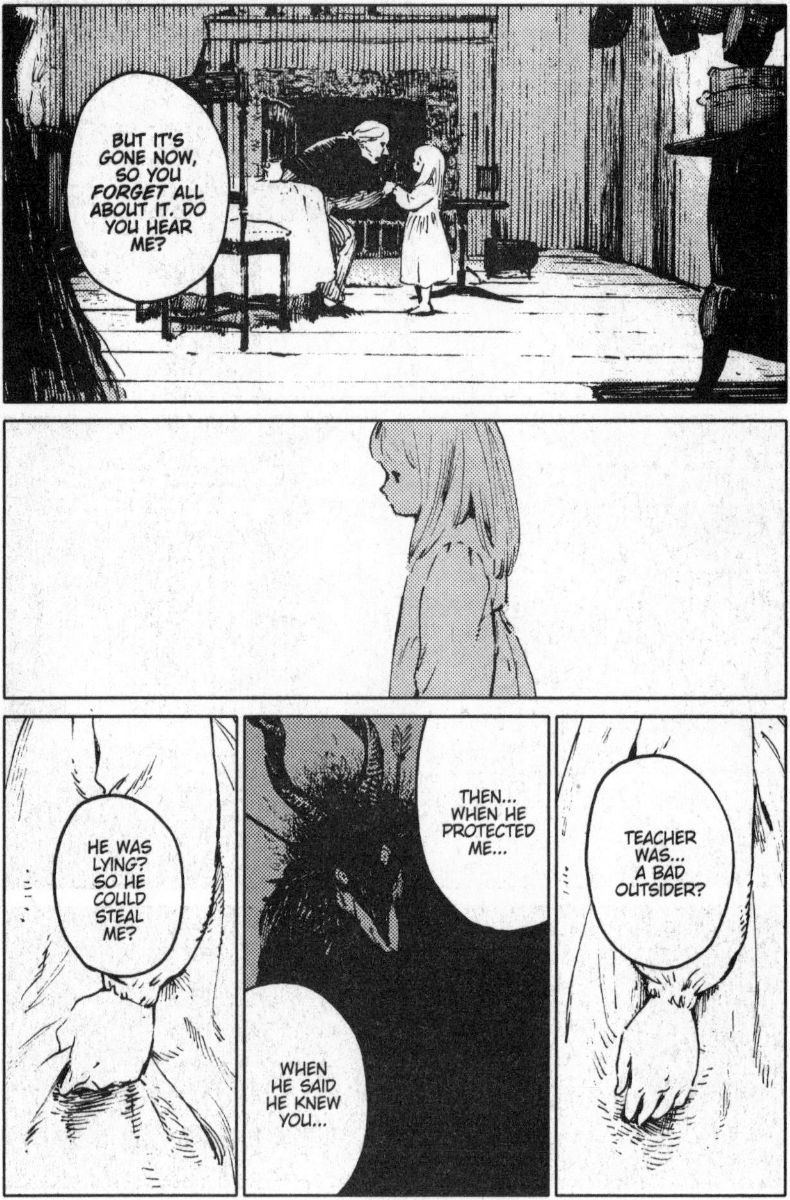
BUT IT'S GONE NOW, SO YOU *FORGET* ALL ABOUT IT. DO YOU HEAR ME?
TEACHER WAS... A BAD OUTSIDER?
THEN... WHEN HE PROTECTED ME...
WHEN HE SAID HE KNEW YOU...
HE WAS LYING? SO HE COULD STEAL ME?

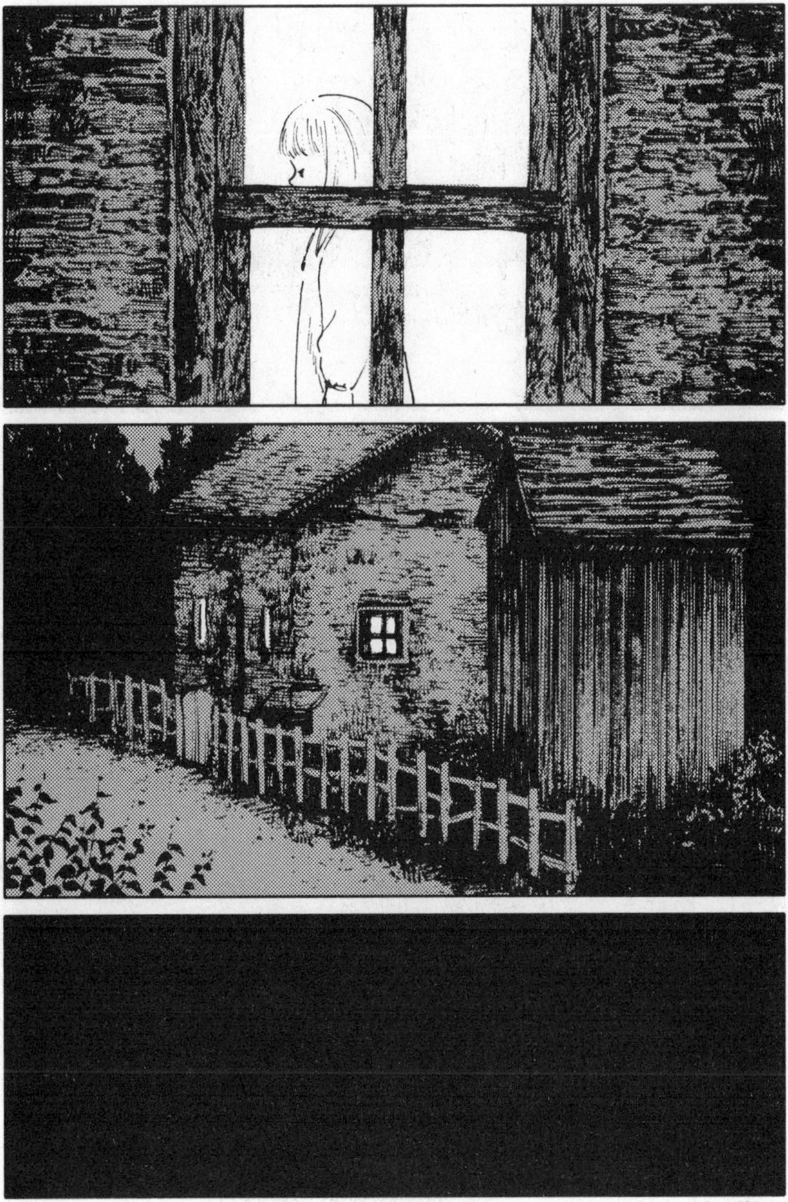

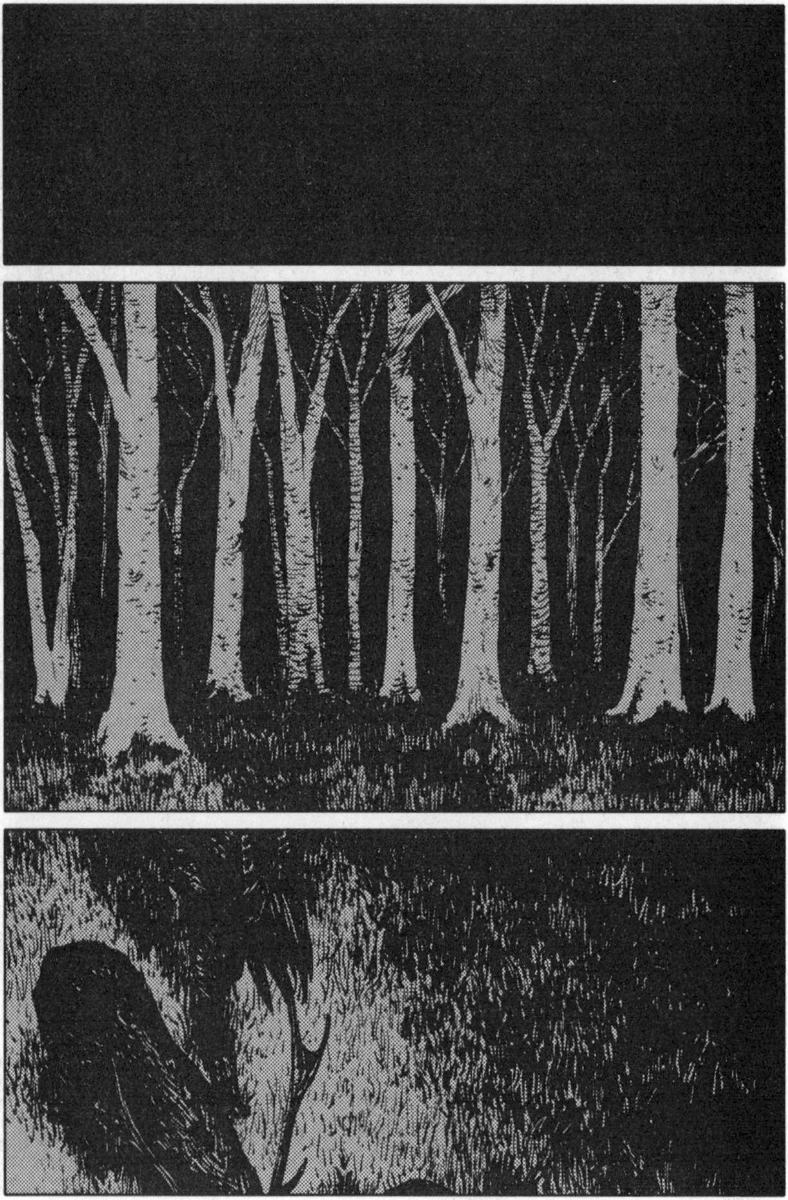

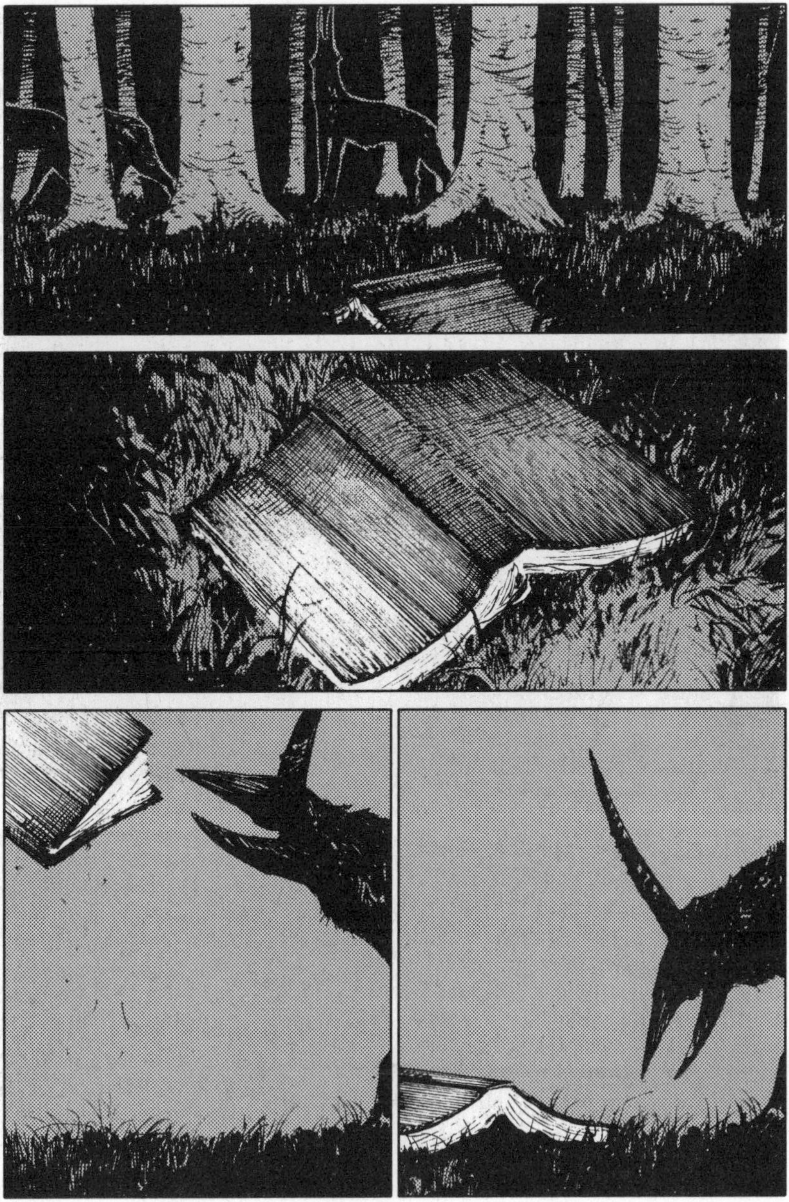

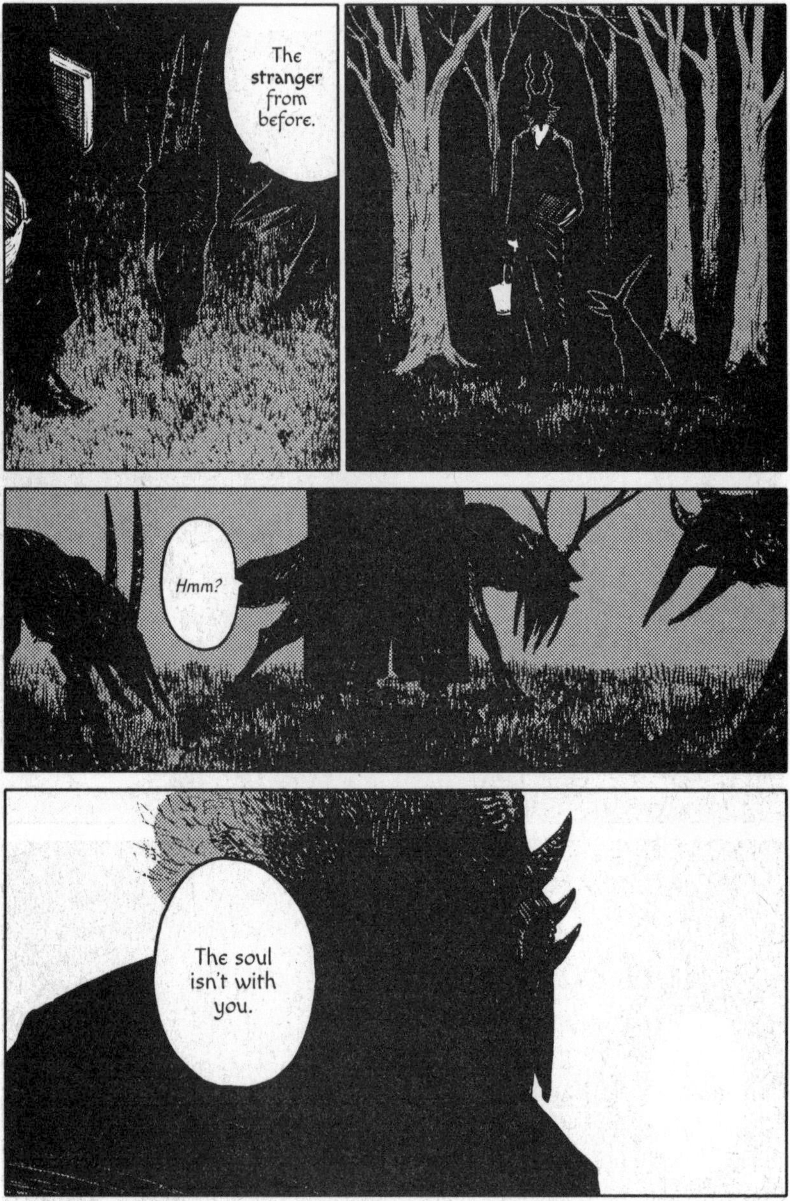
The stranger from before.
Hmm?
The soul isn't with you.

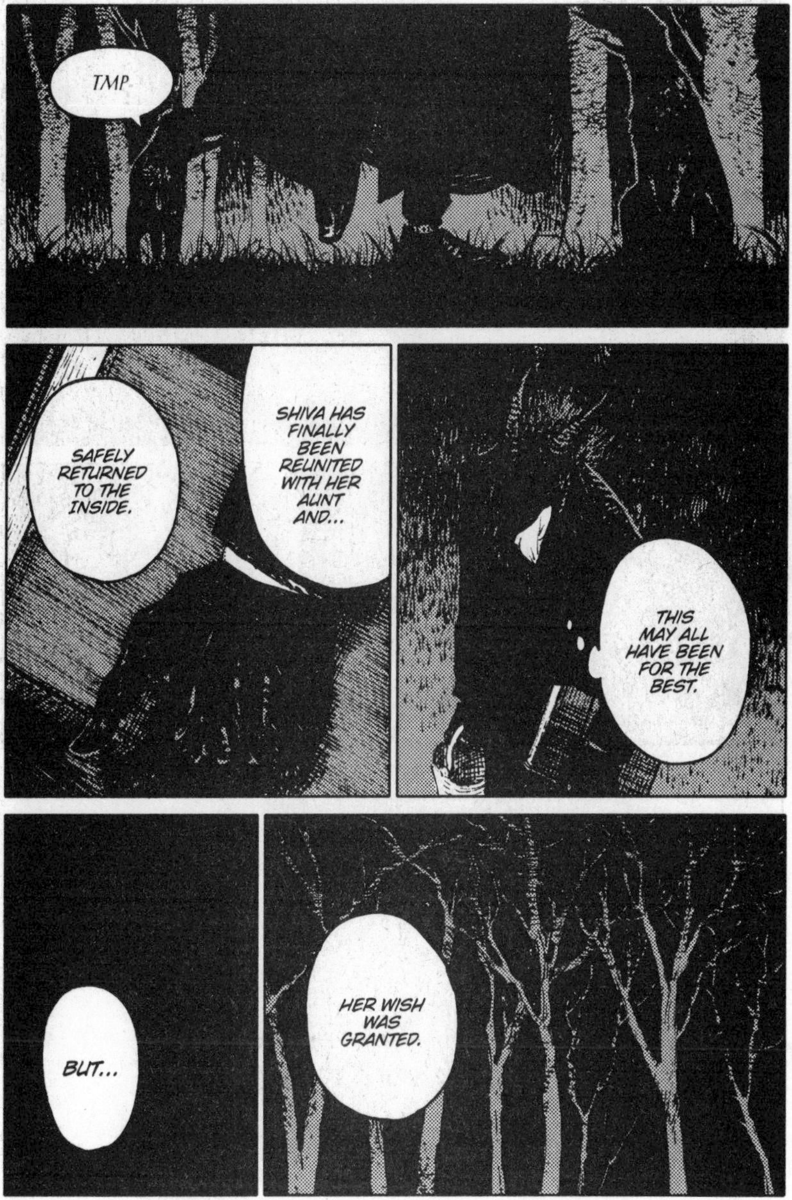
TMP
THIS MAY ALL HAVE BEEN FOR THE BEST.
SHIVA HAS FINALLY BEEN REUNITED WITH HER AUNT AND...
SAFELY RETURNED TO THE INSIDE.
HER WISH WAS GRANTED.
BUT...

LAST TIME, THE SOLDIERS TRIED TO KILL HER.
WHAT MADE THEM SUDDENLY DECIDE TO PROTECT HER?
WHY WAS HER AUNT EVEN HERE?
IS SHIVA...
TRULY SAFE WITH THEM...?

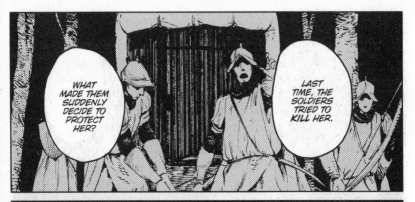

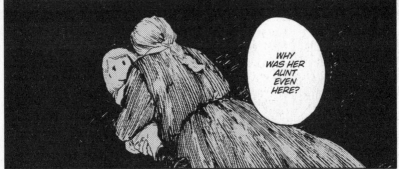

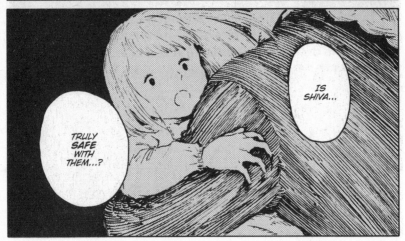

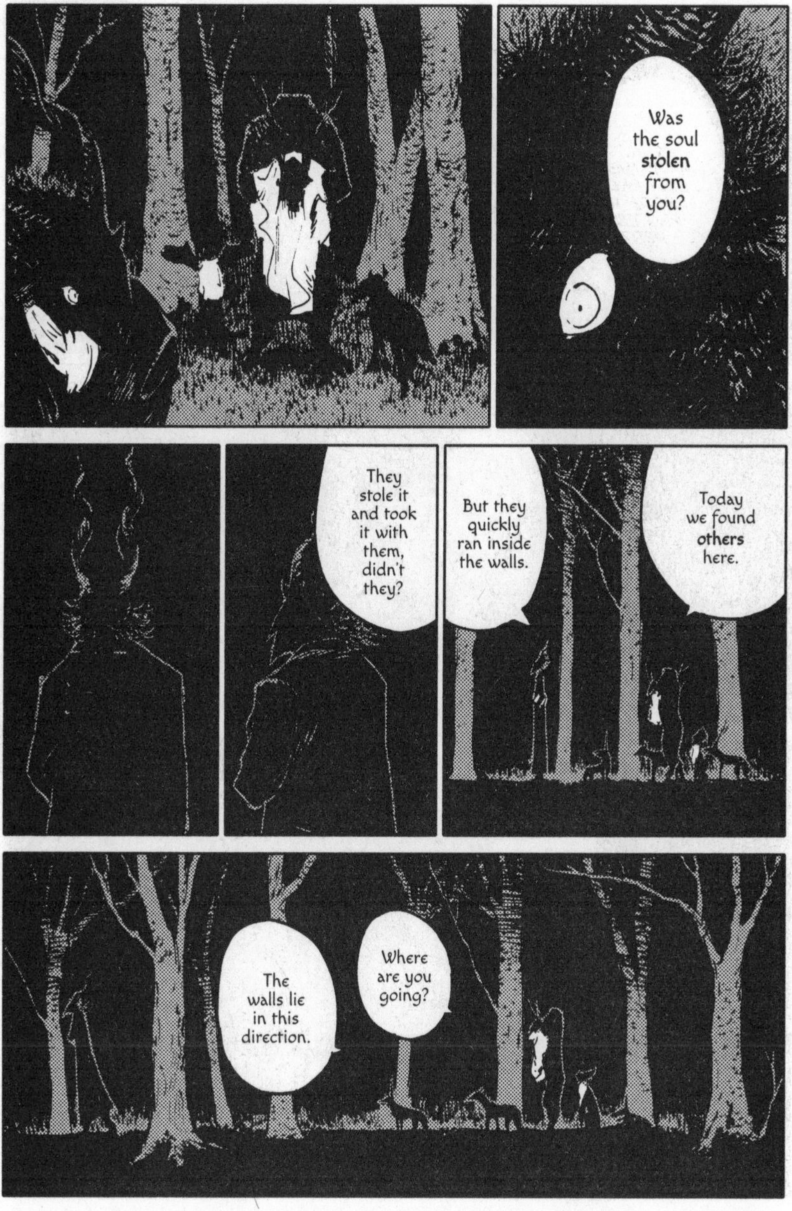
Was the soul stolen from you?
Today we found others here.
But they quickly ran inside the walls.
They stole it and took it with them, didn't they?
Where are you going?
The walls lie in this direction.

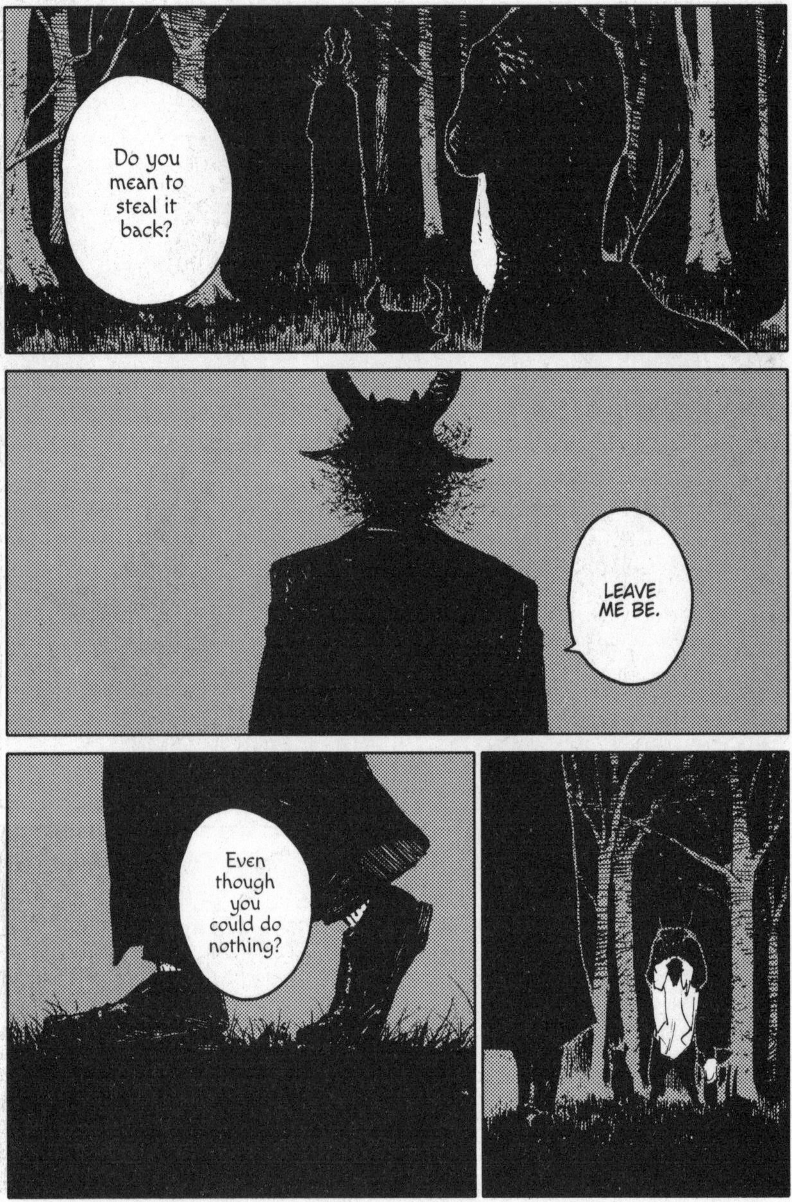
Do you mean to steal it back?
LEAVE ME BE.
Even though you could do nothing?

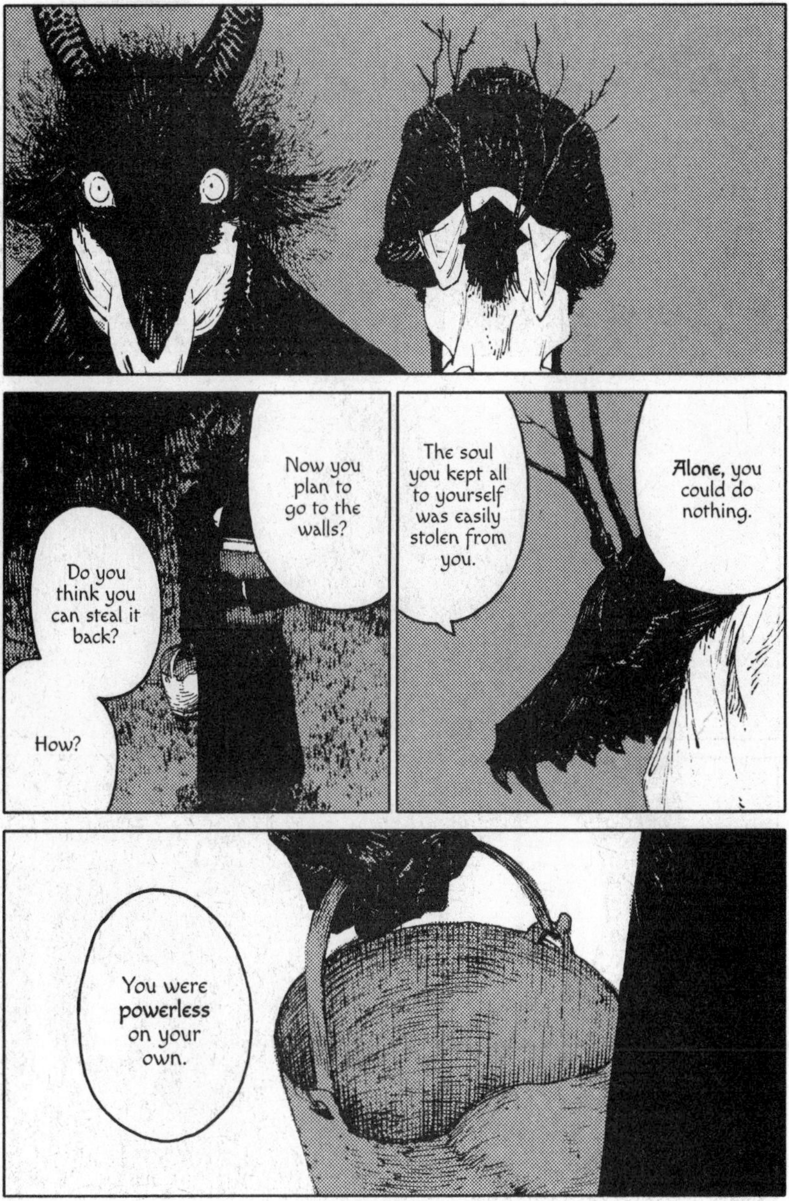
Alone, you could do nothing.
The soul you kept all to yourself was easily stolen from you.
Now you plan to go to the walls?
Do you think you can steal it back?
How?
You were powerless on your own.

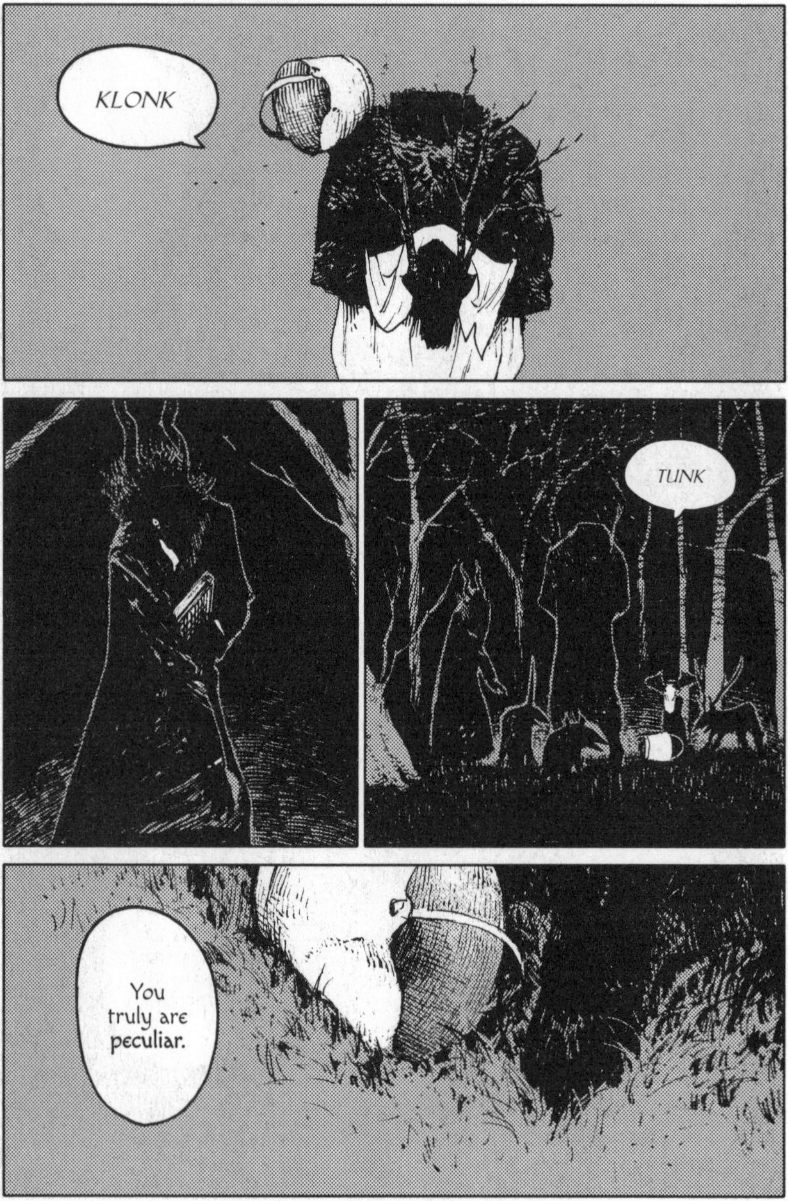
KLONK
TUNK
You truly are peculiar.

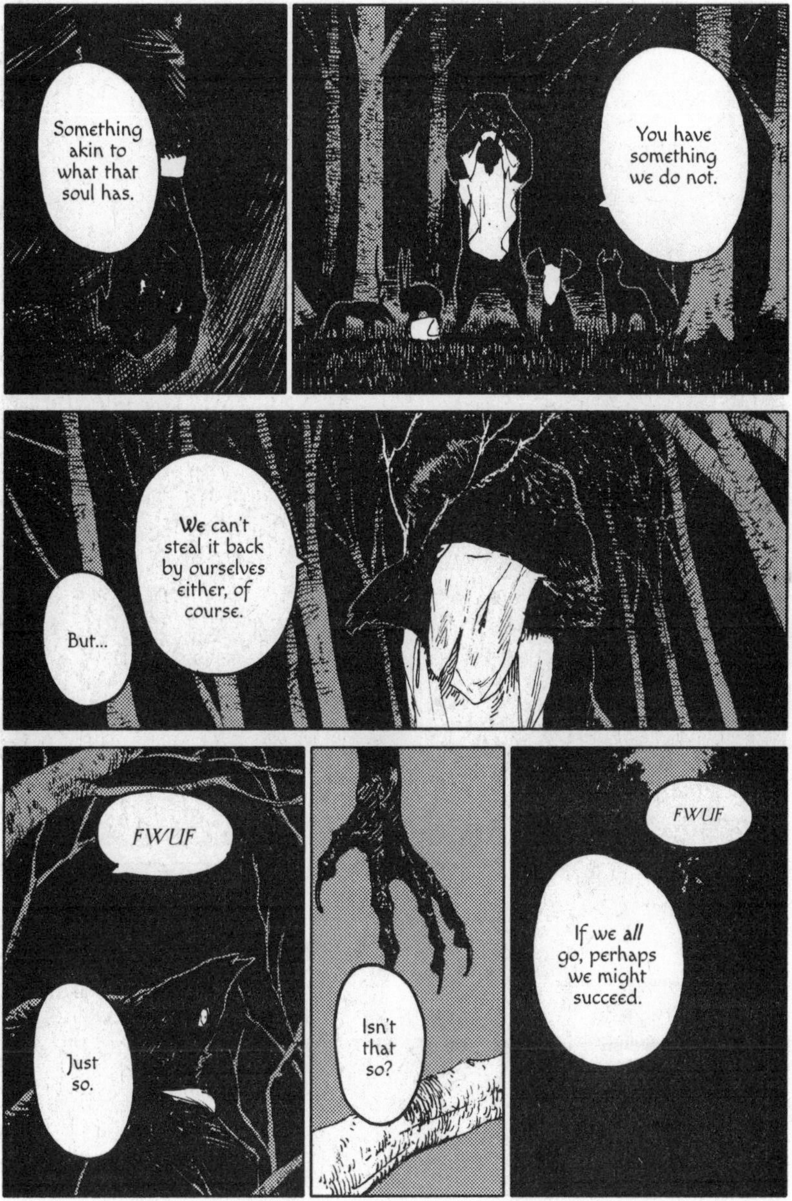
You have something we do not.
Something akin to what that soul has.
We can't steal it back by ourselves either, of course.
But...
FWUF
If we *all* go, perhaps we might succeed.
Isn't that so?
FWUF
Just so.

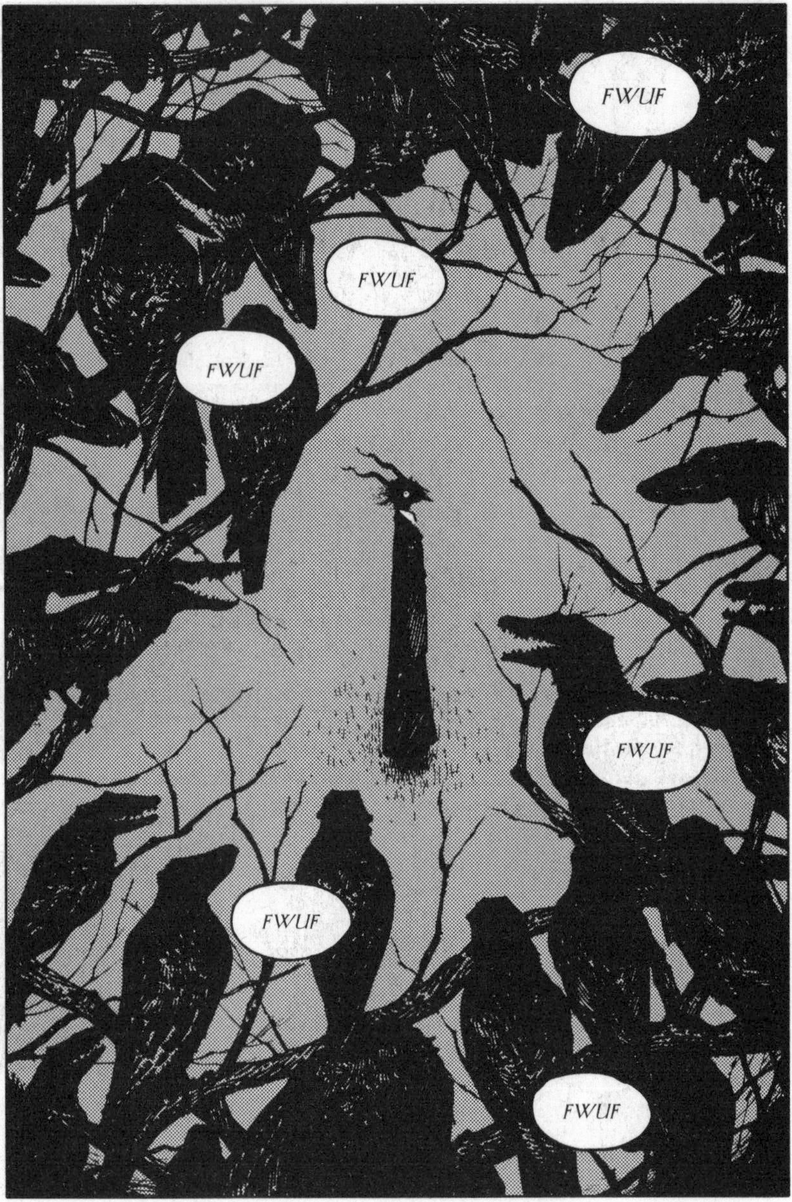
FWUF
FWUF
FWUF
FWUF
FWUF
FWUF

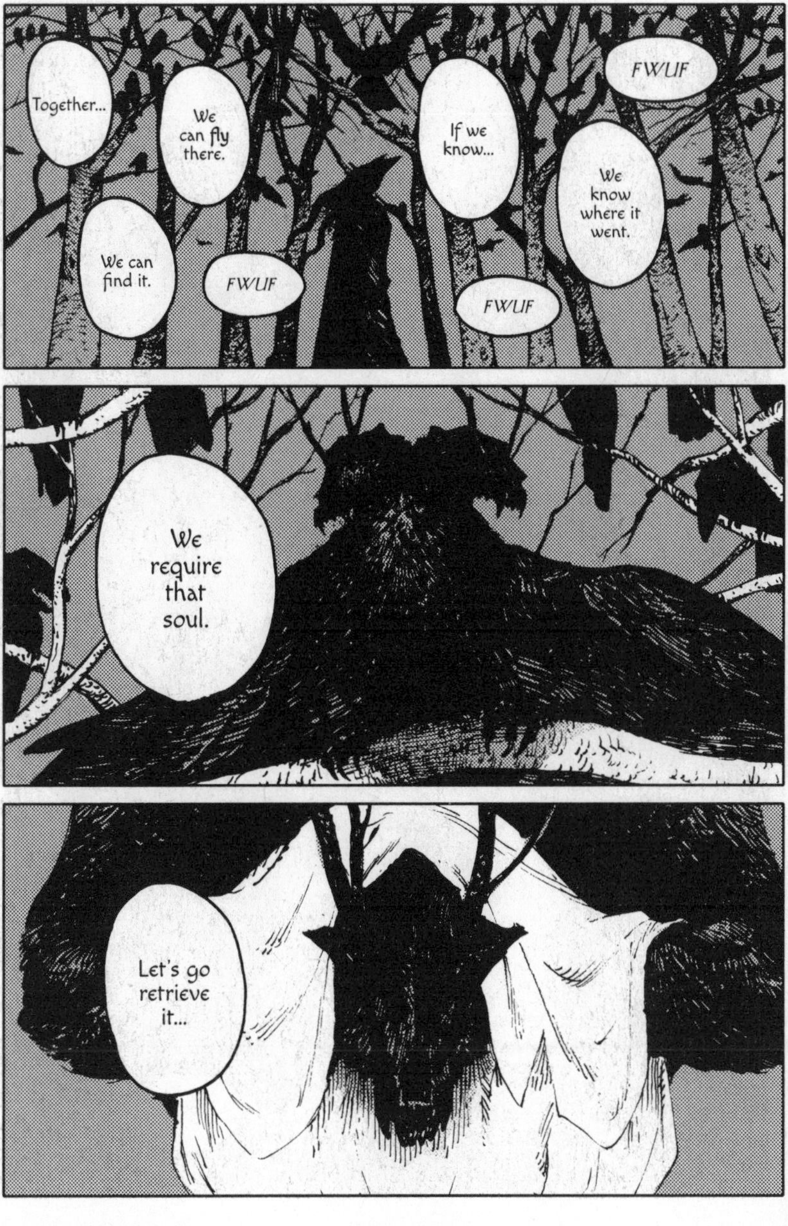
FWUF
We know where it went.
If we know...
FWUF
We can fly there.
FWUF
Together...
We can find it.
We require that soul.
Let's go retrieve it...

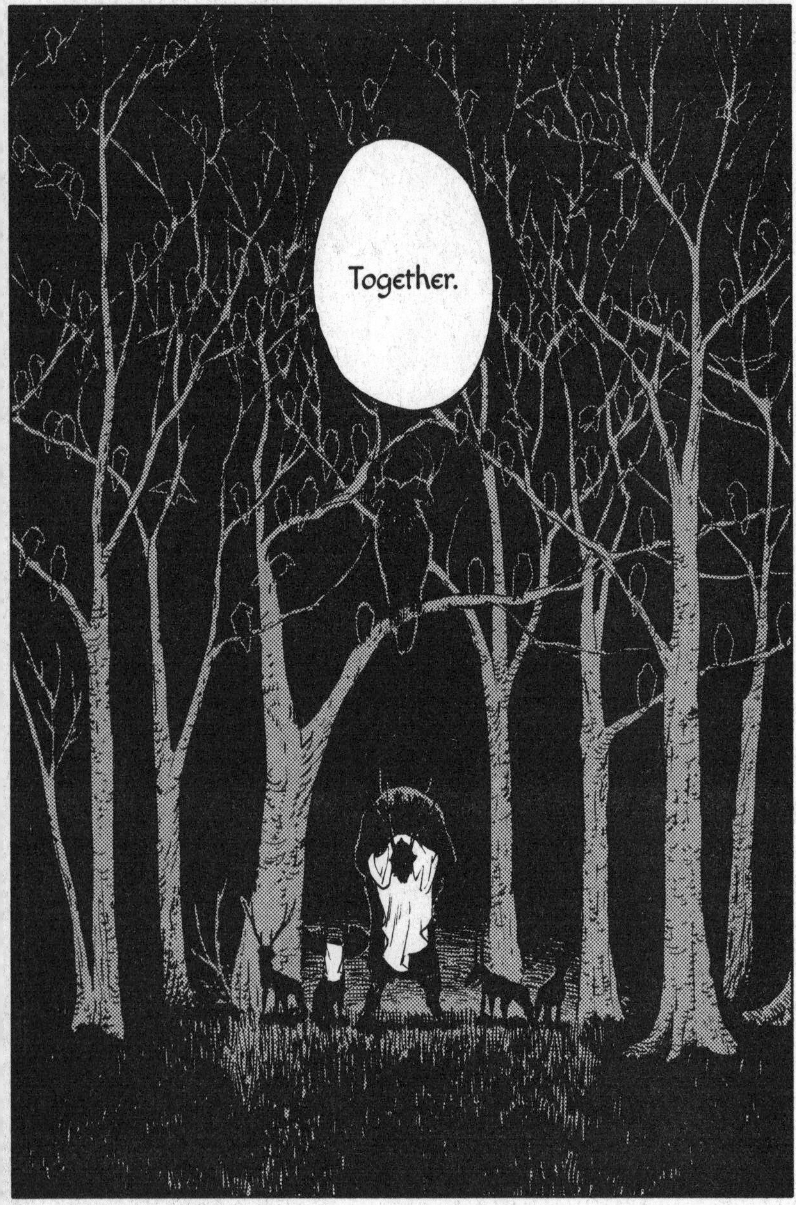
Together.

Siúil, a Rún
The Girl from the Other Side

Siúil, a Rún
The Girl from the Other Side

Chapter 13

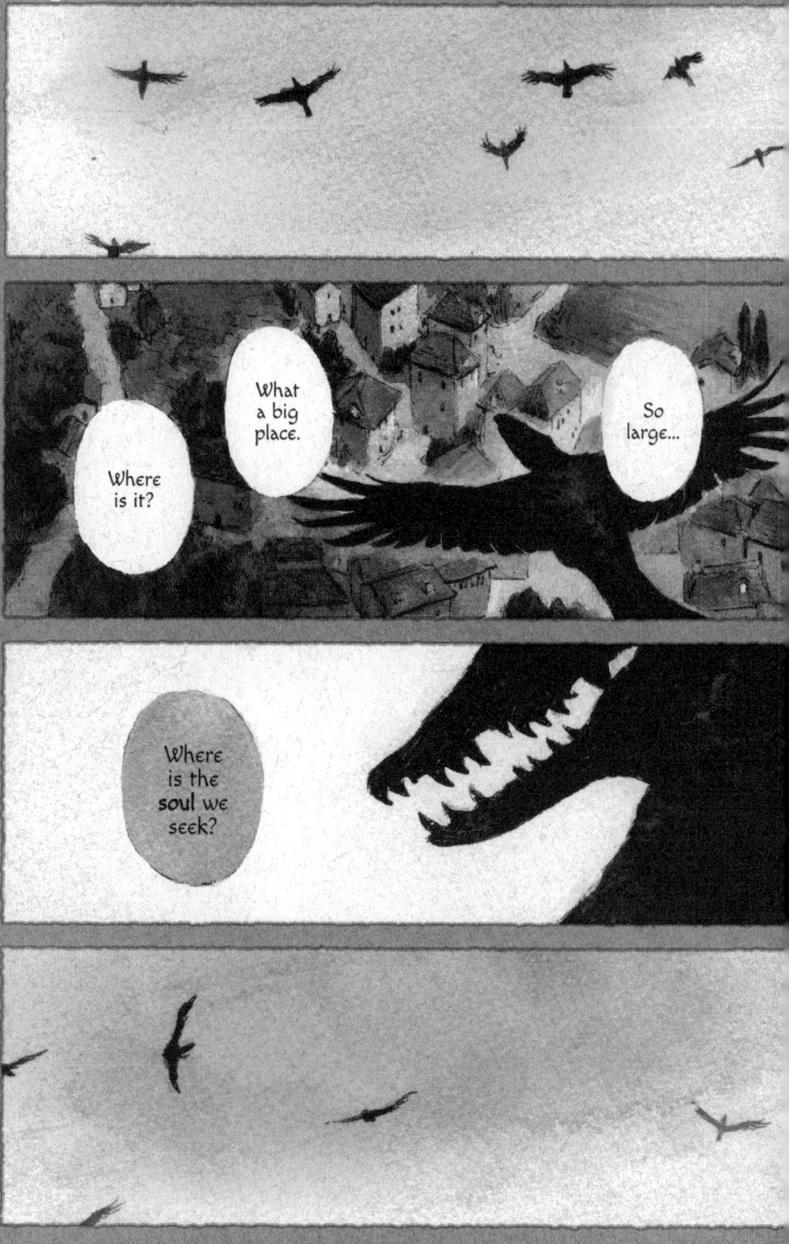

So large...
What a big place.
Where is it?
Where is the soul we seek?

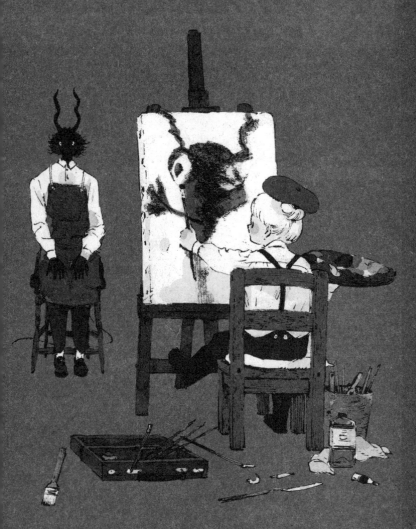

Deeve.

Chapter 13

teacher.

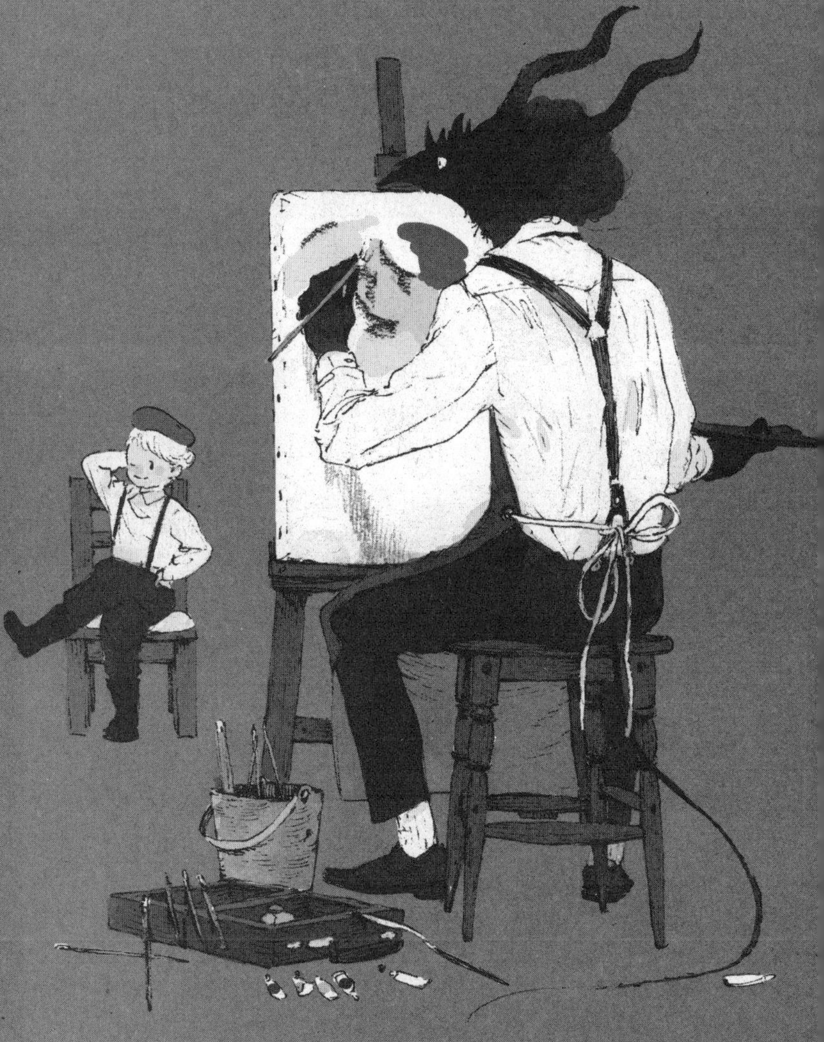

Siúil, a Rún
The Girl from the Other Side

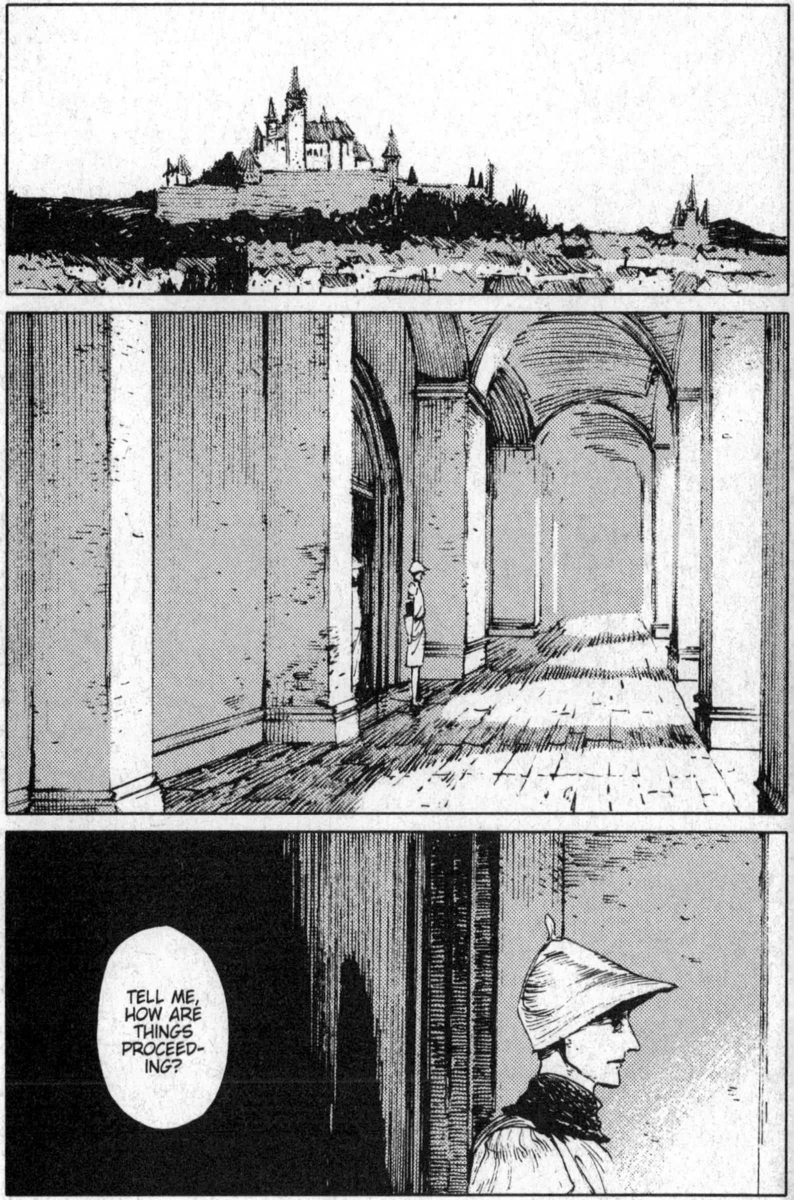
TELL ME, HOW ARE THINGS PROCEED- ING?

IT ALL GOES SMOOTHLY, SIRE.
WE CAPTURED THE GIRL, AS THE REVELATION DECREED...
AND WE HAVE MOVED HER TO THE EASTERN VILLAGE, WHERE WE NOW MONITOR HER.
AND WHAT SAYS OUR HEAVENLY FATHER?
I HAVE NOT YET RECEIVED A NEW REVELATION, SIRE.
I BEG YOU, GRANT US A LITTLE MORE TIME.
I SEE.

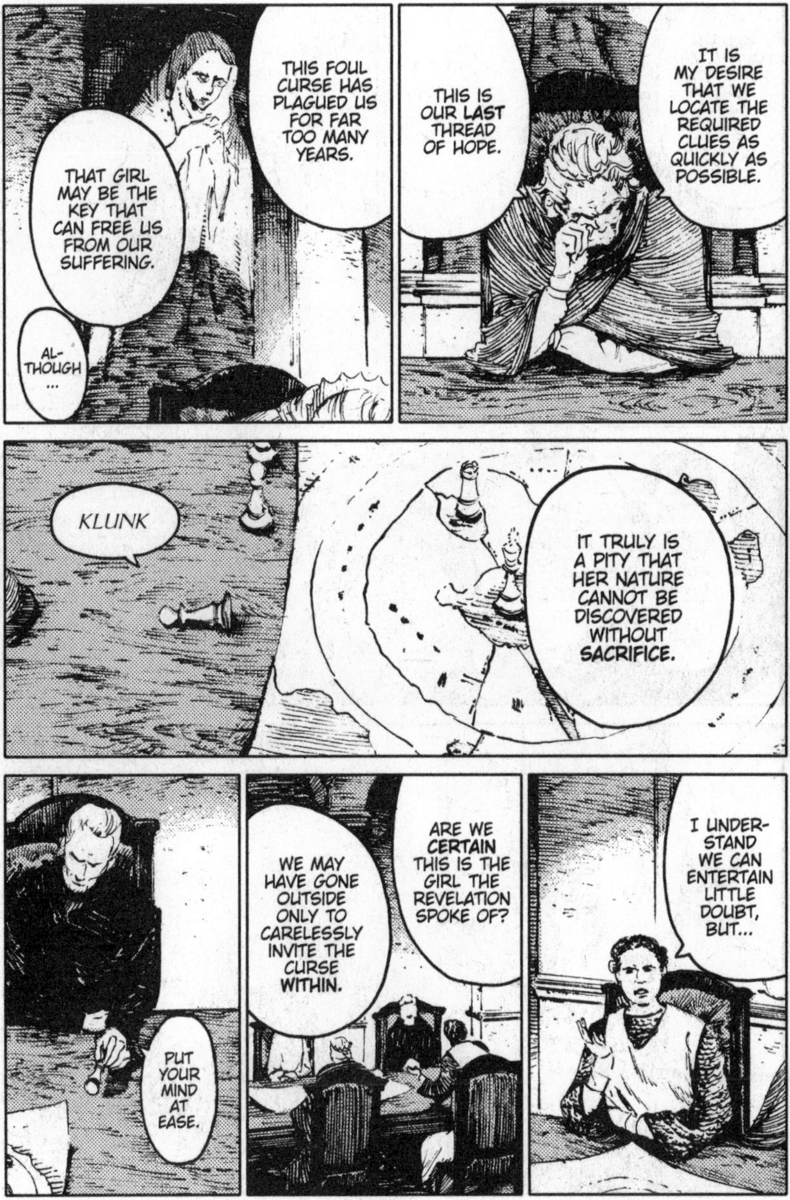
IT IS MY DESIRE THAT WE LOCATE THE REQUIRED CLUES AS QUICKLY AS POSSIBLE.
THIS IS OUR LAST THREAD OF HOPE.
THIS FOUL CURSE HAS PLAGUED US FOR FAR TOO MANY YEARS.
THAT GIRL MAY BE THE KEY THAT CAN FREE US FROM OUR SUFFERING.
AL-THOUGH ...
IT TRULY IS A PITY THAT HER NATURE CANNOT BE DISCOVERED WITHOUT SACRIFICE.
KLUNK
I UNDER-STAND WE CAN ENTERTAIN LITTLE DOUBT, BUT...
ARE WE CERTAIN THIS IS THE GIRL THE REVELATION SPOKE OF?
WE MAY HAVE GONE OUTSIDE ONLY TO CARELESSLY INVITE THE CURSE WITHIN.
PUT YOUR MIND AT EASE.

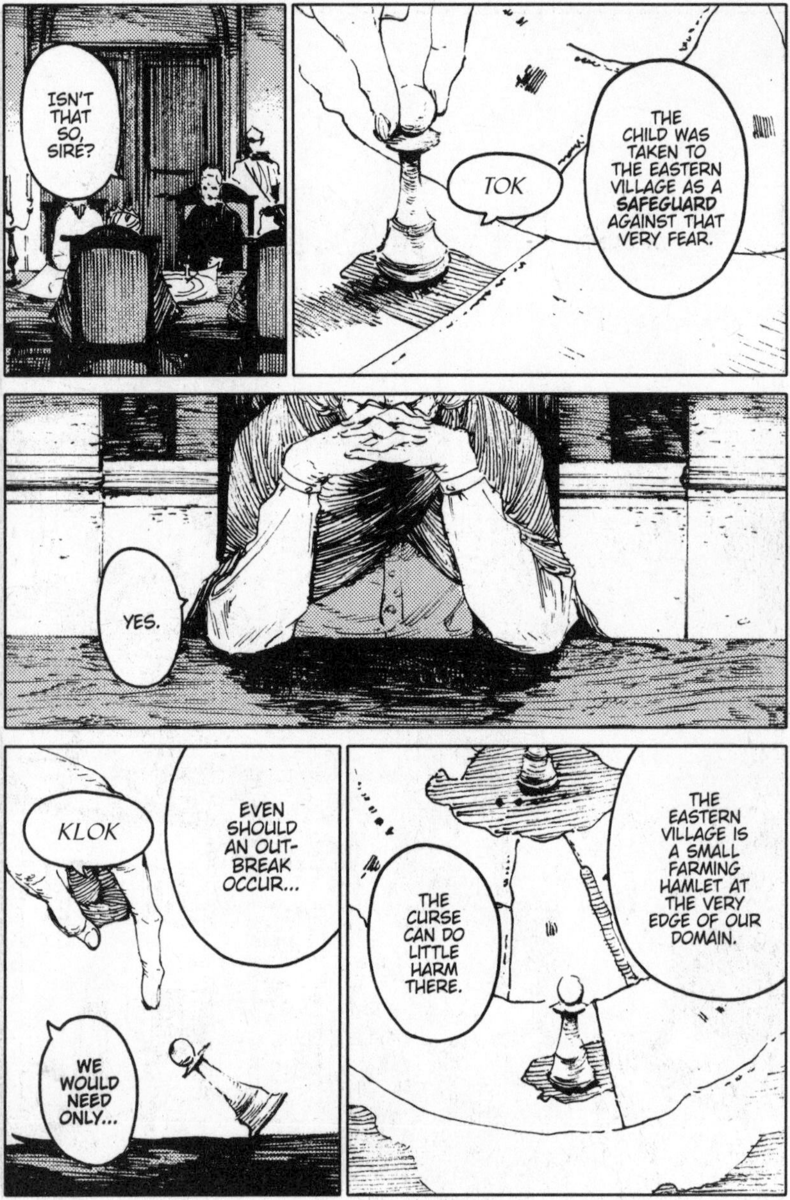
THE CHILD WAS TAKEN TO THE EASTERN VILLAGE AS A **SAFEGUARD** AGAINST THAT VERY FEAR.
TOK
ISN'T THAT SO, SIRE?
YES.
THE EASTERN VILLAGE IS A SMALL FARMING HAMLET AT THE VERY EDGE OF OUR DOMAIN.
THE CURSE CAN DO LITTLE HARM THERE.
EVEN SHOULD AN OUT-BREAK OCCUR...
KLOK
WE WOULD NEED ONLY...

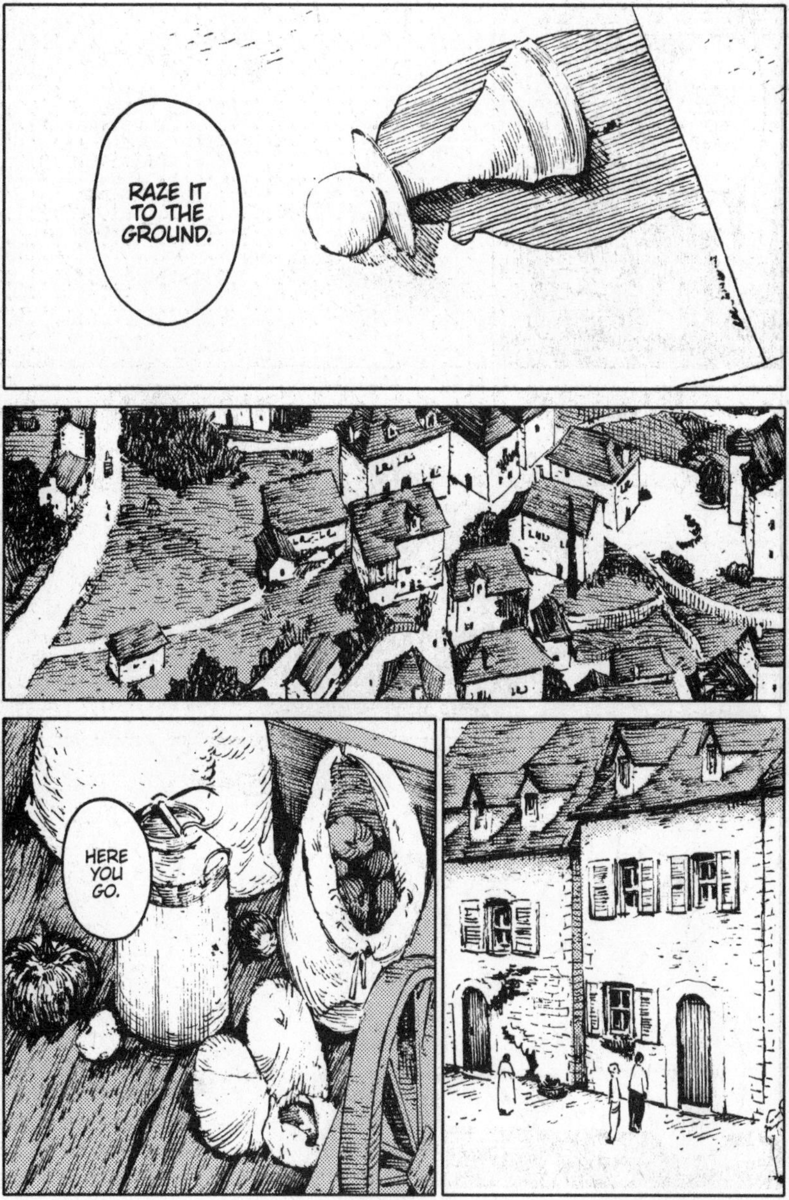
RAZE IT TO THE GROUND.
HERE YOU GO.

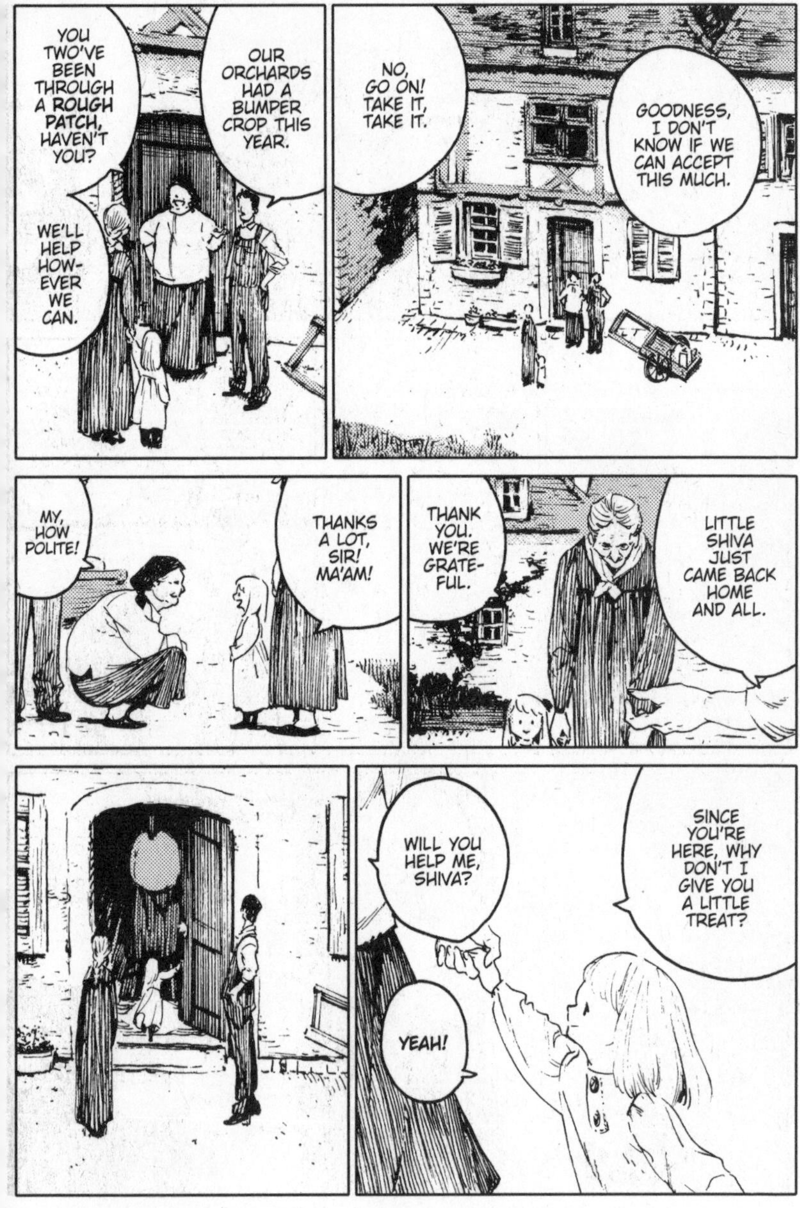
GOODNESS, I DON'T KNOW IF WE CAN ACCEPT THIS MUCH.
NO, GO ON! TAKE IT, TAKE IT.
OUR ORCHARDS HAD A BUMPER CROP THIS YEAR.
YOU TWO'VE BEEN THROUGH A ROUGH PATCH, HAVEN'T YOU?
WE'LL HELP HOW-EVER WE CAN.
LITTLE SHIVA JUST CAME BACK HOME AND ALL.
THANK YOU. WE'RE GRATE-FUL.
THANKS A LOT, SIR! MA'AM!
MY, HOW POLITE!
SINCE YOU'RE HERE, WHY DON'T I GIVE YOU A LITTLE TREAT?
WILL YOU HELP ME, SHIVA?
YEAH!

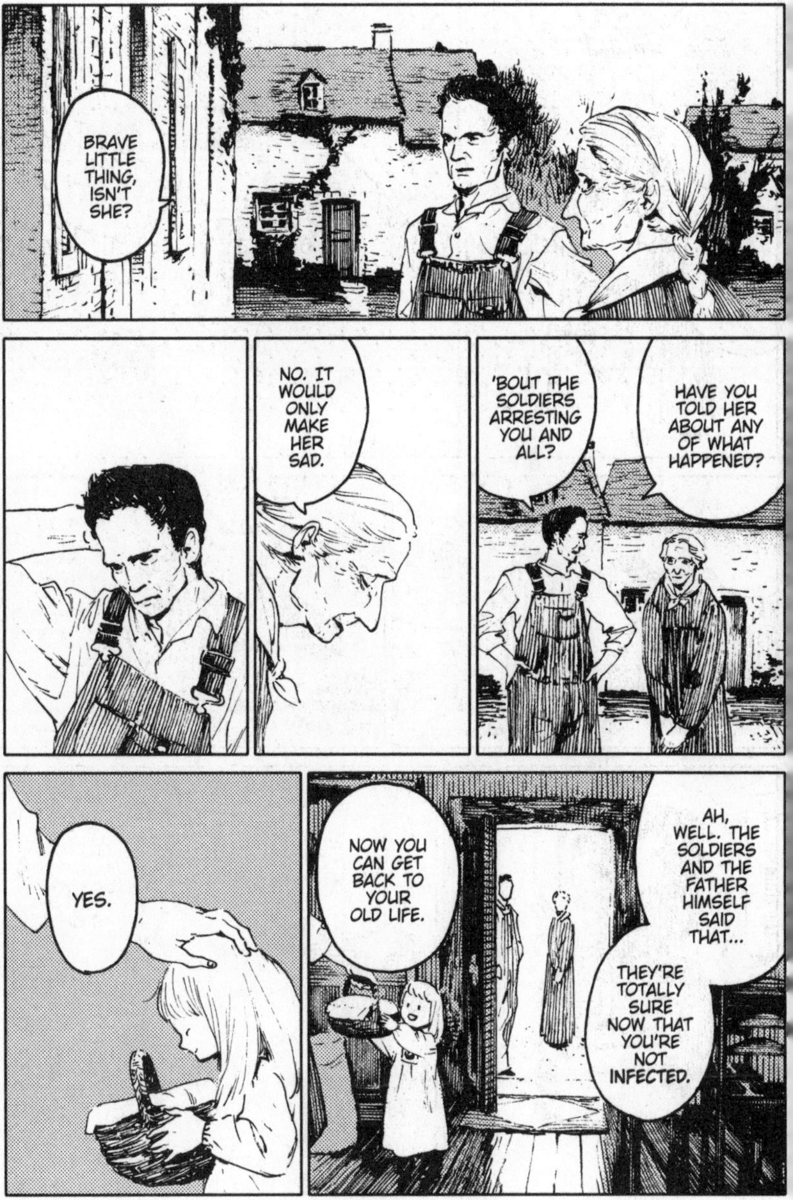
BRAVE LITTLE THING, ISN'T SHE?
HAVE YOU TOLD HER ABOUT ANY OF WHAT HAPPENED?
'BOUT THE SOLDIERS ARRESTING YOU AND ALL?
NO. IT WOULD ONLY MAKE HER SAD.
AH, WELL. THE SOLDIERS AND THE FATHER HIMSELF SAID THAT...
THEY'RE TOTALLY SURE NOW THAT YOU'RE NOT INFECTED.
NOW YOU CAN GET BACK TO YOUR OLD LIFE.
YES.

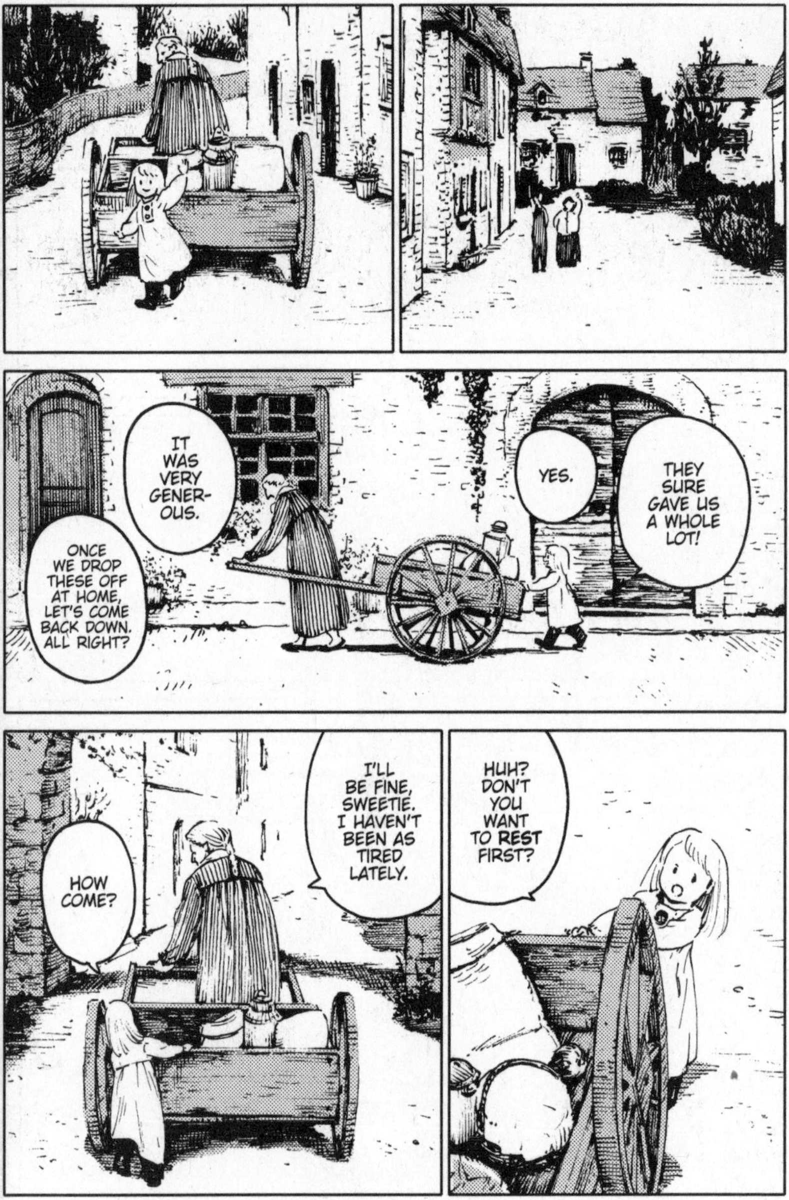
THEY SURE GAVE US A WHOLE LOT!
YES.
IT WAS VERY GENER-OUS.
ONCE WE DROP THESE OFF AT HOME, LET'S COME BACK DOWN. ALL RIGHT?
HUH? DON'T YOU WANT TO REST FIRST?
I'LL BE FINE, SWEETIE. I HAVEN'T BEEN AS TIRED LATELY.
HOW COME?

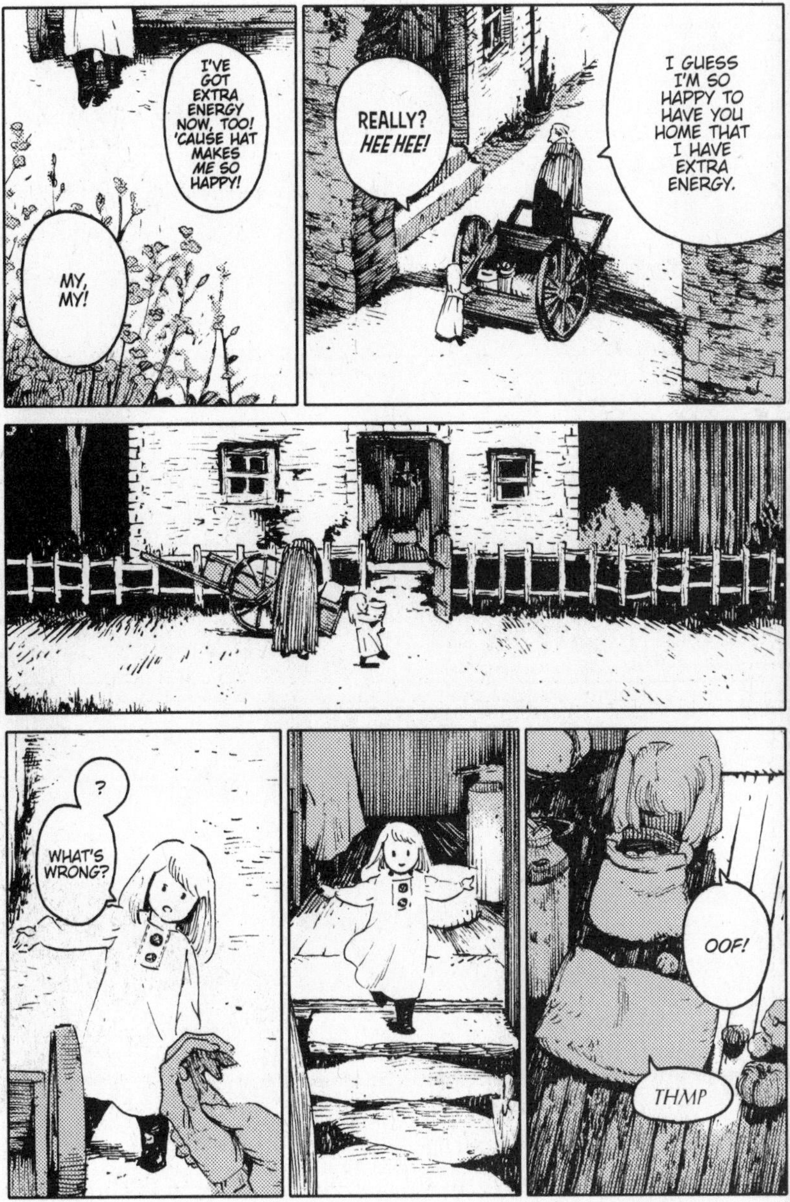
I GUESS I'M SO HAPPY TO HAVE YOU HOME THAT I HAVE EXTRA ENERGY.
REALLY? HEE HEE!
I'VE GOT EXTRA ENERGY NOW, TOO! 'CAUSE HAT MAKES ME SO HAPPY!
MY, MY!
OOF!
THMP
?
WHAT'S WRONG?

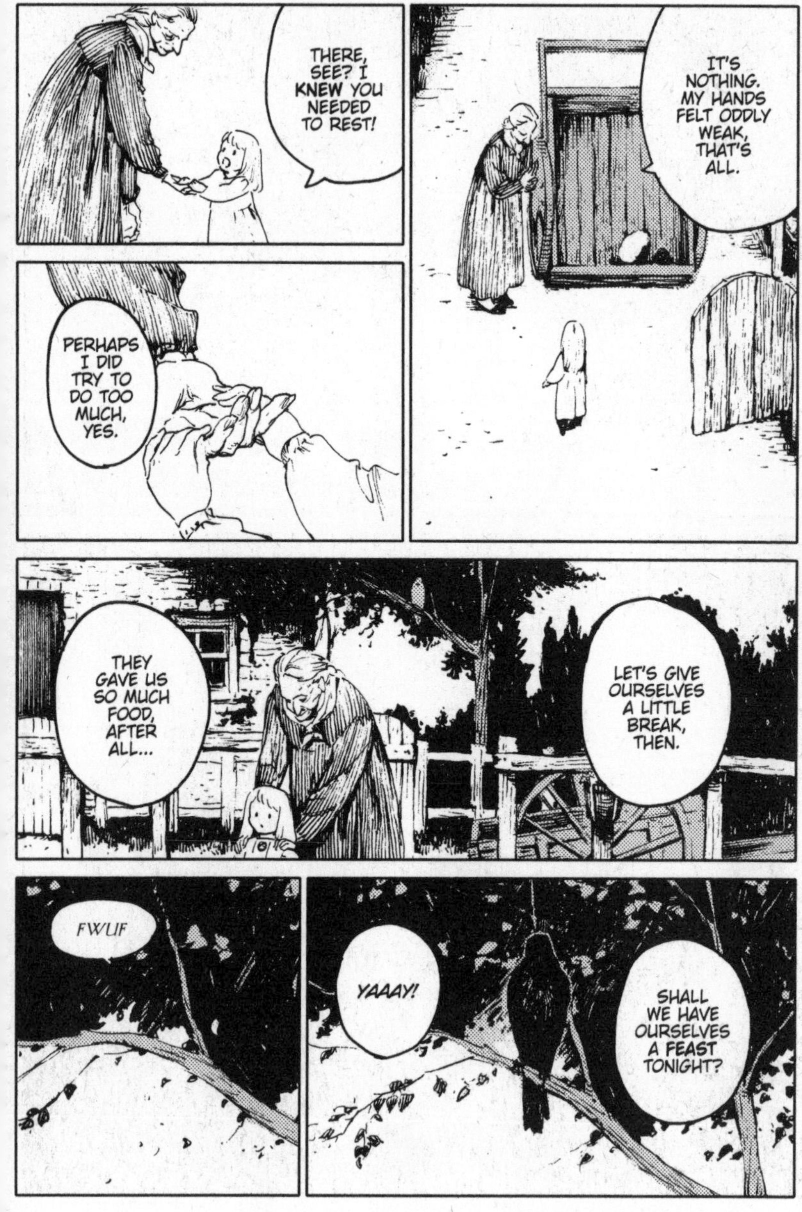
IT'S NOTHING. MY HANDS FELT ODDLY WEAK, THAT'S ALL.
THERE, SEE? I KNEW YOU NEEDED TO REST!
PERHAPS I DID TRY TO DO TOO MUCH, YES.
LET'S GIVE OURSELVES A LITTLE BREAK, THEN.
THEY GAVE US SO MUCH FOOD, AFTER ALL...
SHALL WE HAVE OURSELVES A FEAST TONIGHT?
YAAAY!
FWUF

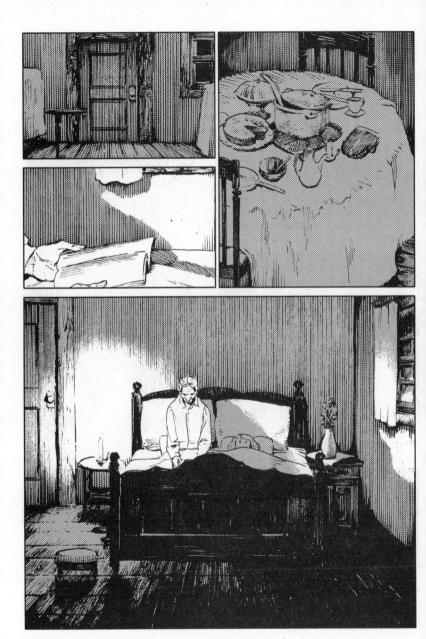

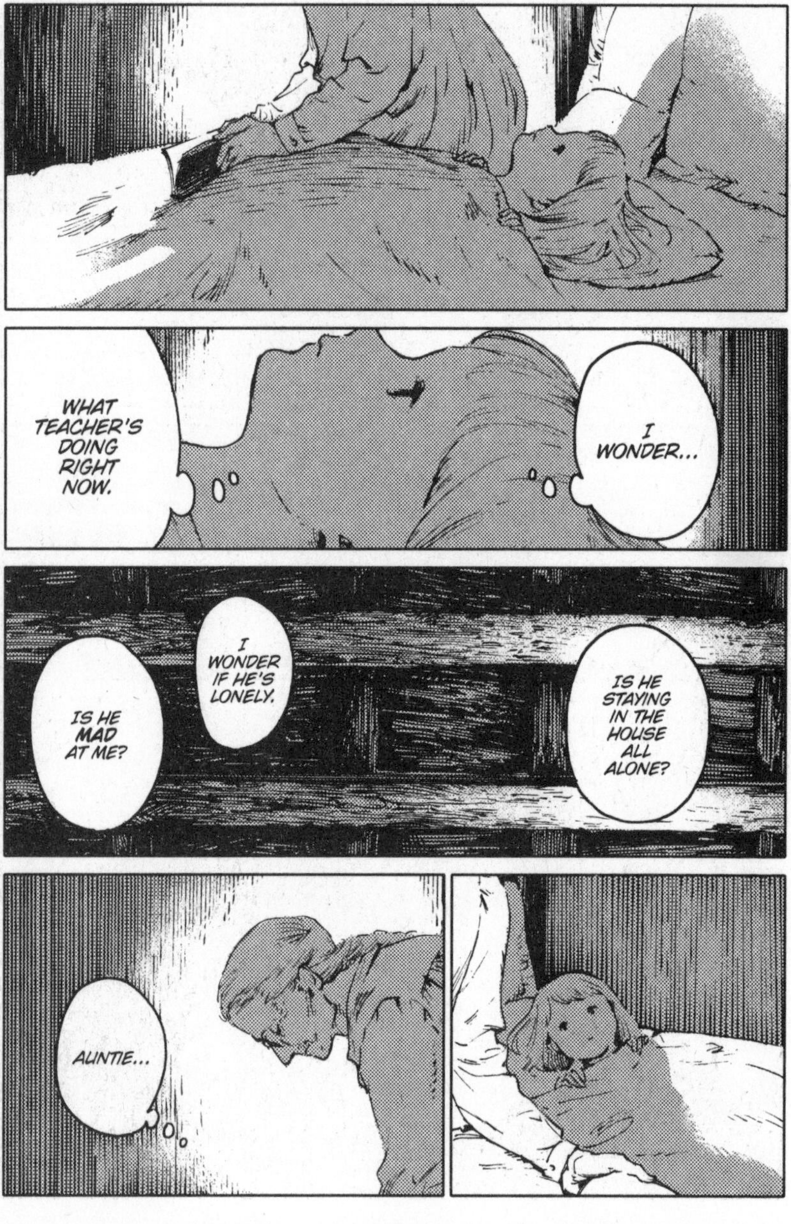
I WONDER...
WHAT TEACHER'S DOING RIGHT NOW.
IS HE STAYING IN THE HOUSE ALL ALONE?
I WONDER IF HE'S LONELY.
IS HE MAD AT ME?
AUNTIE...

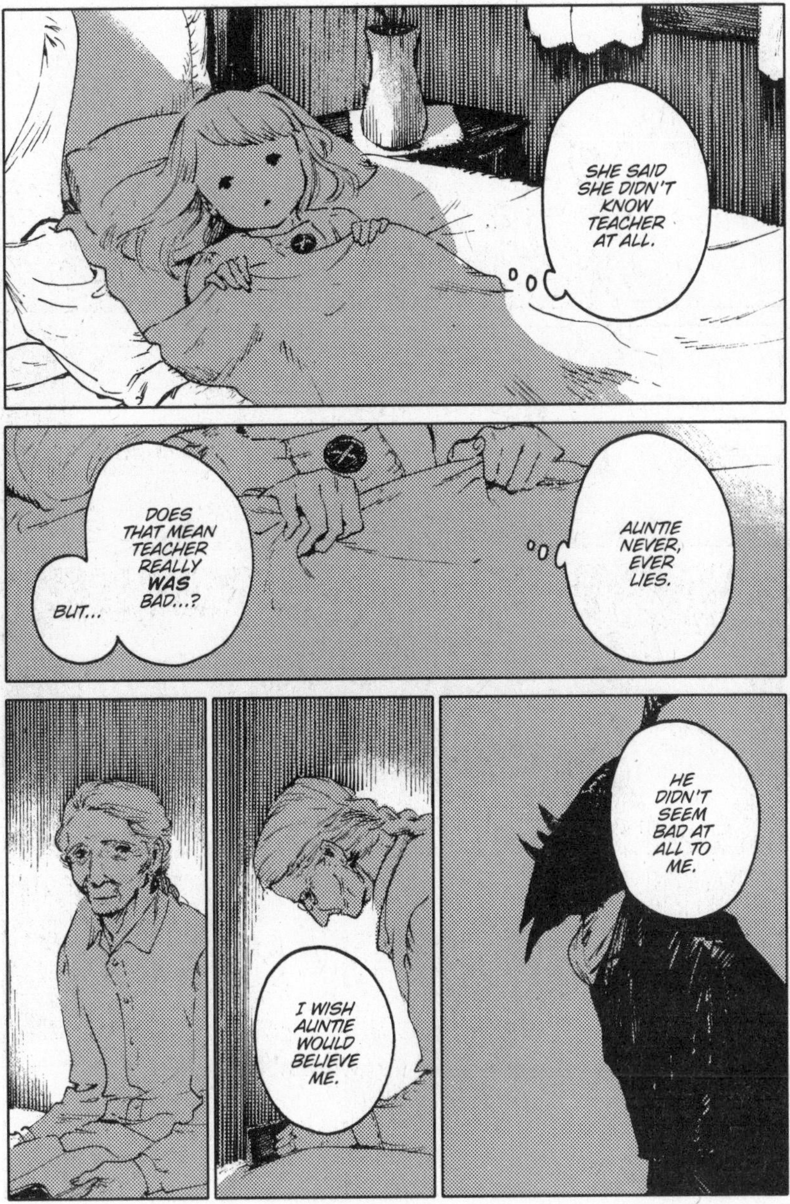
SHE SAID SHE DIDN'T KNOW TEACHER AT ALL.
AUNTIE NEVER, EVER LIES.
DOES THAT MEAN TEACHER REALLY **WAS** BAD...?
BUT...
HE DIDN'T SEEM BAD AT ALL TO ME.
I WISH AUNTIE WOULD BELIEVE ME.

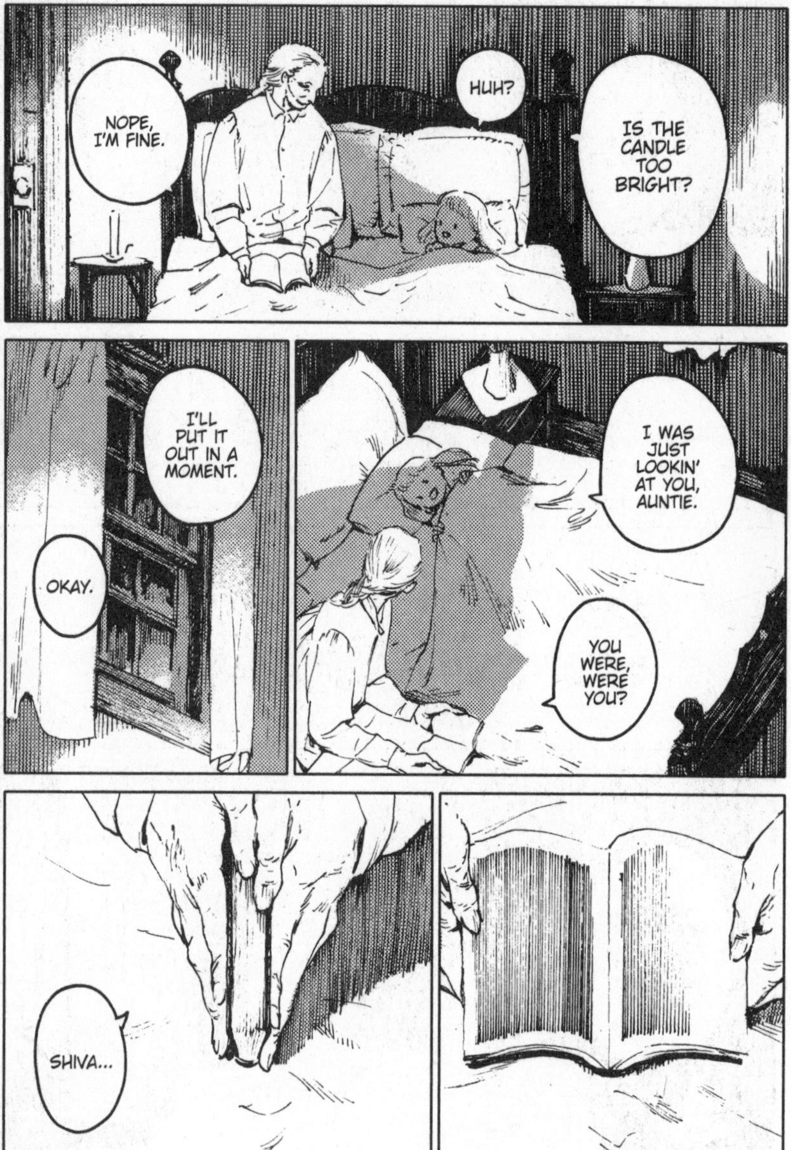
IS THE CANDLE TOO BRIGHT?
HUH?
NOPE, I'M FINE.
I WAS JUST LOOKIN' AT YOU, AUNTIE.
YOU WERE, WERE YOU?
I'LL PUT IT OUT IN A MOMENT.
OKAY.
SHIVA...

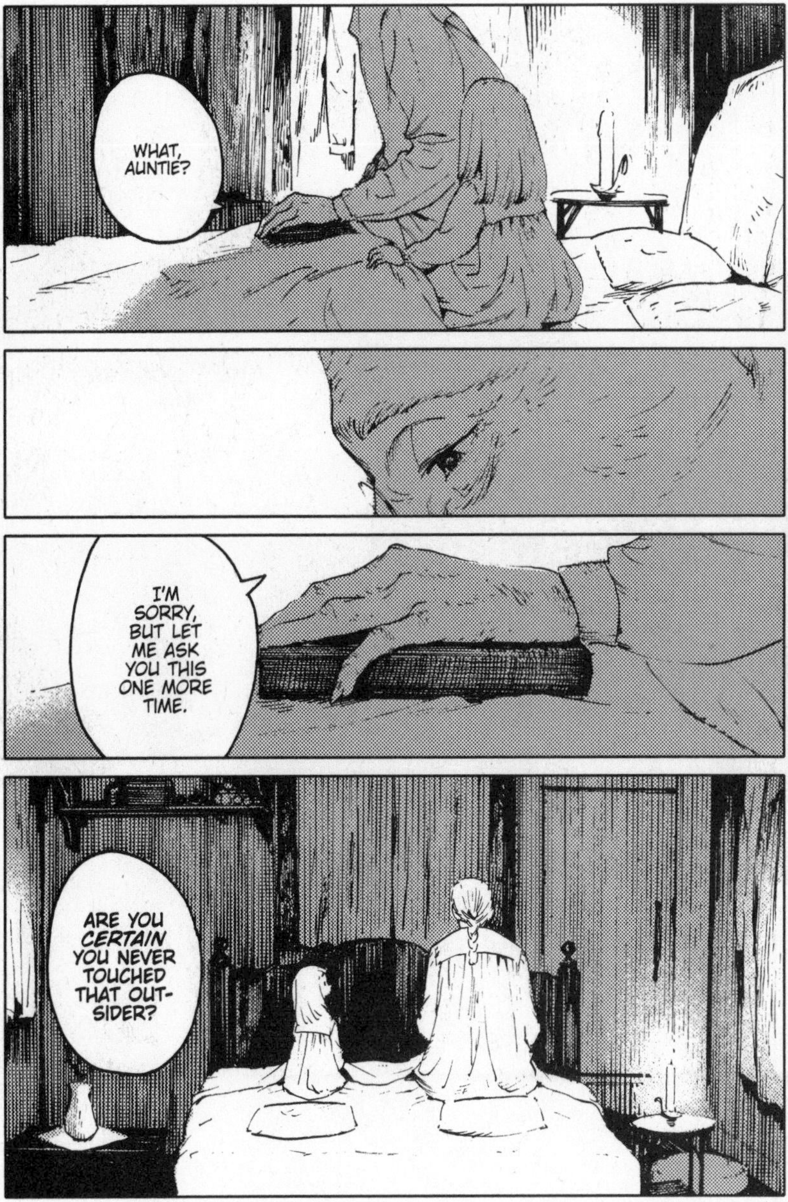
WHAT, AUNTIE?
I'M SORRY, BUT LET ME ASK YOU THIS ONE MORE TIME.
ARE YOU *CERTAIN* YOU NEVER TOUCHED THAT OUT-SIDER?

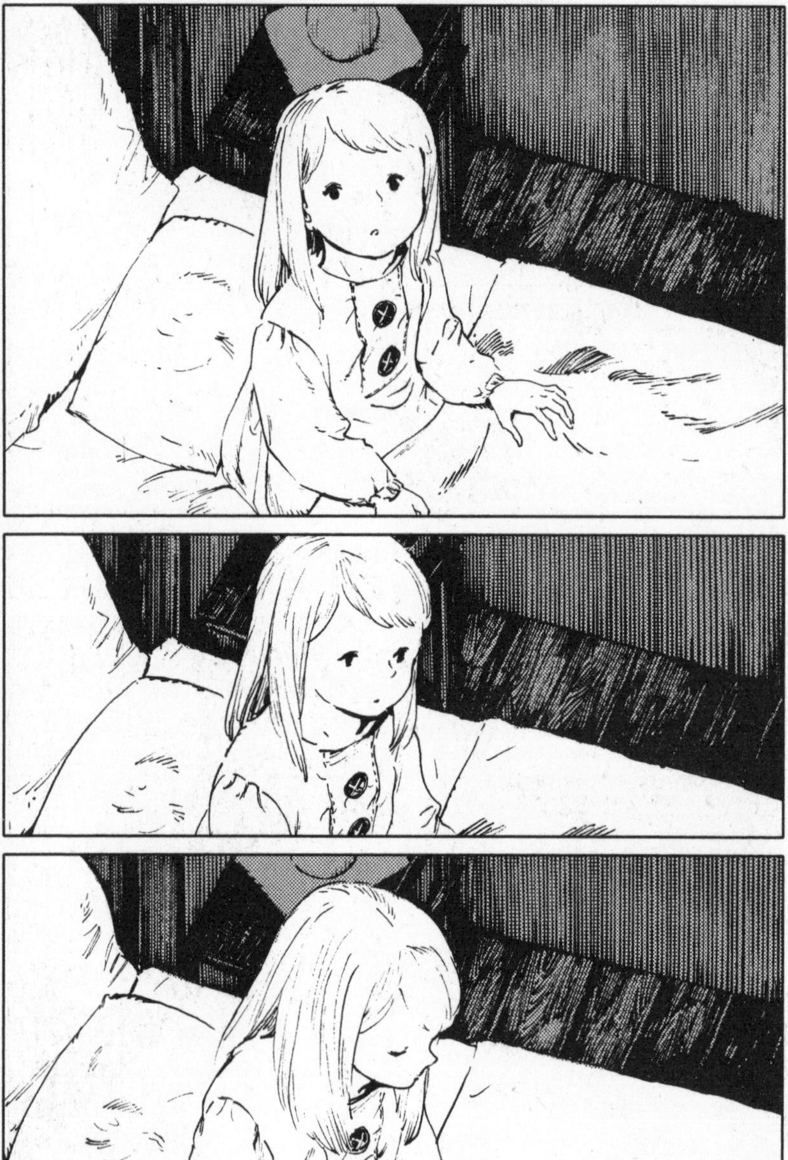

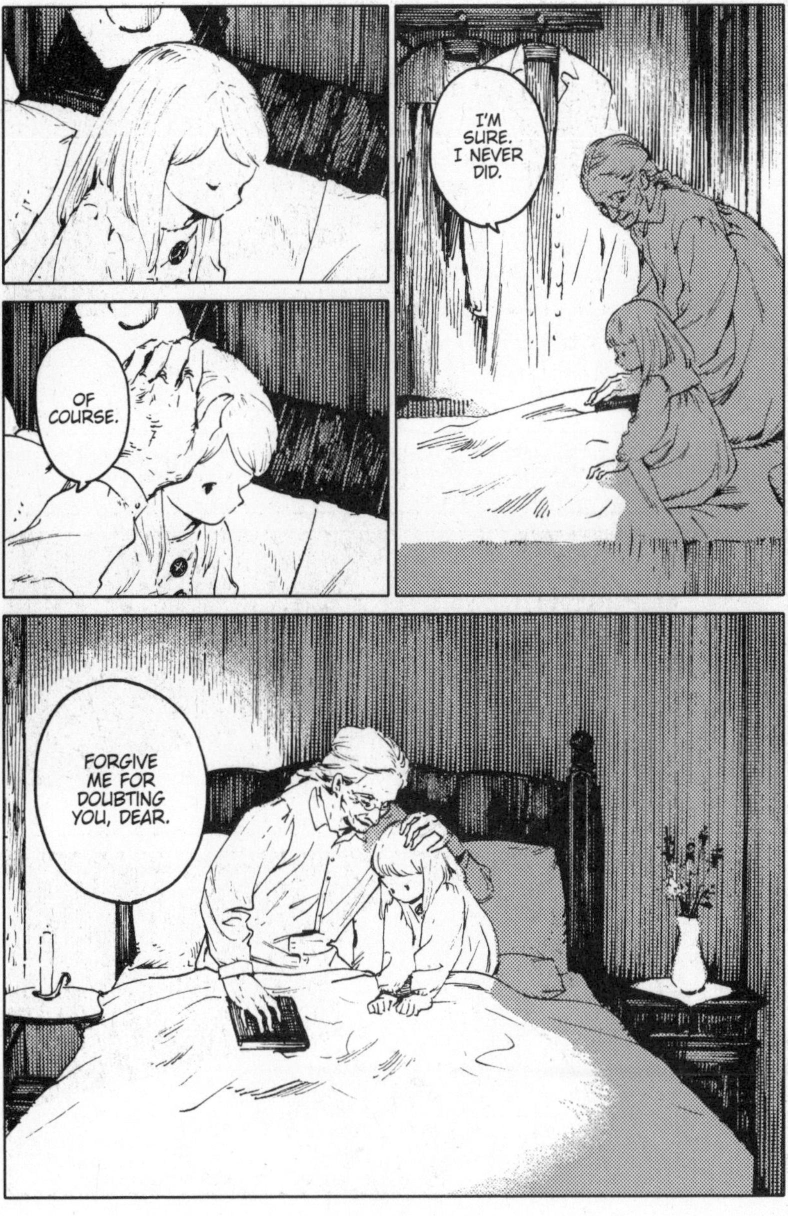
I'M SURE. I NEVER DID.
OF COURSE.
FORGIVE ME FOR DOUBTING YOU, DEAR.

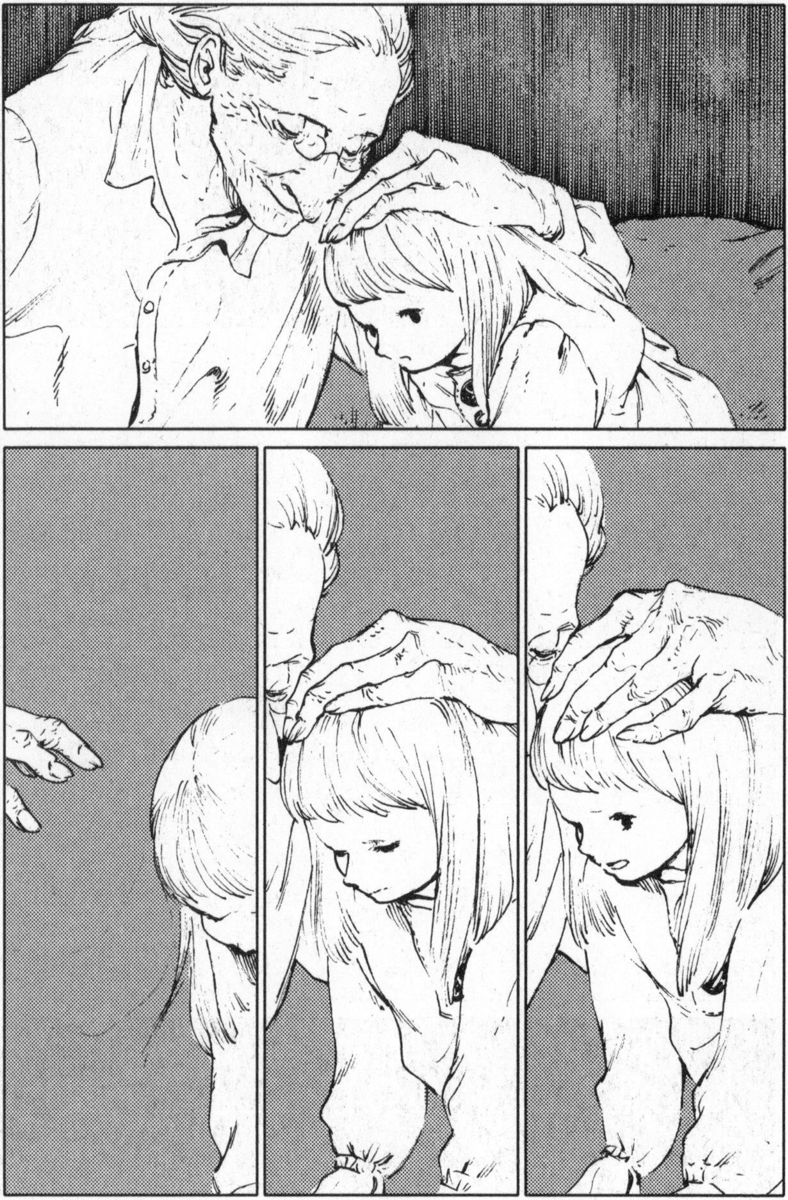

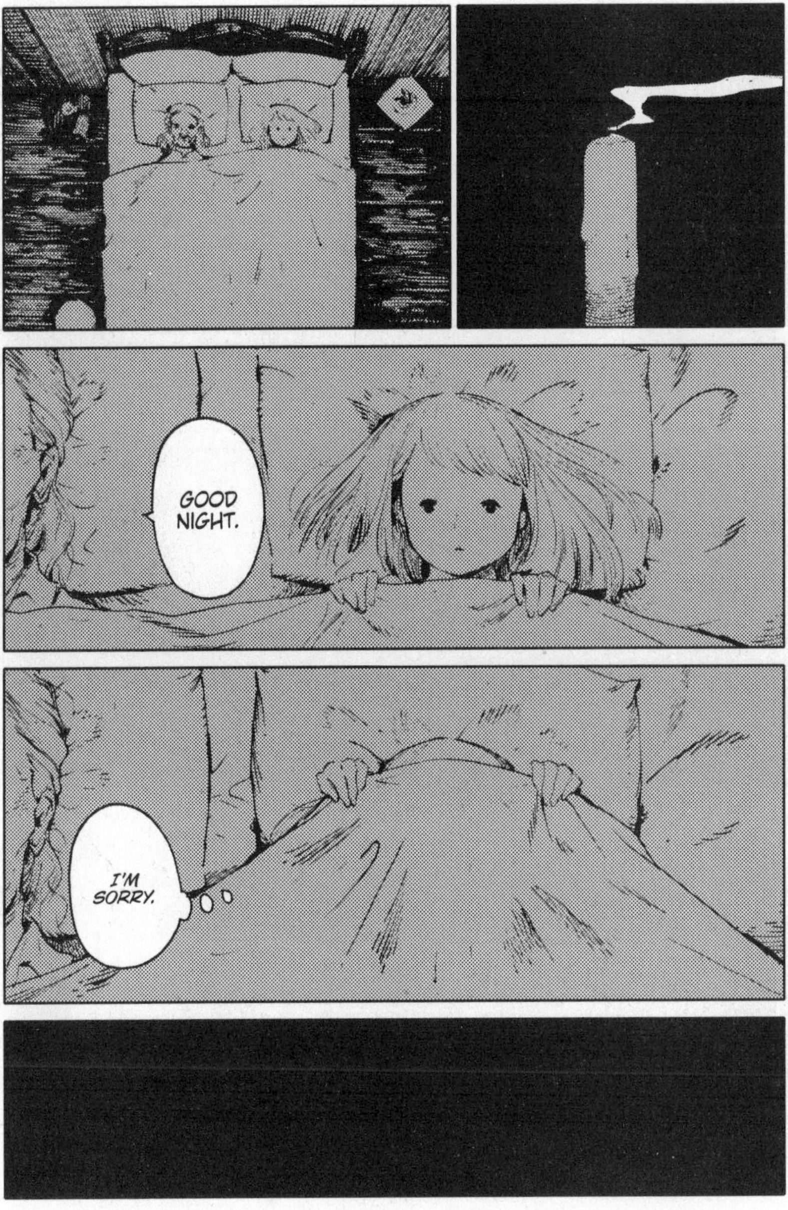
GOOD NIGHT.
I'M SORRY.

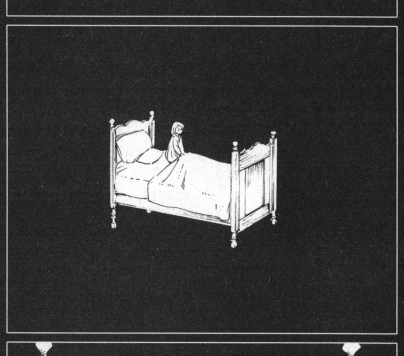

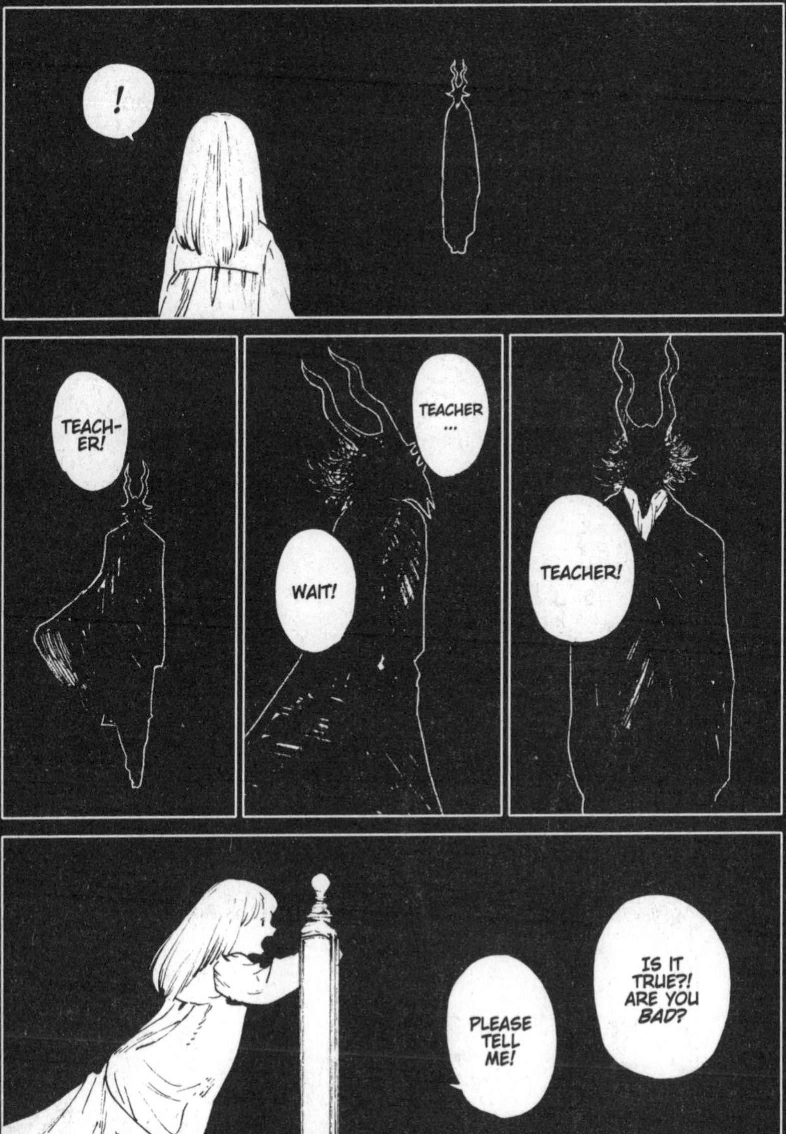
!
TEACHER!
TEACHER ...
WAIT!
TEACH-ER!
IS IT TRUE?! ARE YOU BAD?
PLEASE TELL ME!

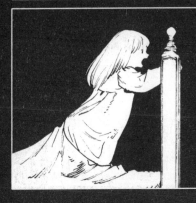

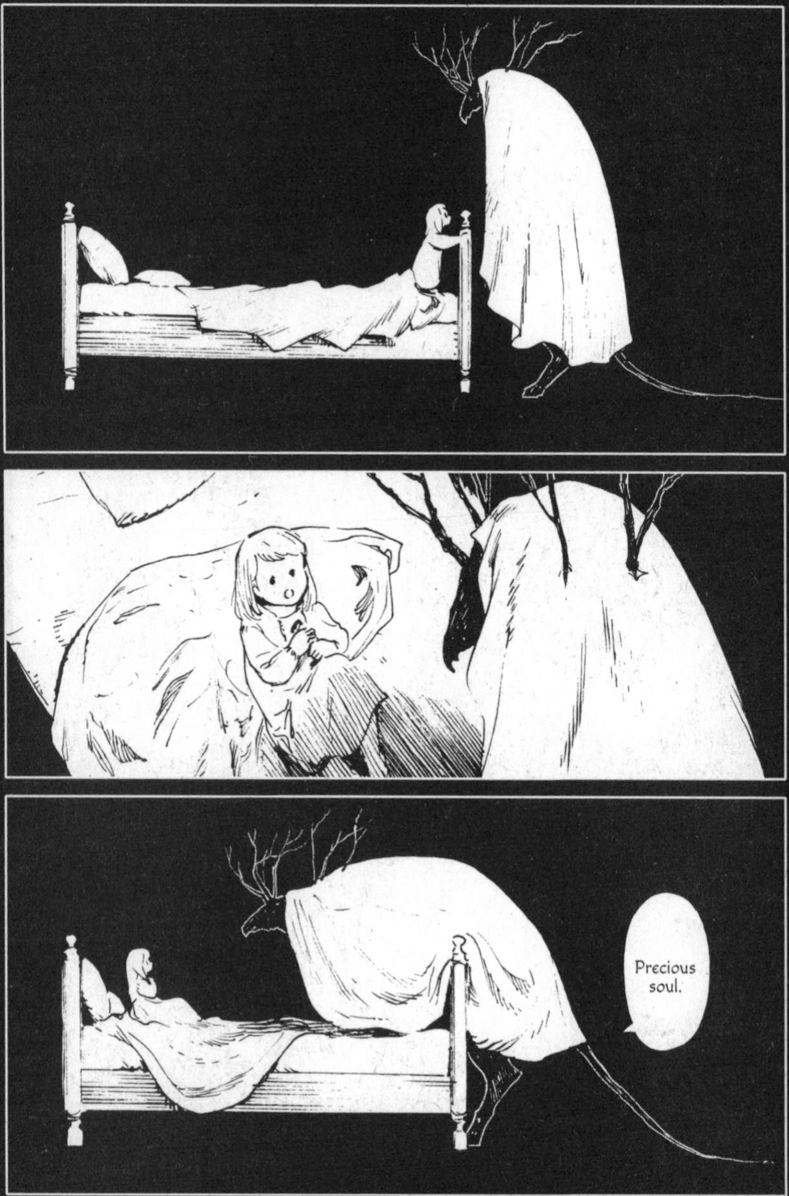
Precious soul.

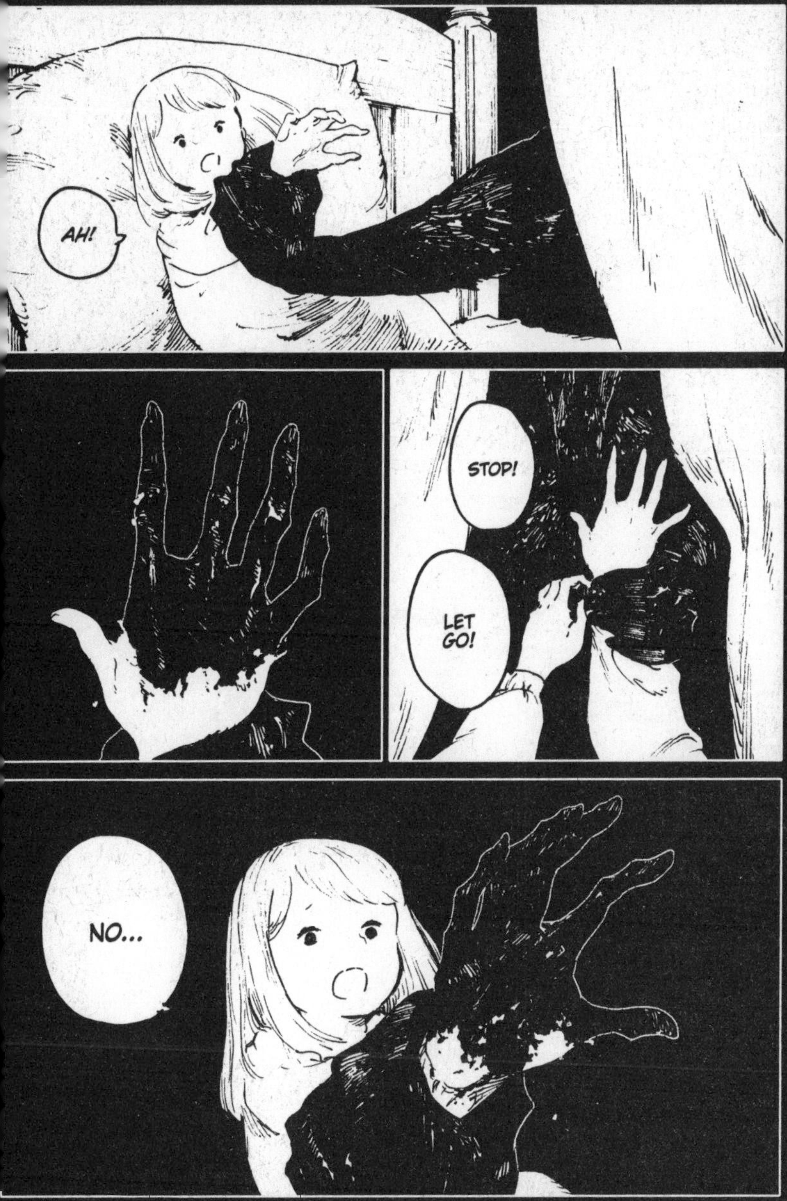
AH!
STOP!
LET GO!
NO...

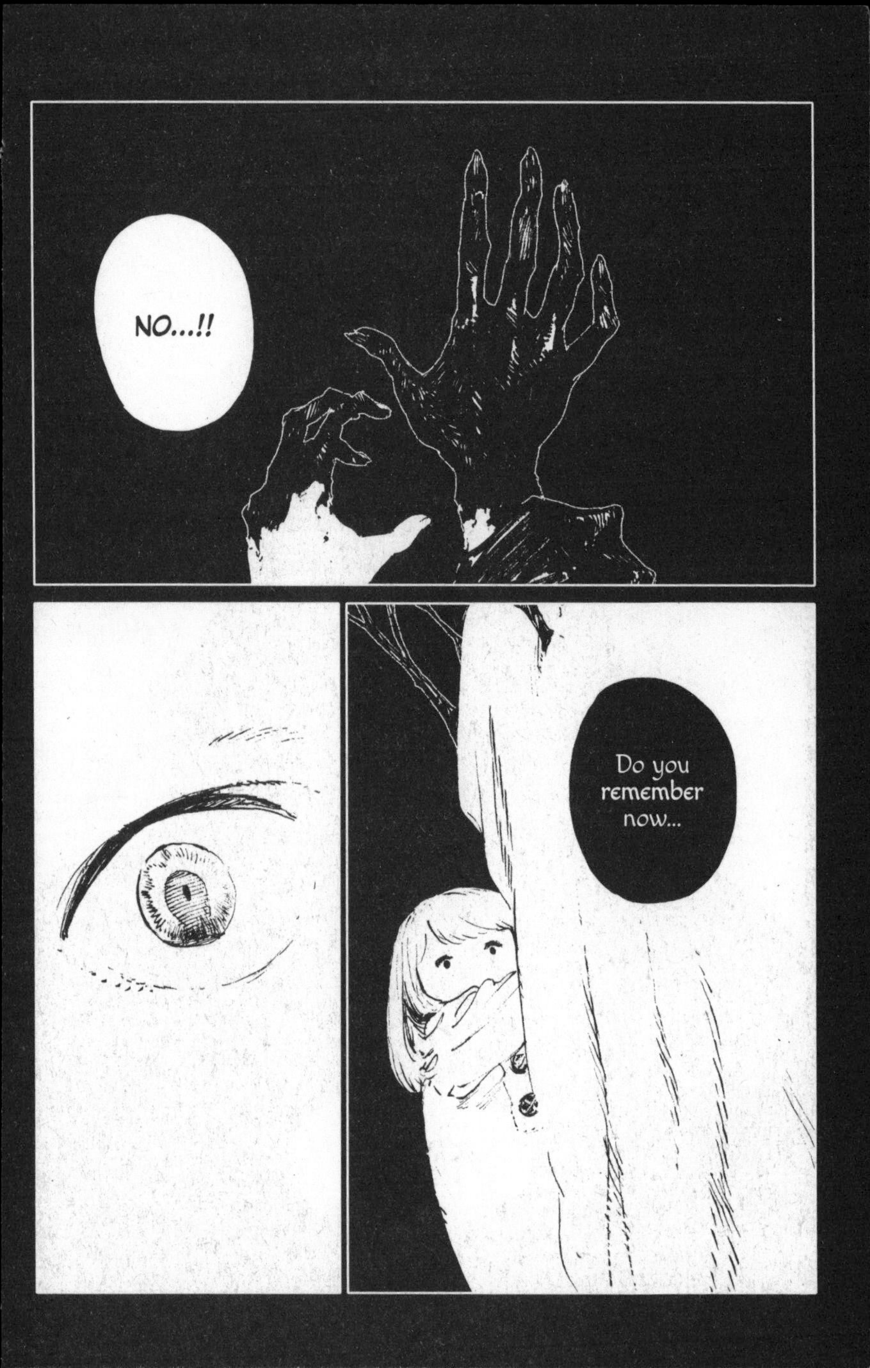
NO...!!
Do you remember now...

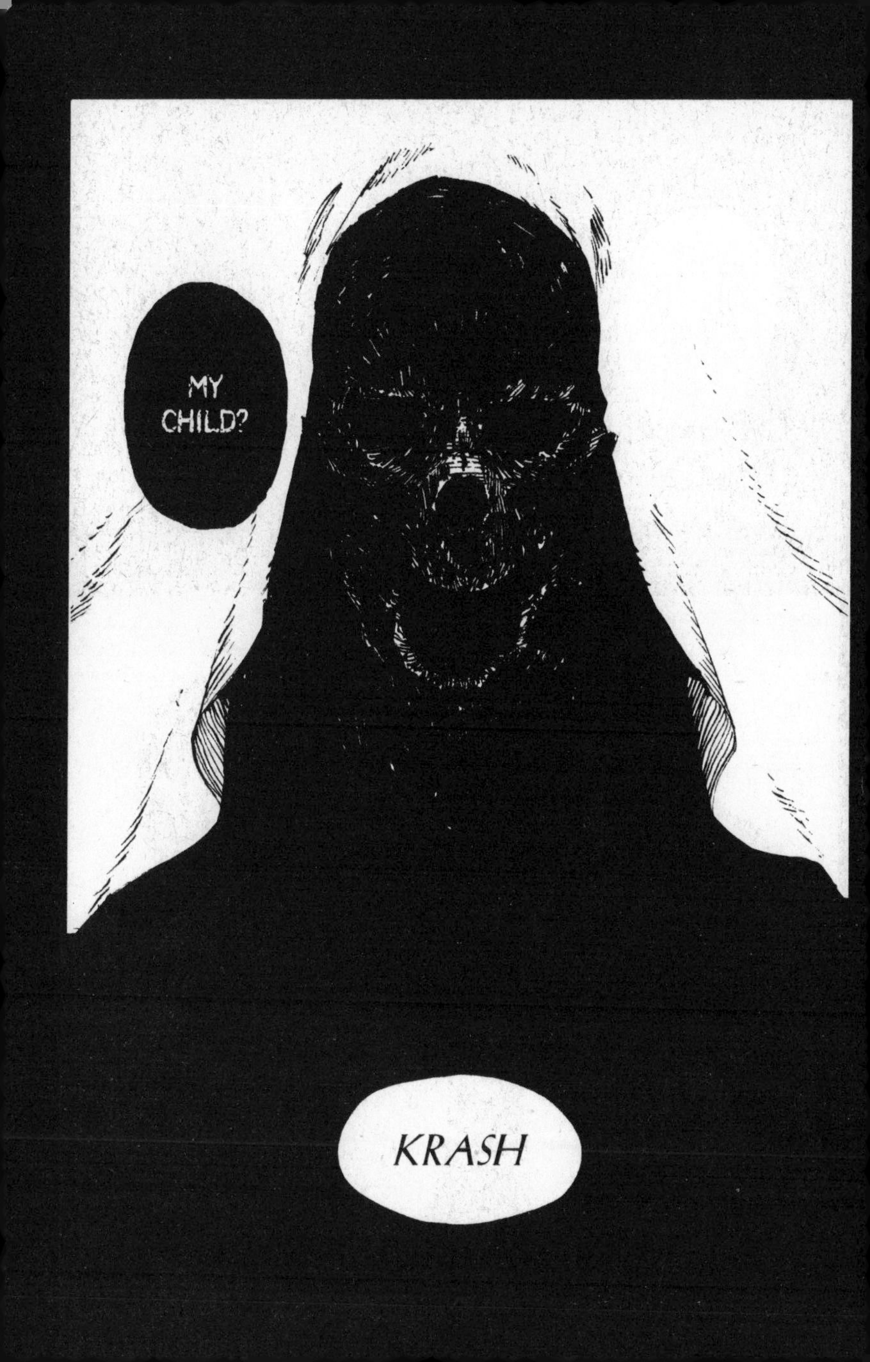
MY CHILD?
KRASH

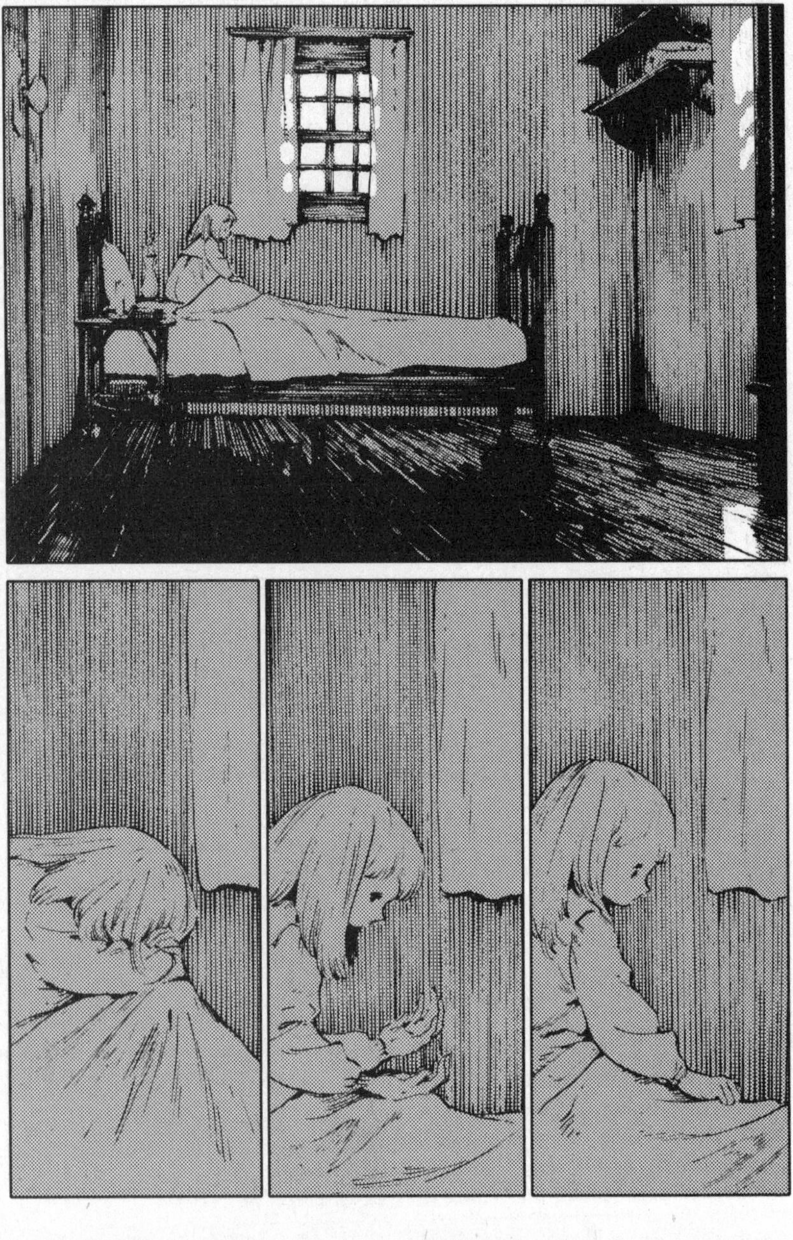

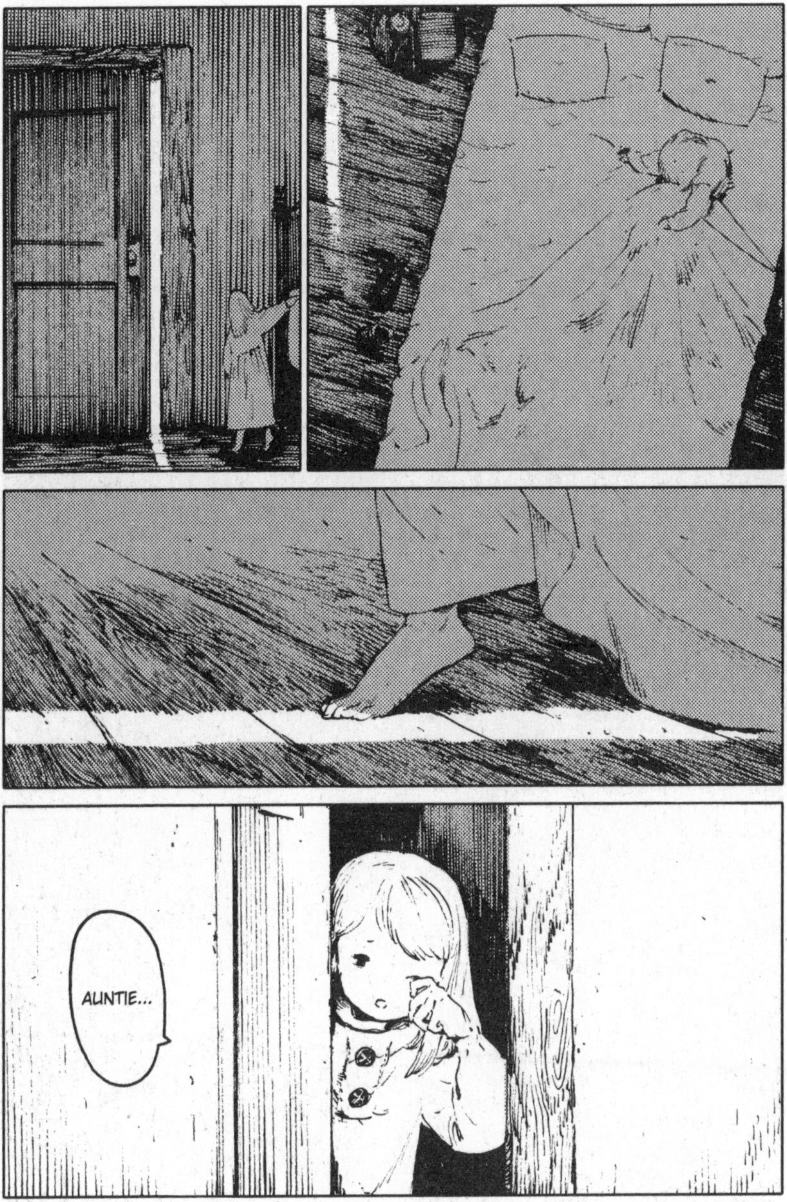
AUNTIE...

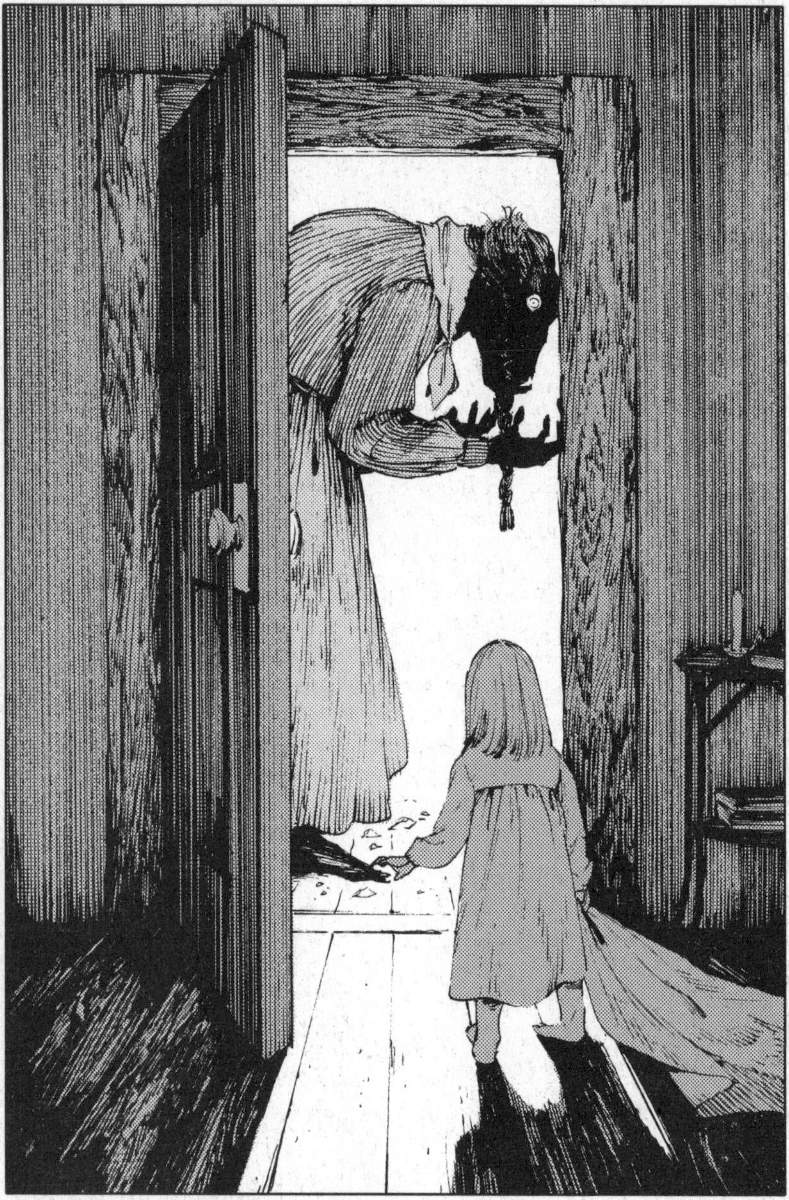

Siúil, a Rún
The Girl from the Other Side

Siúil, a Rún
The Girl from the Other Side

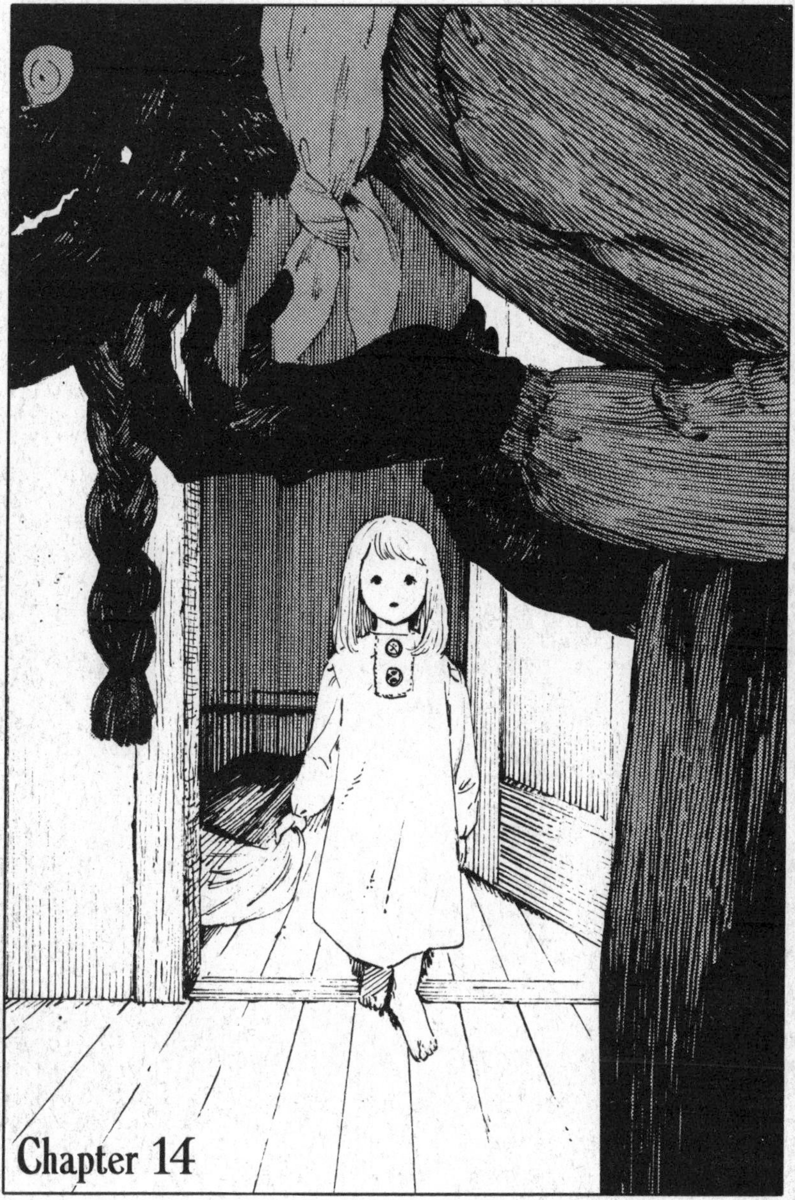
Chapter 14

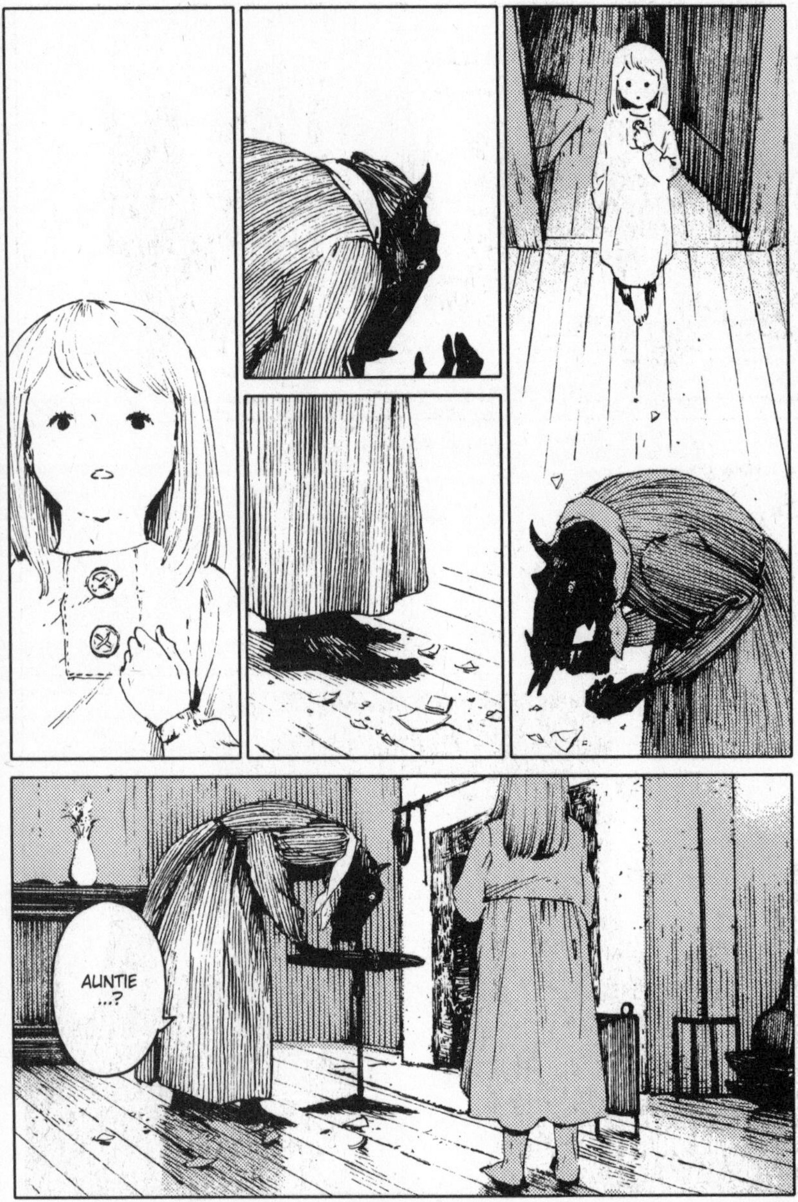
AUNTIE ...?

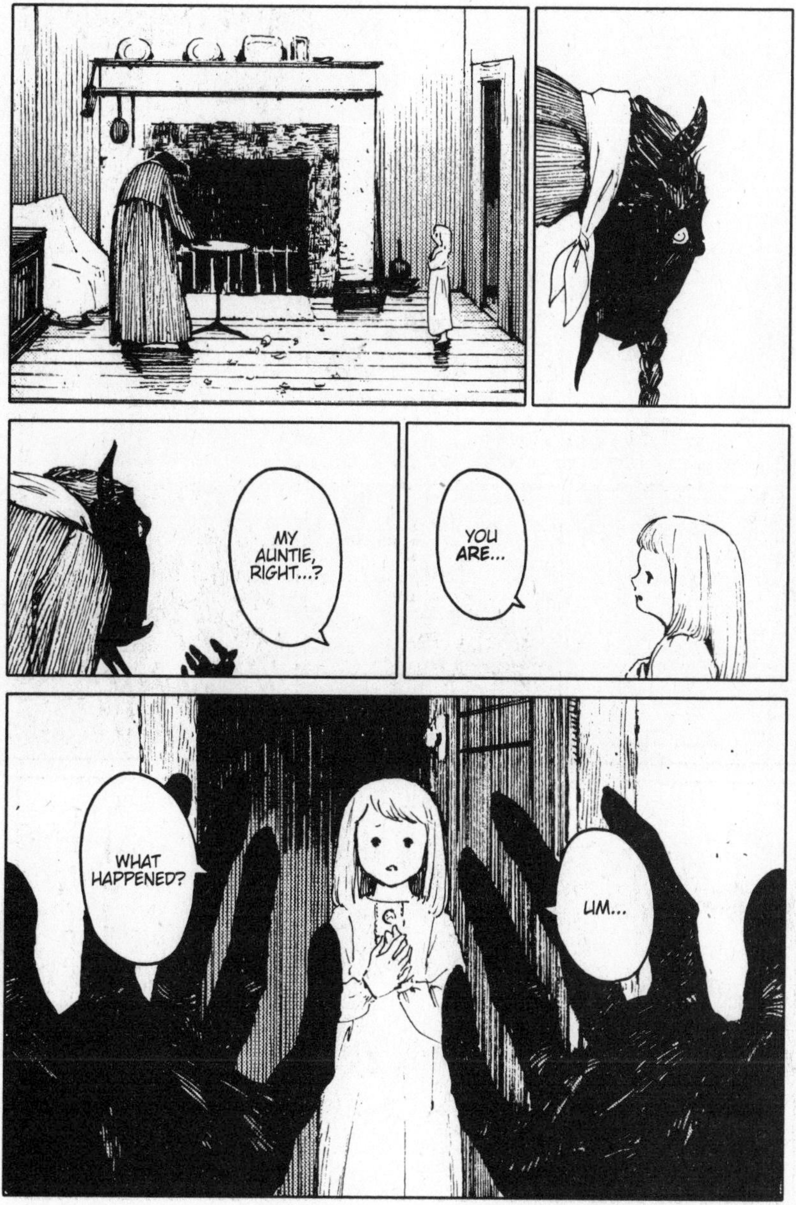
YOU ARE...
MY AUNTIE, RIGHT...?
UM...
WHAT HAPPENED?

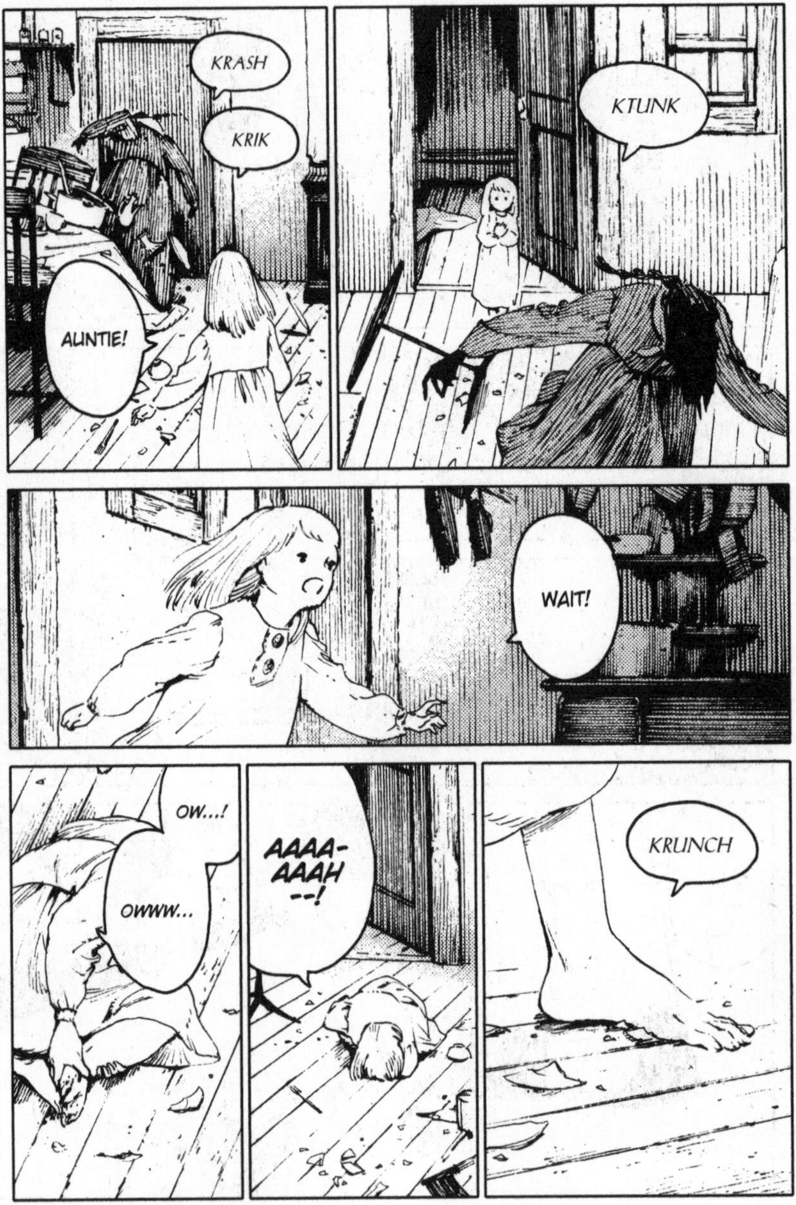
KTUNK
KRASH
KRIK
AUNTIE!
WAIT!
KRUNCH
AAAA-AAAH--!
OW...!
OWWW...

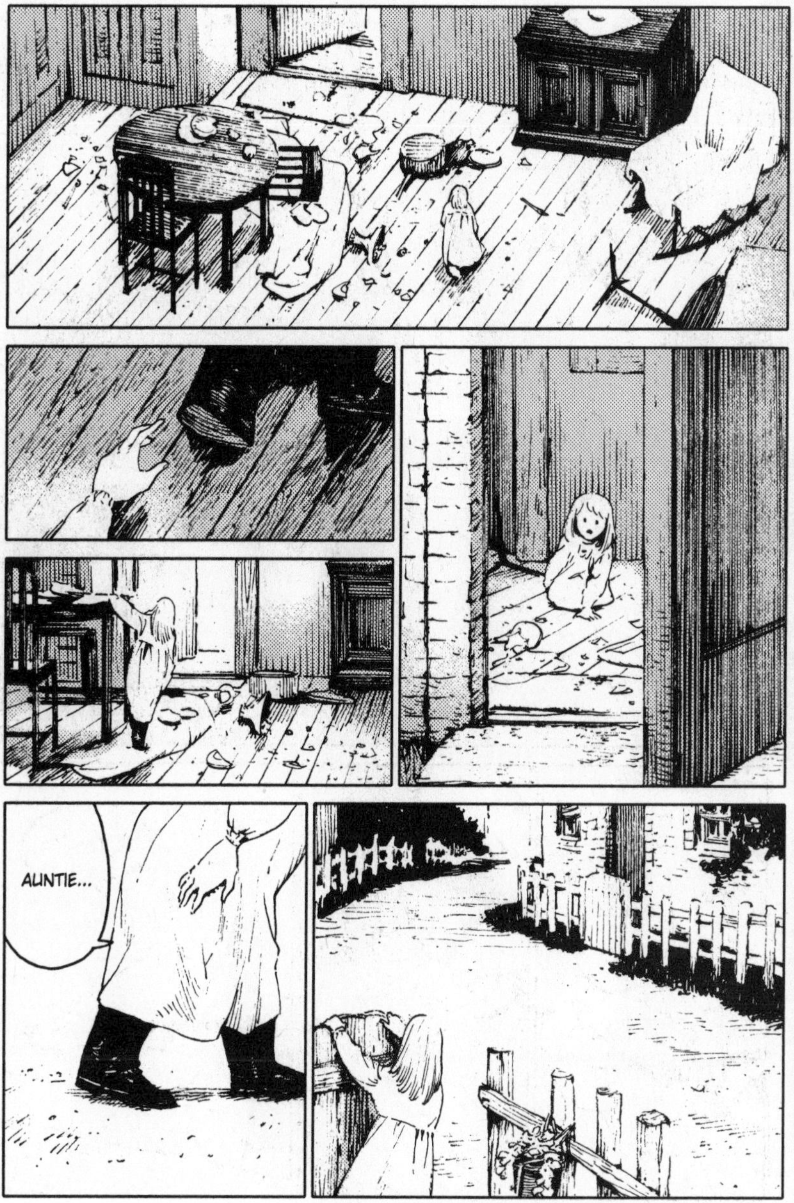
AUNTIE...

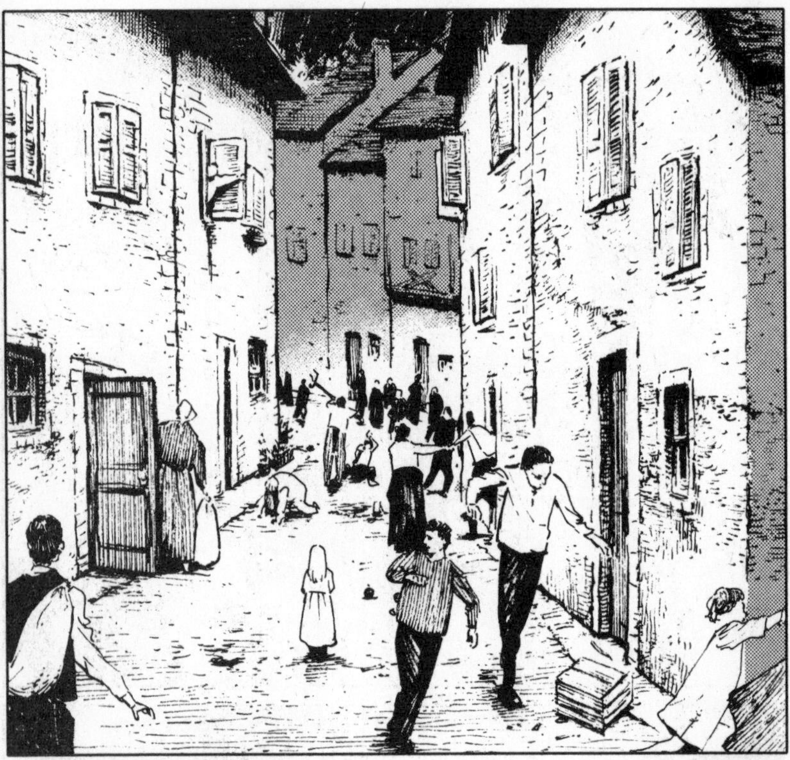
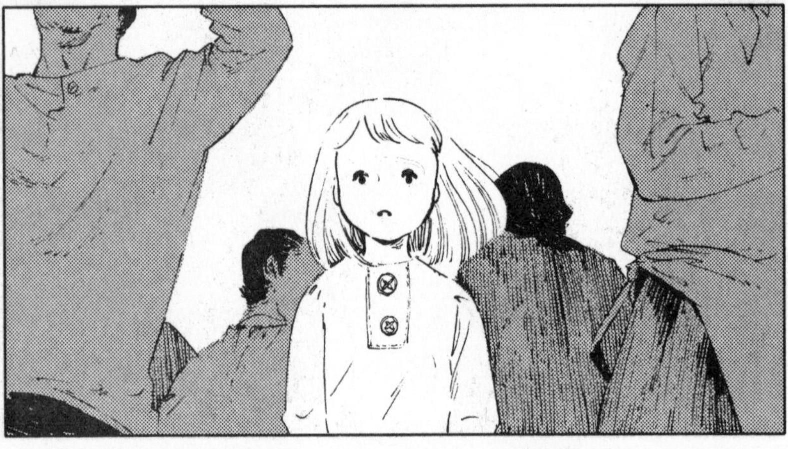

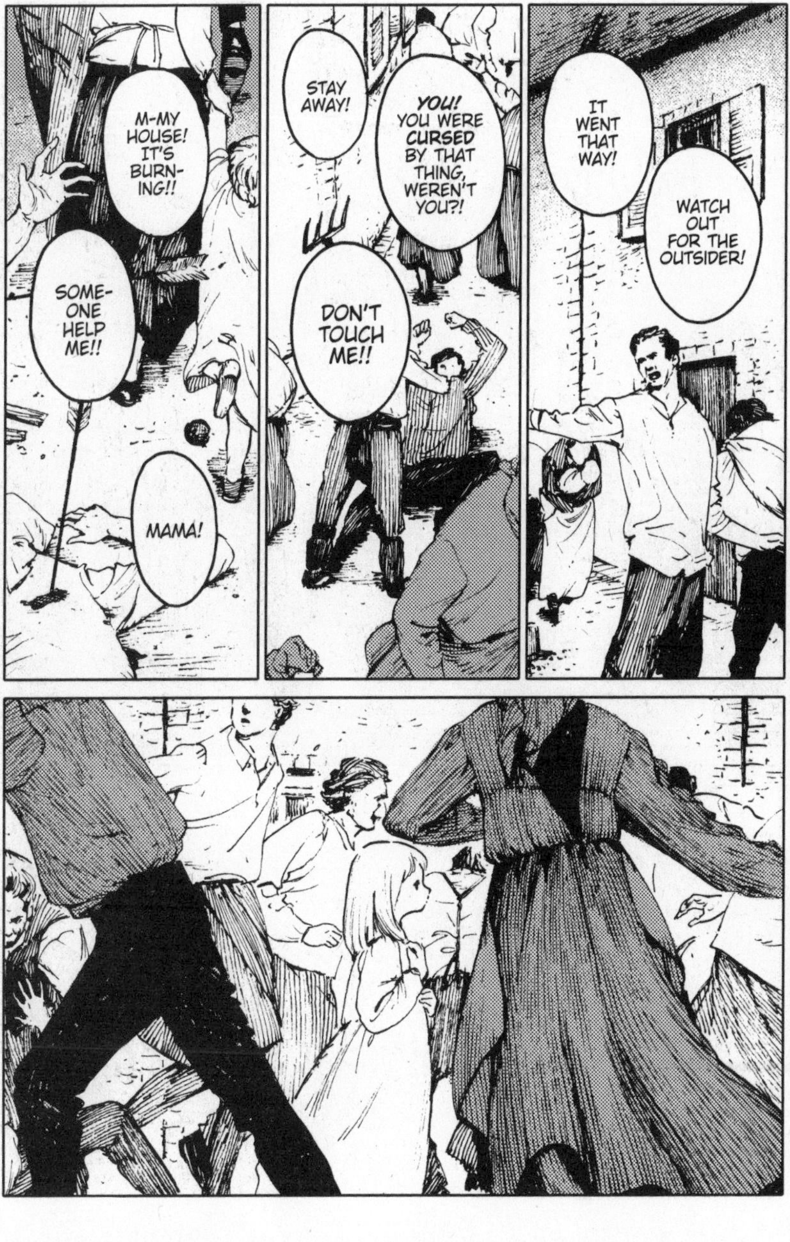
IT WENT THAT WAY!
WATCH OUT FOR THE OUTSIDER!
YOU! YOU WERE **CURSED** BY THAT THING, WEREN'T YOU?!
STAY AWAY!
DON'T TOUCH ME!!
M-MY HOUSE! IT'S BURNING!!
SOME-ONE HELP ME!!
MAMA!

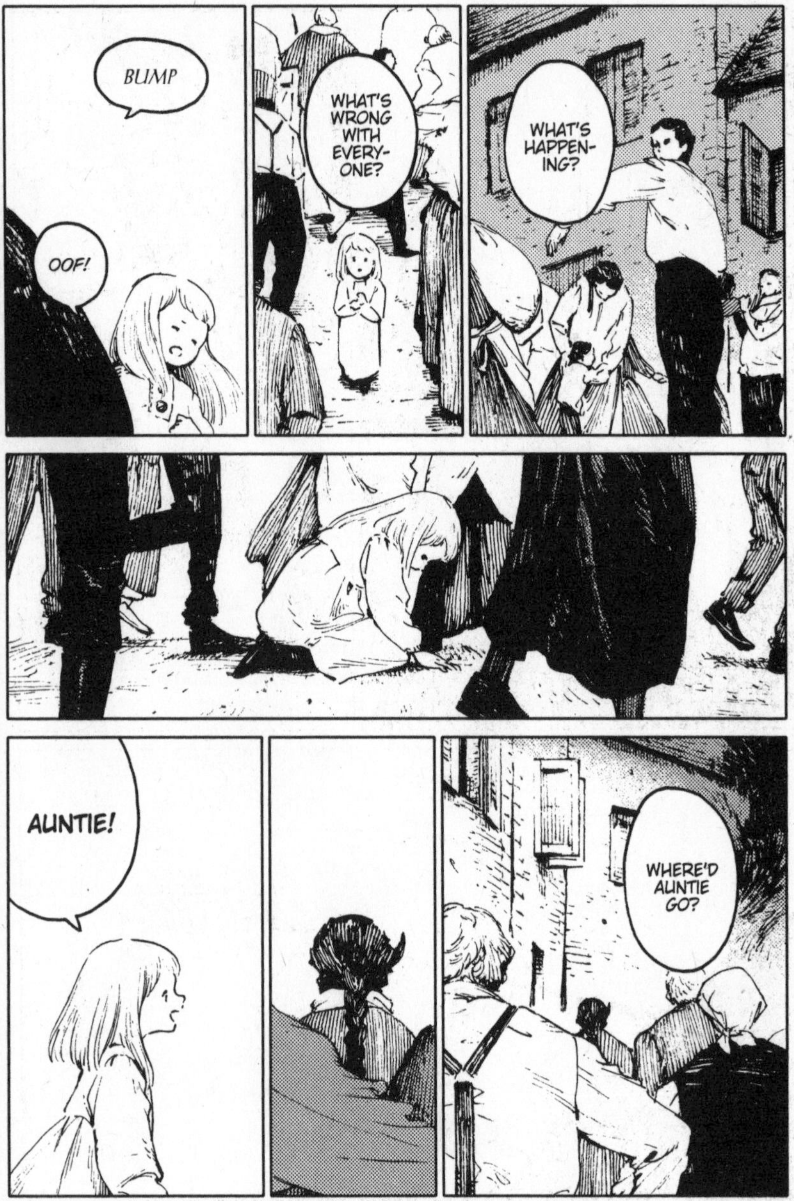
WHAT'S HAPPEN-ING?
WHAT'S WRONG WITH EVERY-ONE?
BUMP
OOF!
WHERE'D AUNTIE GO?
AUNTIE!

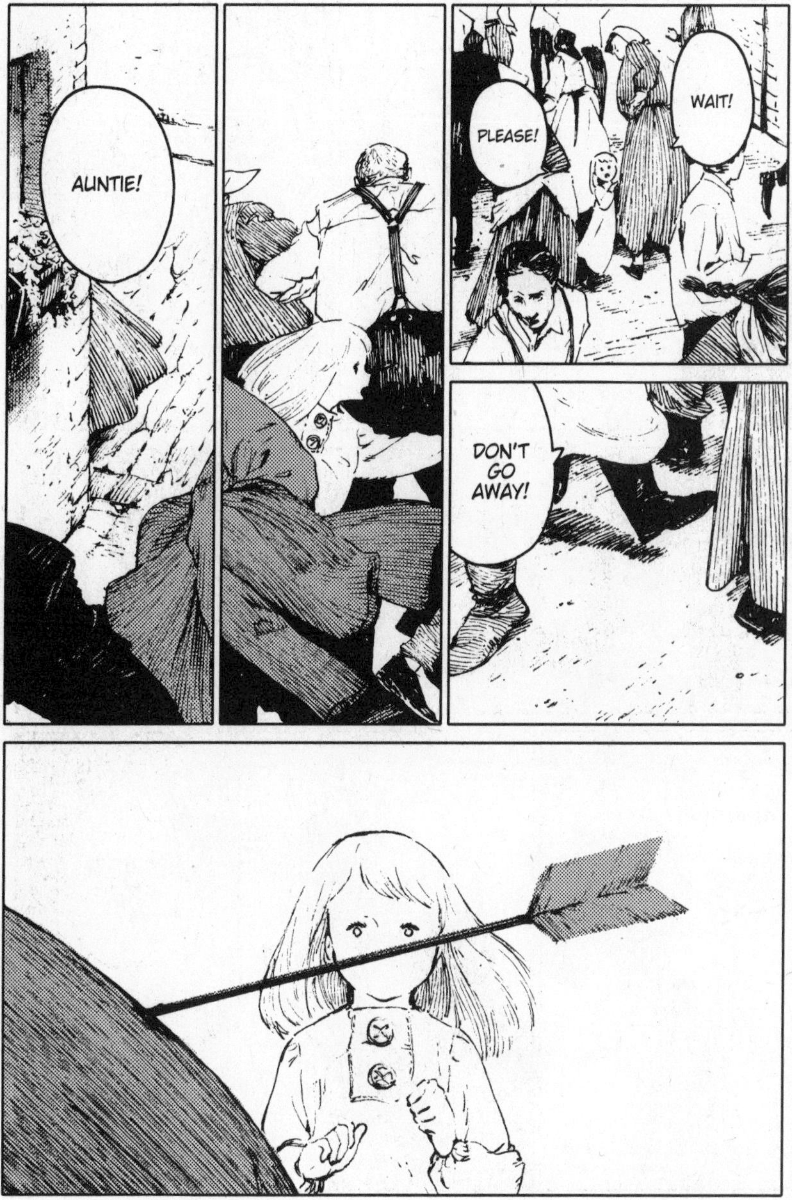
WAIT!
PLEASE!
DON'T GO AWAY!
AUNTIE!

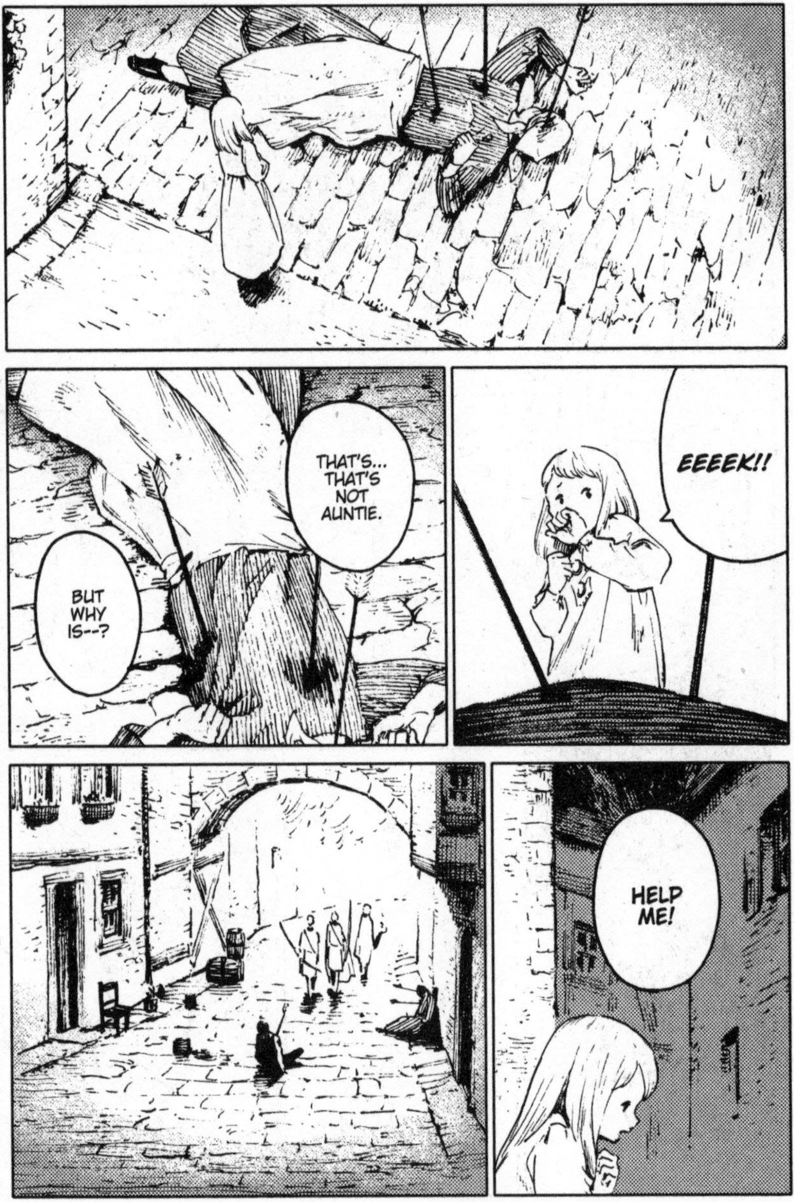
EEEEK!!
THAT'S... THAT'S NOT AUNTIE.
BUT WHY IS--?
HELP ME!

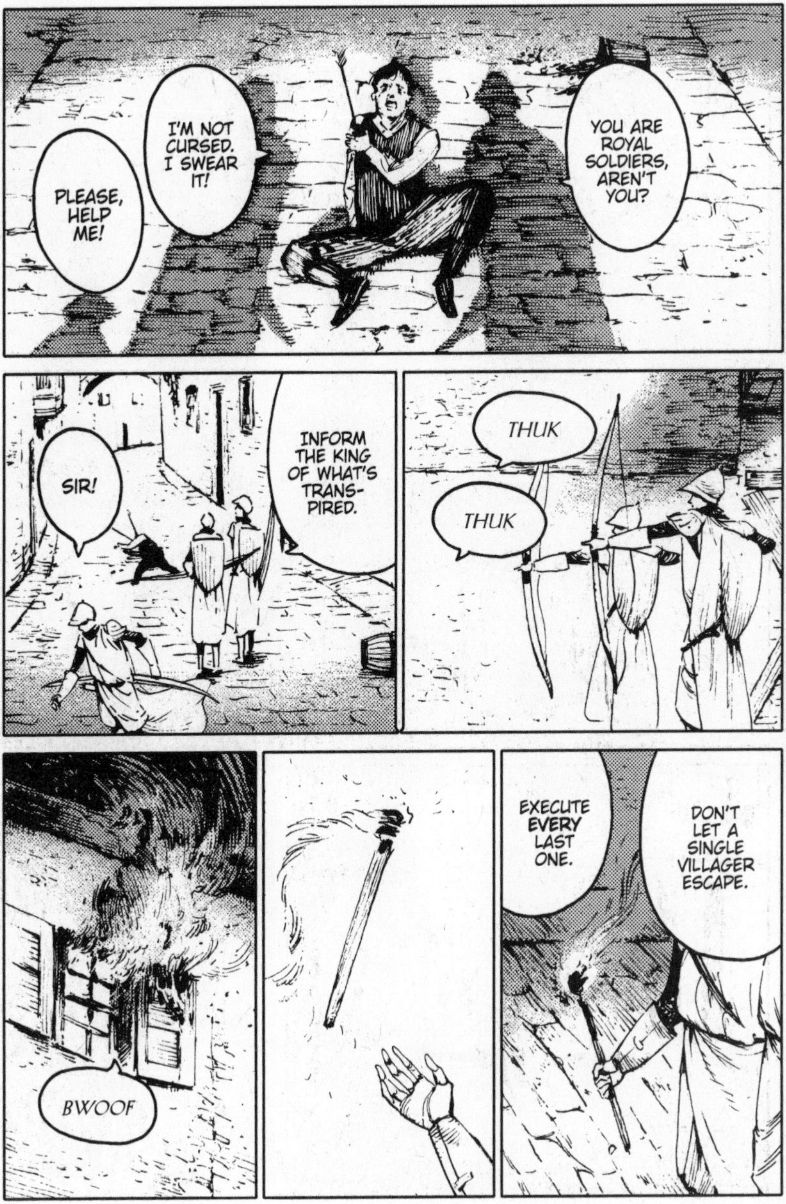
YOU ARE ROYAL SOLDIERS, AREN'T YOU?
I'M NOT CURSED. I SWEAR IT!
PLEASE, HELP ME!
THUK
THUK
INFORM THE KING OF WHAT'S TRANS-PIRED.
SIR!
DON'T LET A SINGLE VILLAGER ESCAPE.
EXECUTE EVERY LAST ONE.
BWOOF

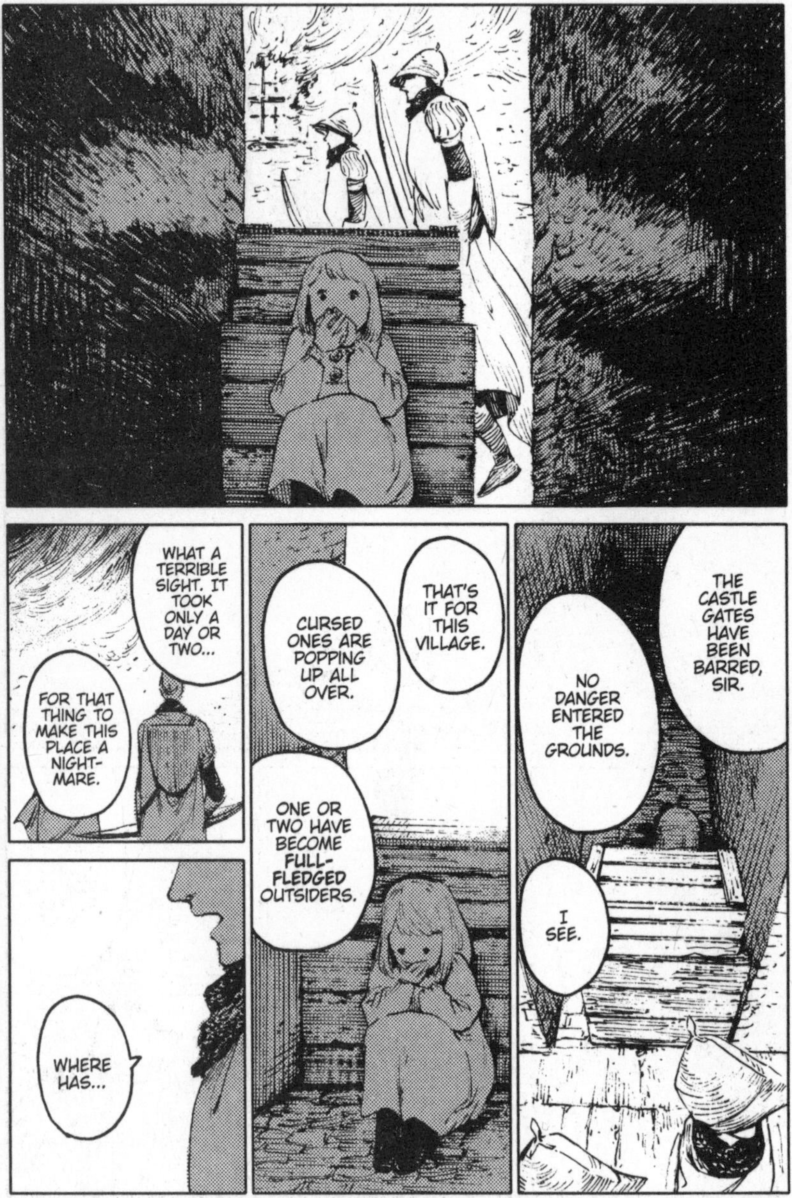
THE CASTLE GATES HAVE BEEN BARRED, SIR.
NO DANGER ENTERED THE GROUNDS.
I SEE.
THAT'S IT FOR THIS VILLAGE.
CURSED ONES ARE POPPING UP ALL OVER.
ONE OR TWO HAVE BECOME FULL-FLEDGED OUTSIDERS.
WHAT A TERRIBLE SIGHT. IT TOOK ONLY A DAY OR TWO...
FOR THAT THING TO MAKE THIS PLACE A NIGHT-MARE.
WHERE HAS...

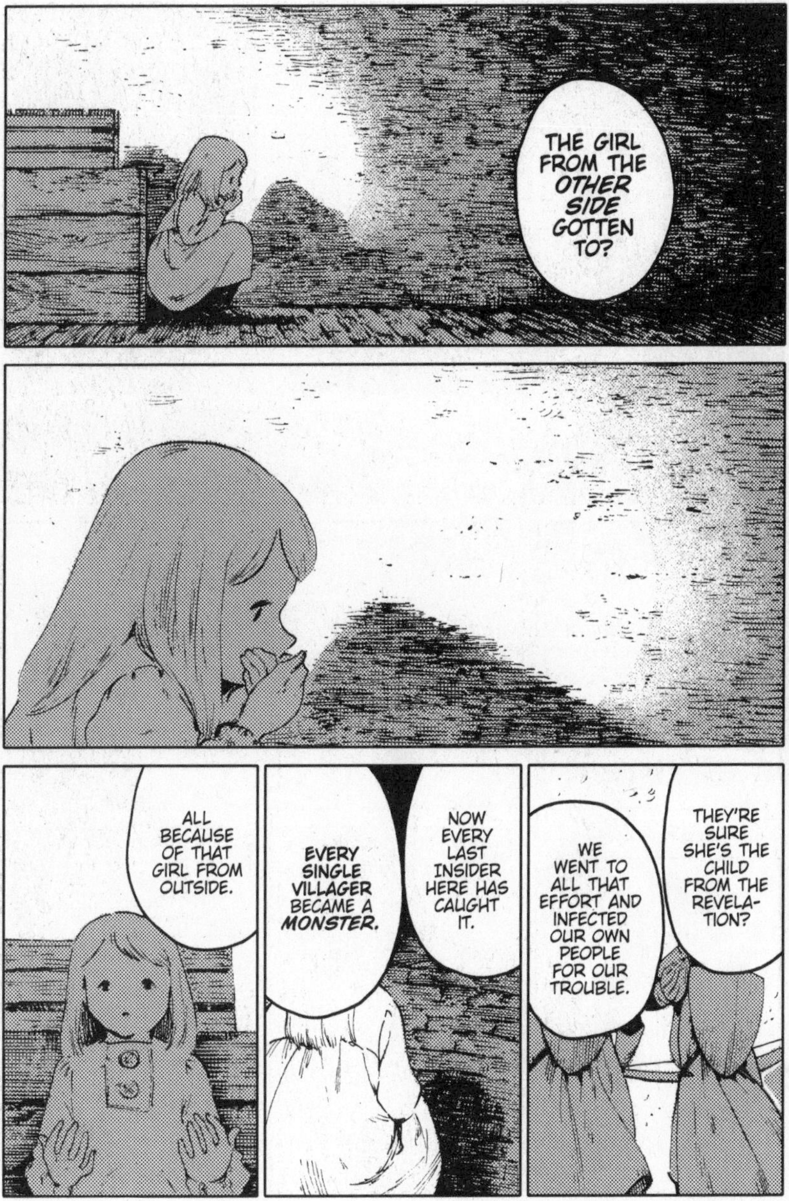
THE GIRL FROM THE *OTHER SIDE* GOTTEN TO?
THEY'RE SURE SHE'S THE CHILD FROM THE REVELA-TION?
WE WENT TO ALL THAT EFFORT AND INFECTED OUR OWN PEOPLE FOR OUR TROUBLE.
NOW EVERY LAST INSIDER HERE HAS CAUGHT IT.
EVERY SINGLE VILLAGER BECAME A *MONSTER*.
ALL BECAUSE OF THAT GIRL FROM OUTSIDE.

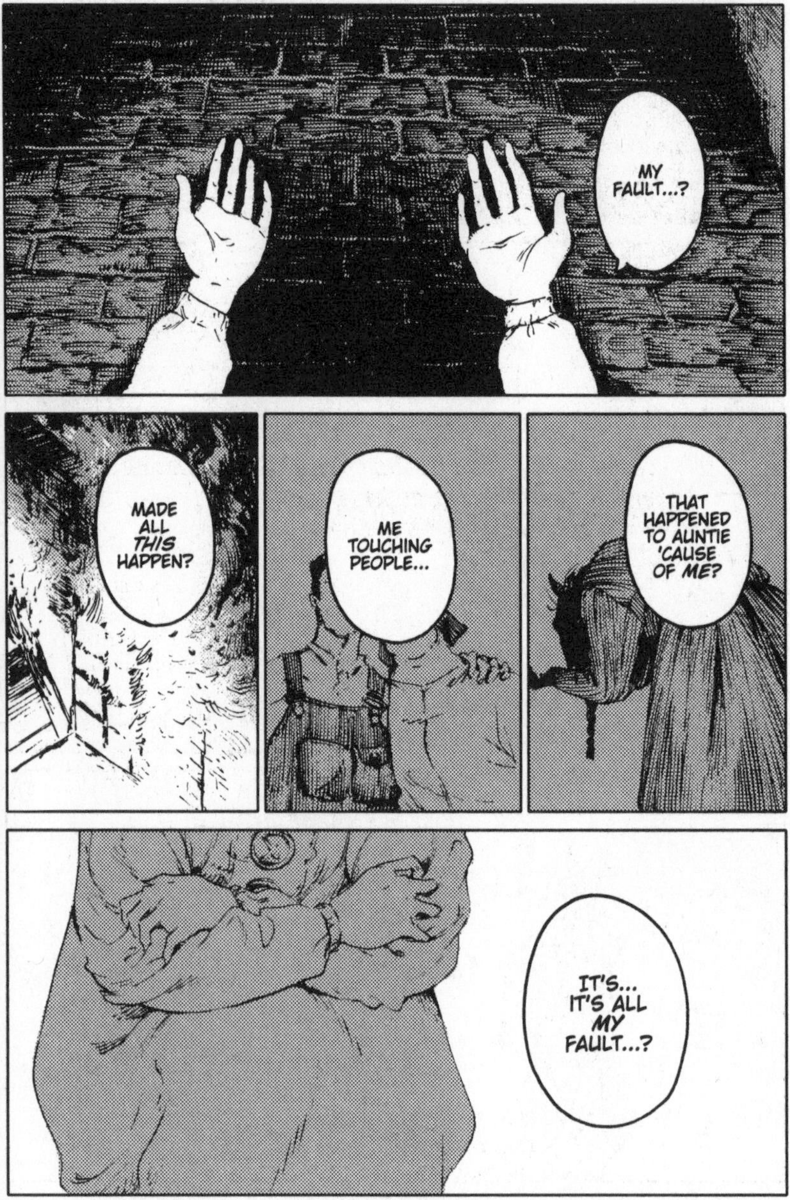
MY FAULT...?
THAT HAPPENED TO AUNTIE 'CAUSE OF *ME*?
ME TOUCHING PEOPLE...
MADE ALL *THIS* HAPPEN?
IT'S... IT'S ALL *MY* FAULT...?

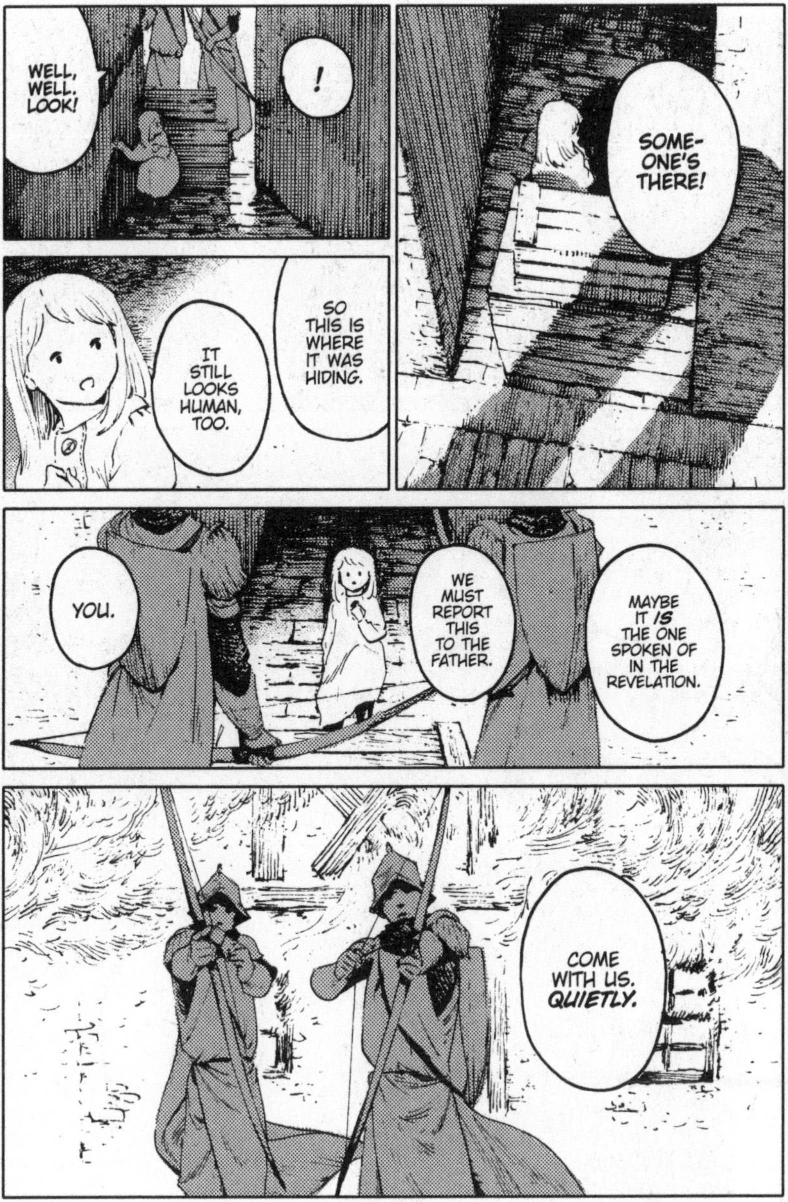
SOME-ONE'S THERE!
WELL, WELL. LOOK!
!
SO THIS IS WHERE IT WAS HIDING.
IT STILL LOOKS HUMAN, TOO.
MAYBE IT *IS* THE ONE SPOKEN OF IN THE REVELATION.
WE MUST REPORT THIS TO THE FATHER.
YOU.
COME WITH US. ***QUIETLY.***

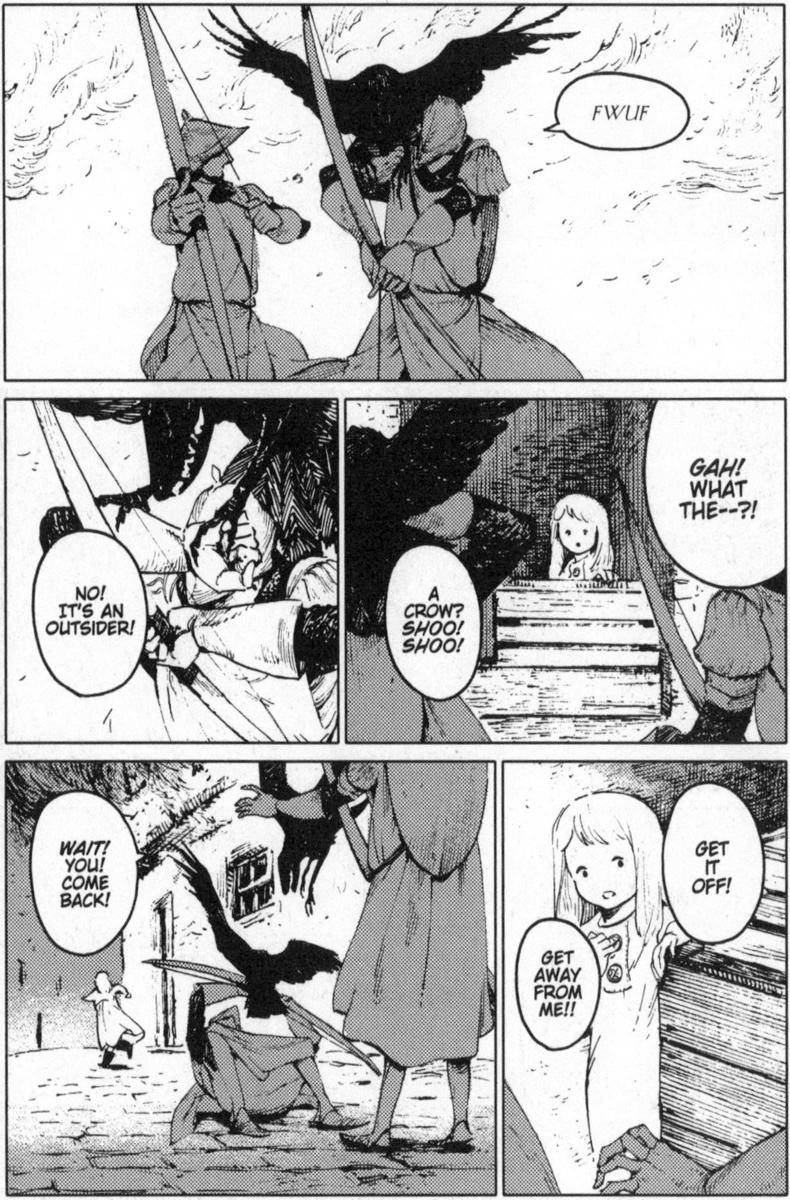
FWUF
GAH! WHAT THE--?!
A CROW? SHOO! SHOO!
NO! IT'S AN OUTSIDER!
GET IT OFF!
GET AWAY FROM ME!!
WAIT! YOU! COME BACK!

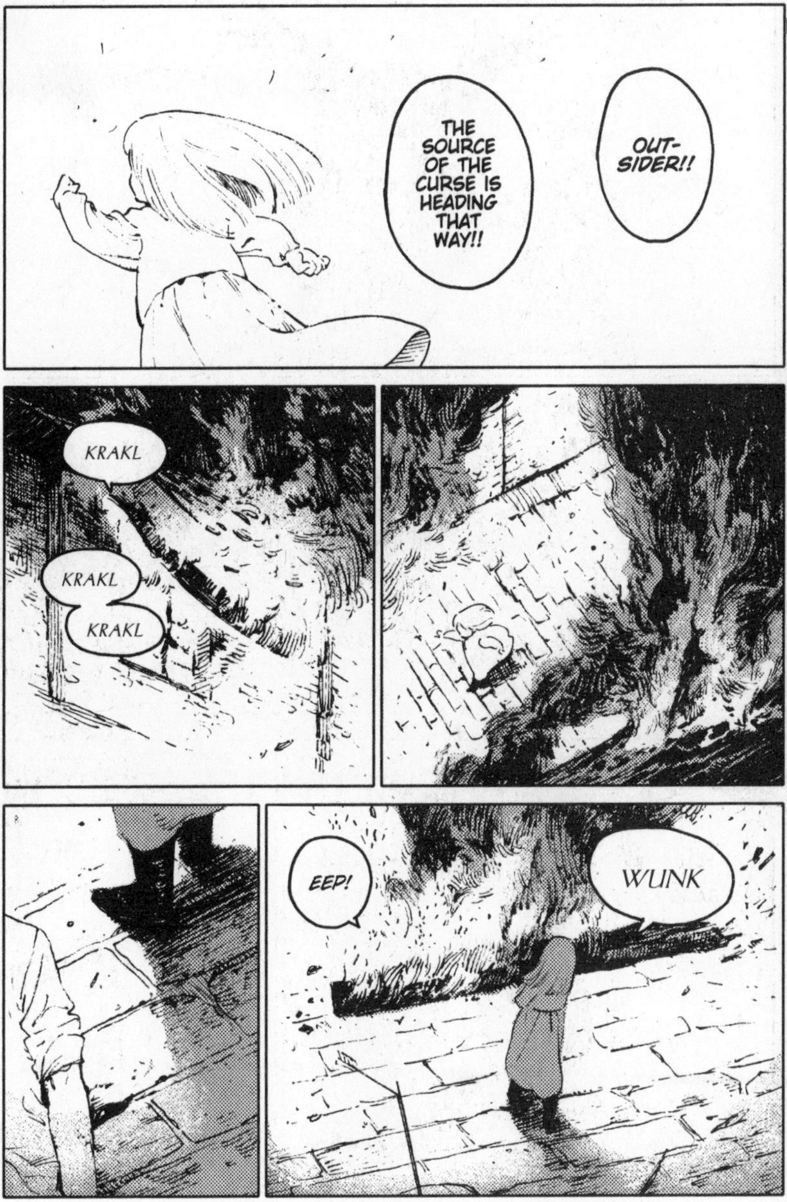
OUT-SIDER!!
THE SOURCE OF THE CURSE IS HEADING THAT WAY!!
KRAKL
KRAKL
KRAKL
WUNK
EEP!

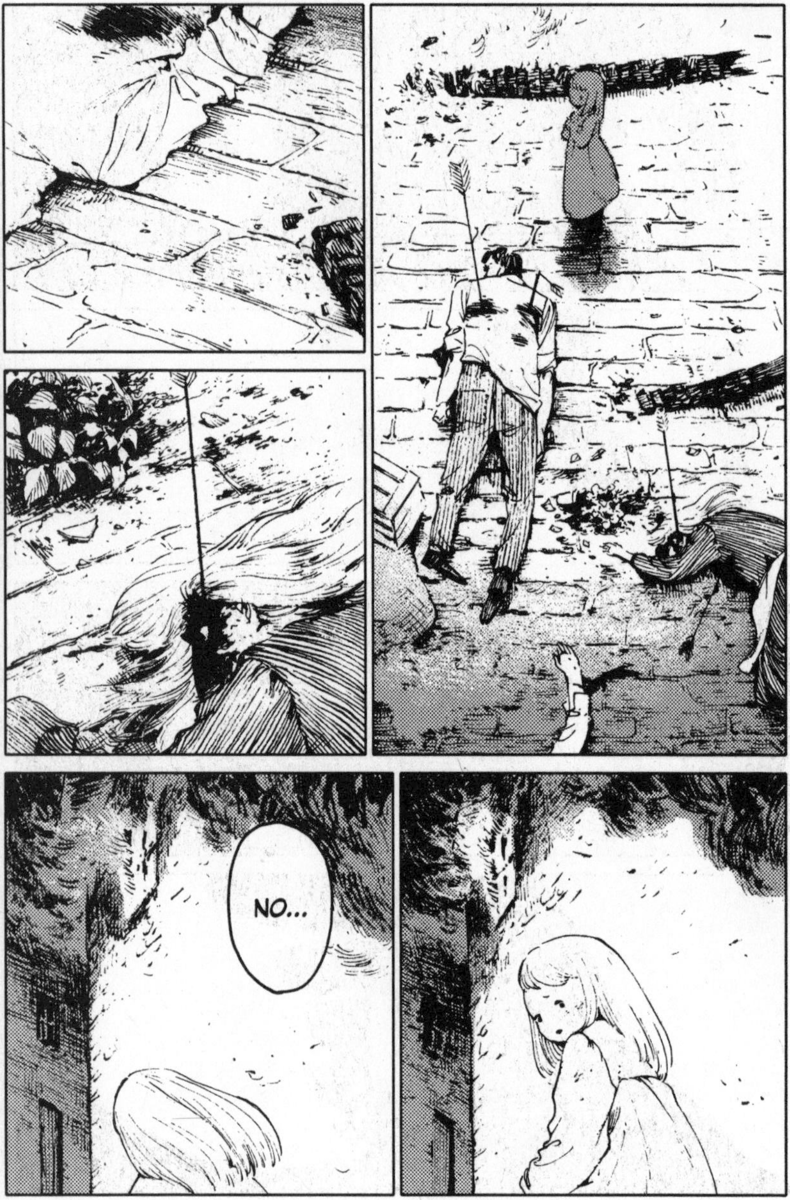
NO...

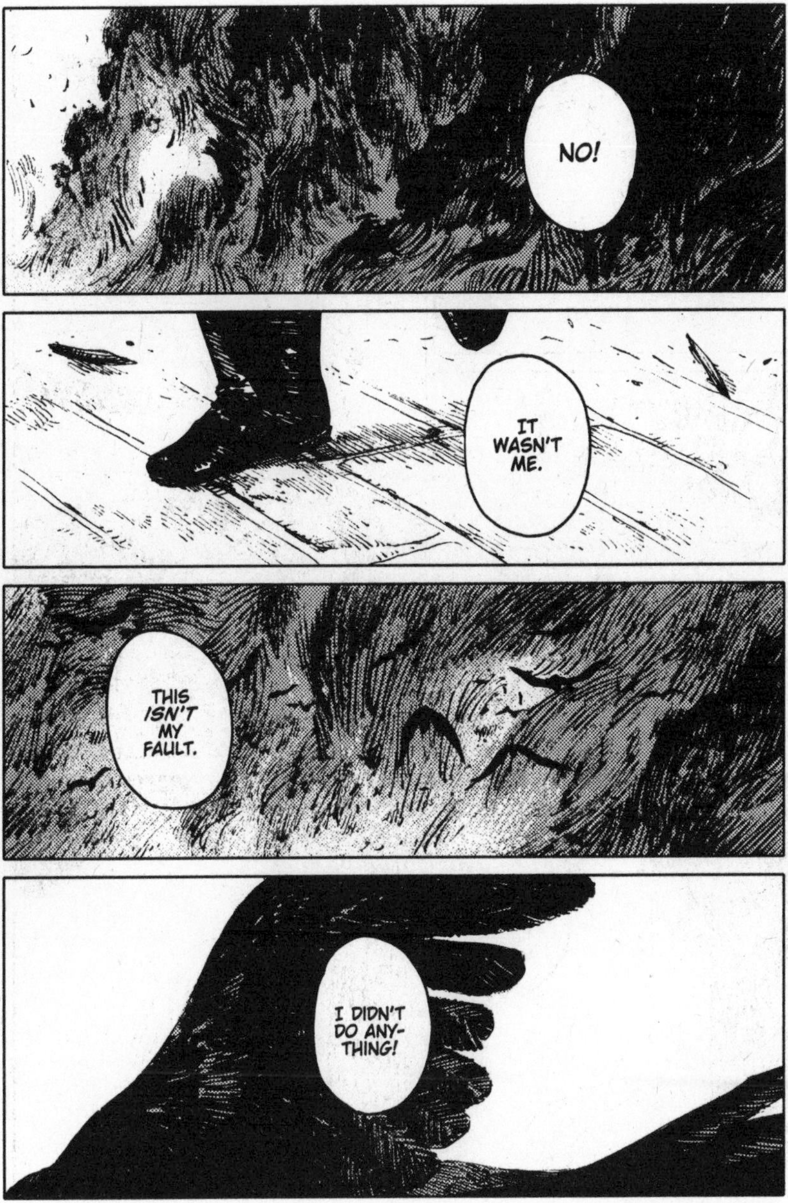
NO!
IT WASN'T ME.
THIS ISN'T MY FAULT.
I DIDN'T DO ANY-THING!

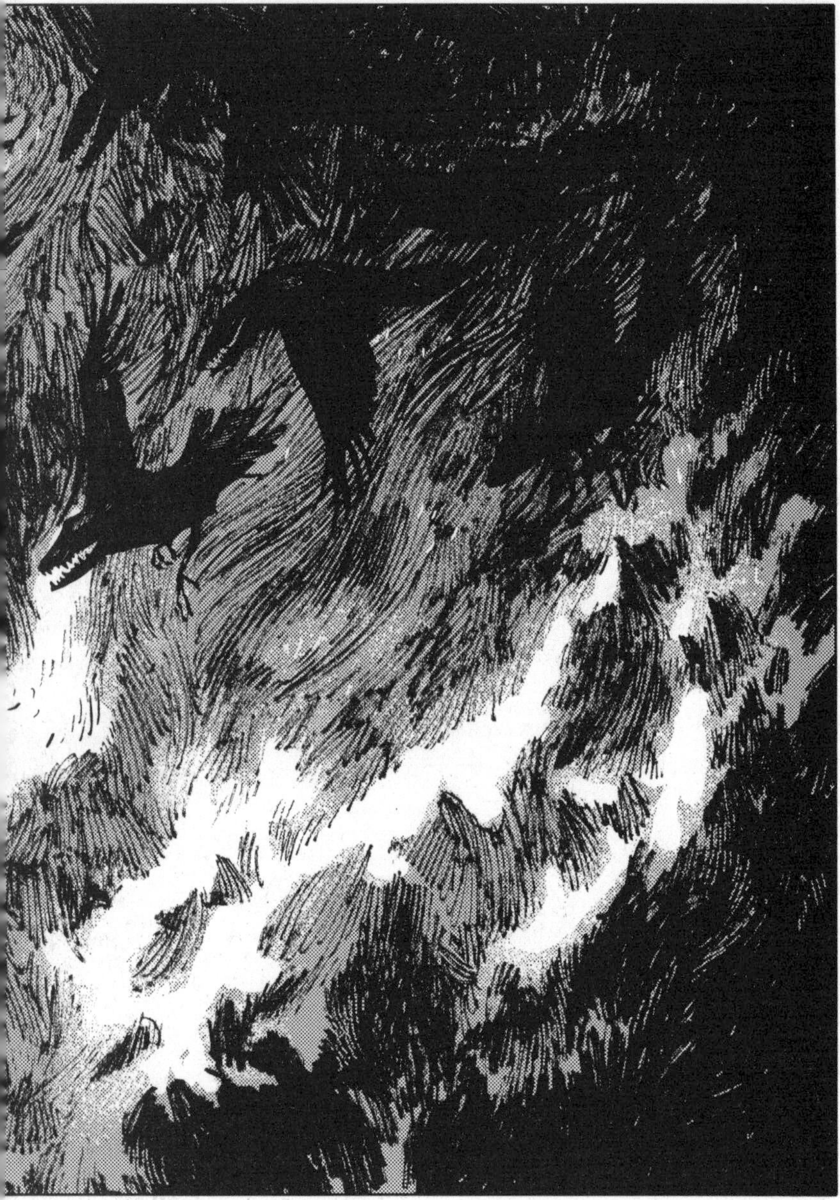

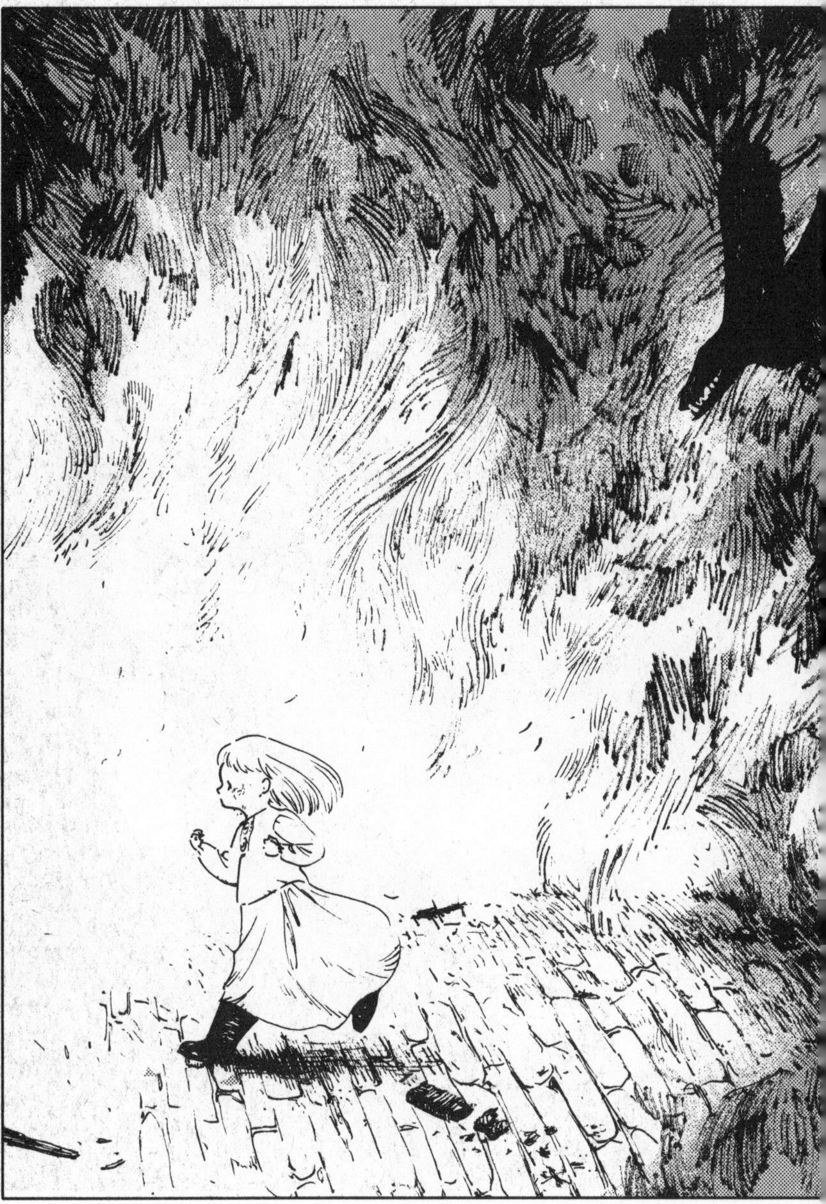

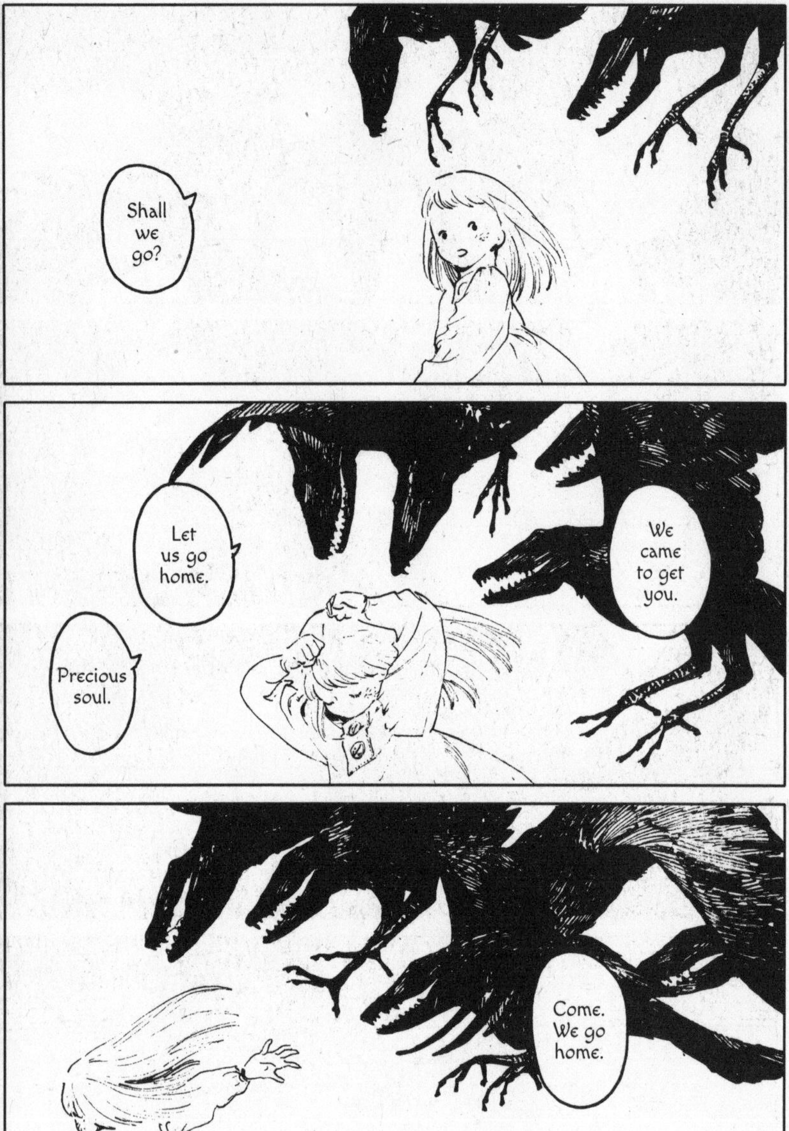
Shall we go?
We came to get you.
Let us go home.
Precious soul.
Come. We go home.

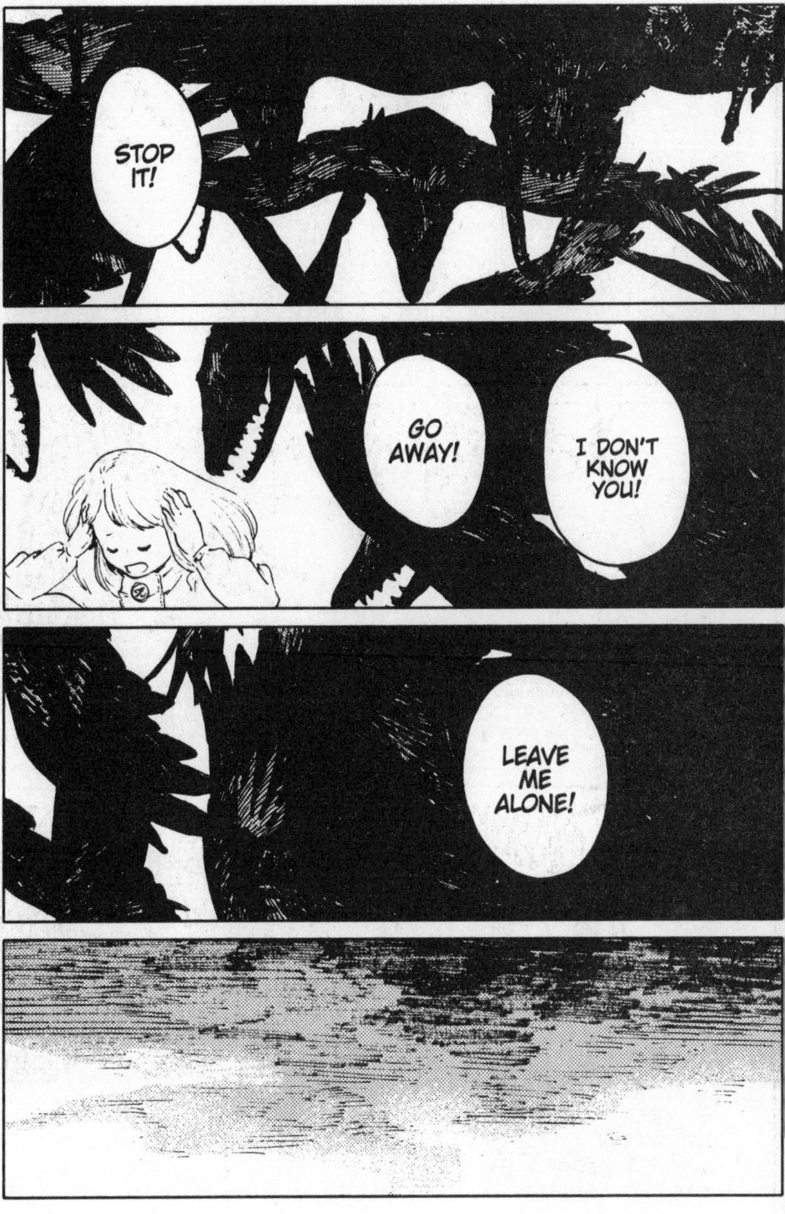
STOP IT!
I DON'T KNOW YOU!
GO AWAY!
LEAVE ME ALONE!

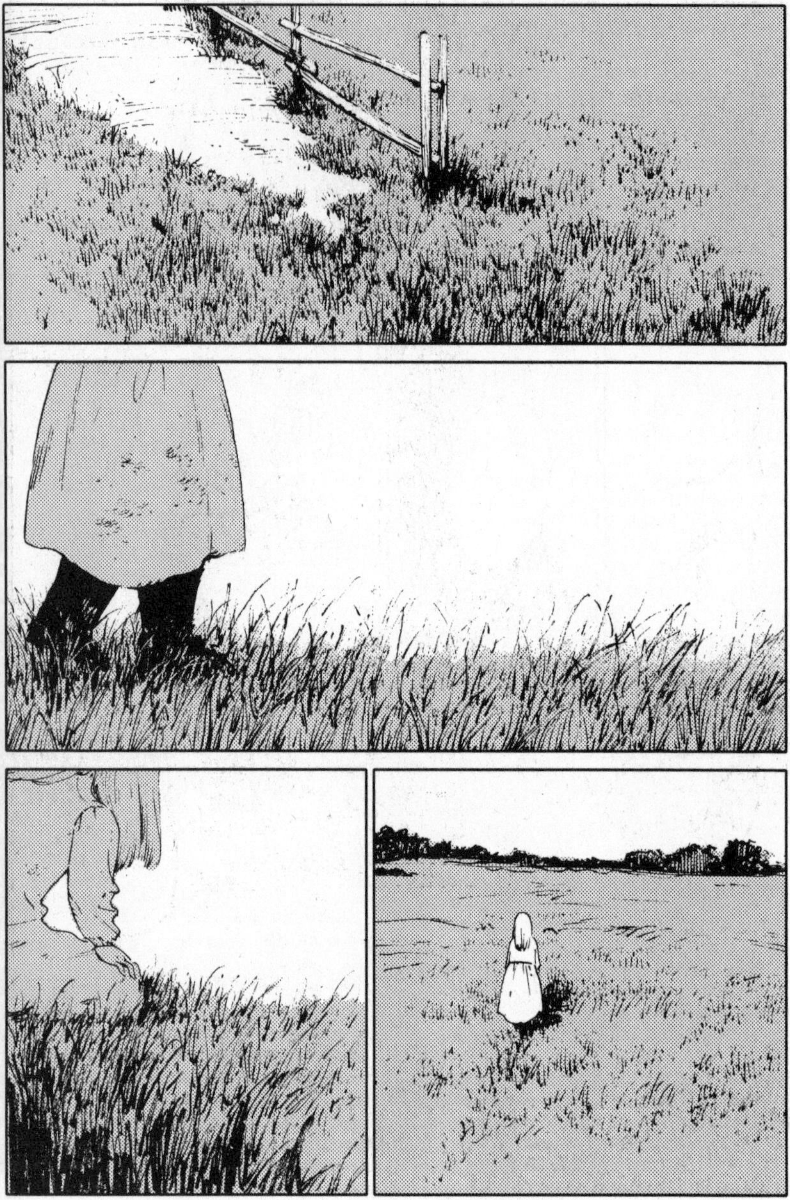

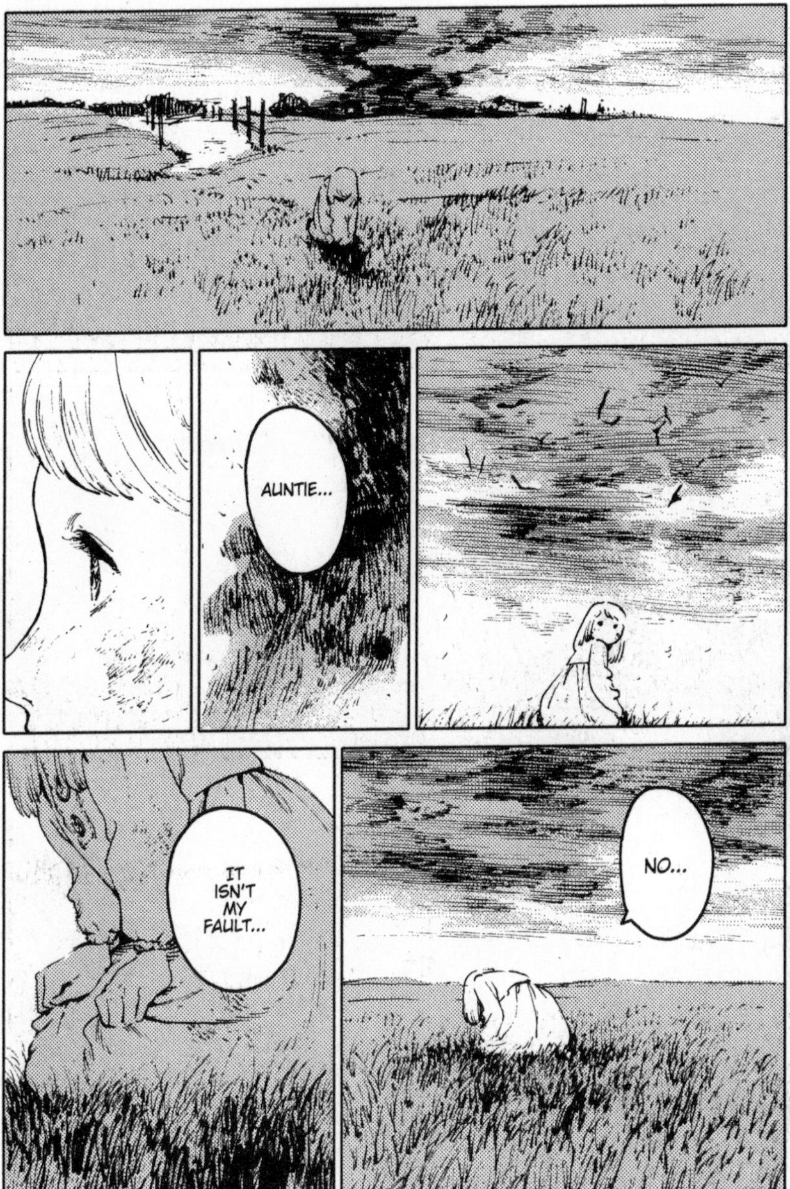
AUNTIE...
NO...
IT ISN'T MY FAULT...

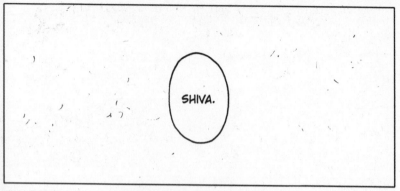

SHIVA.

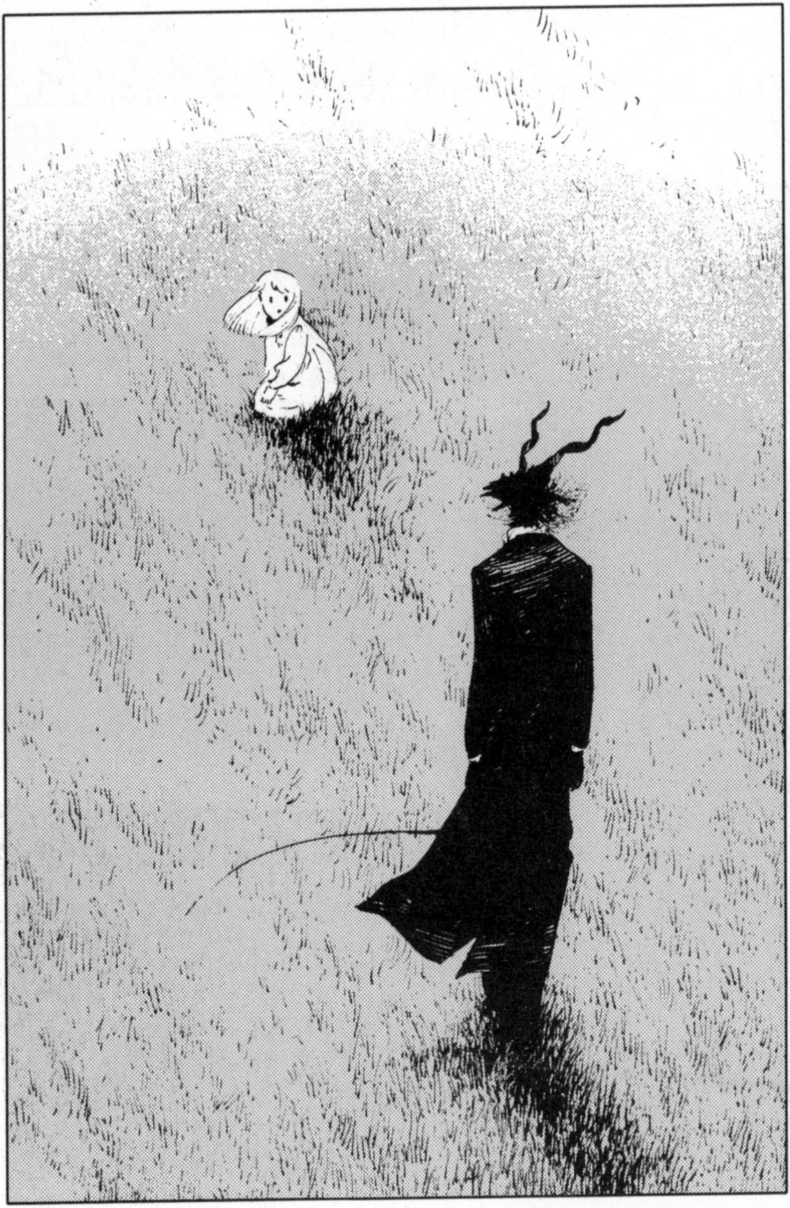

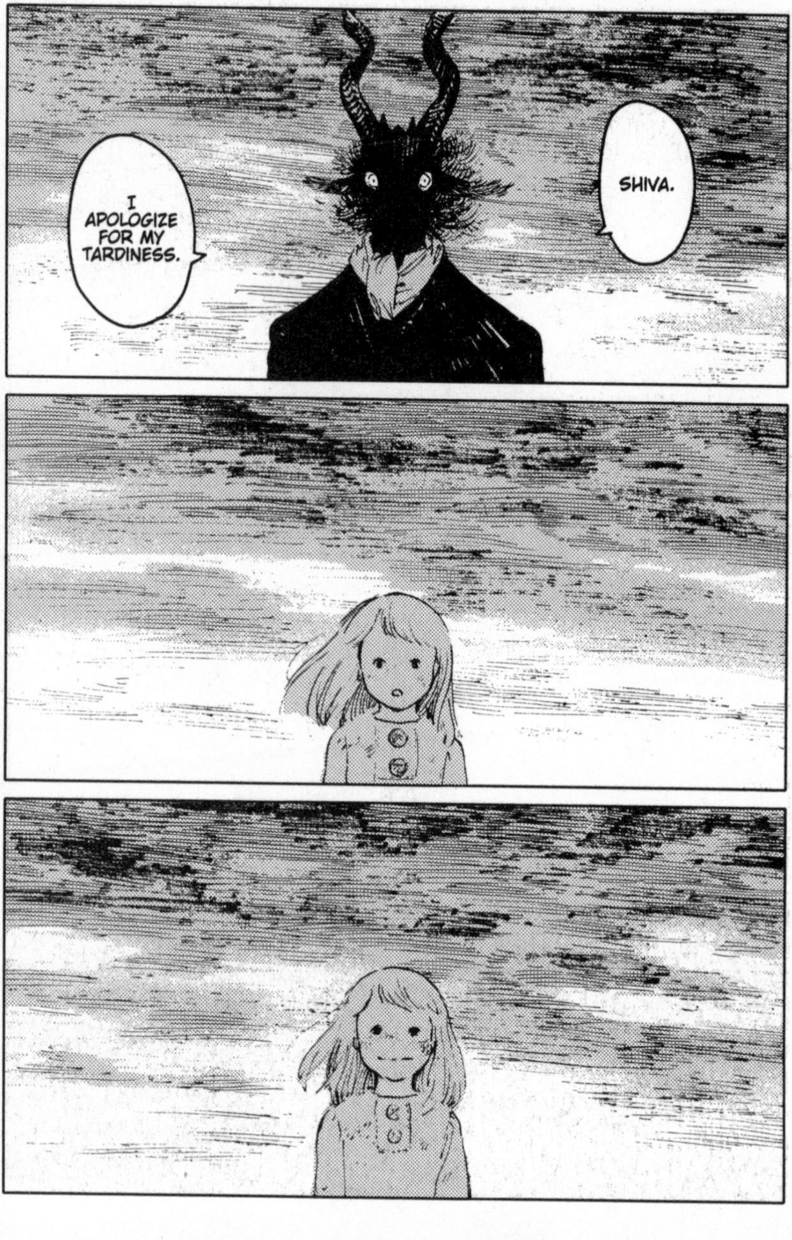
SHIVA.
I APOLOGIZE FOR MY TARDINESS.

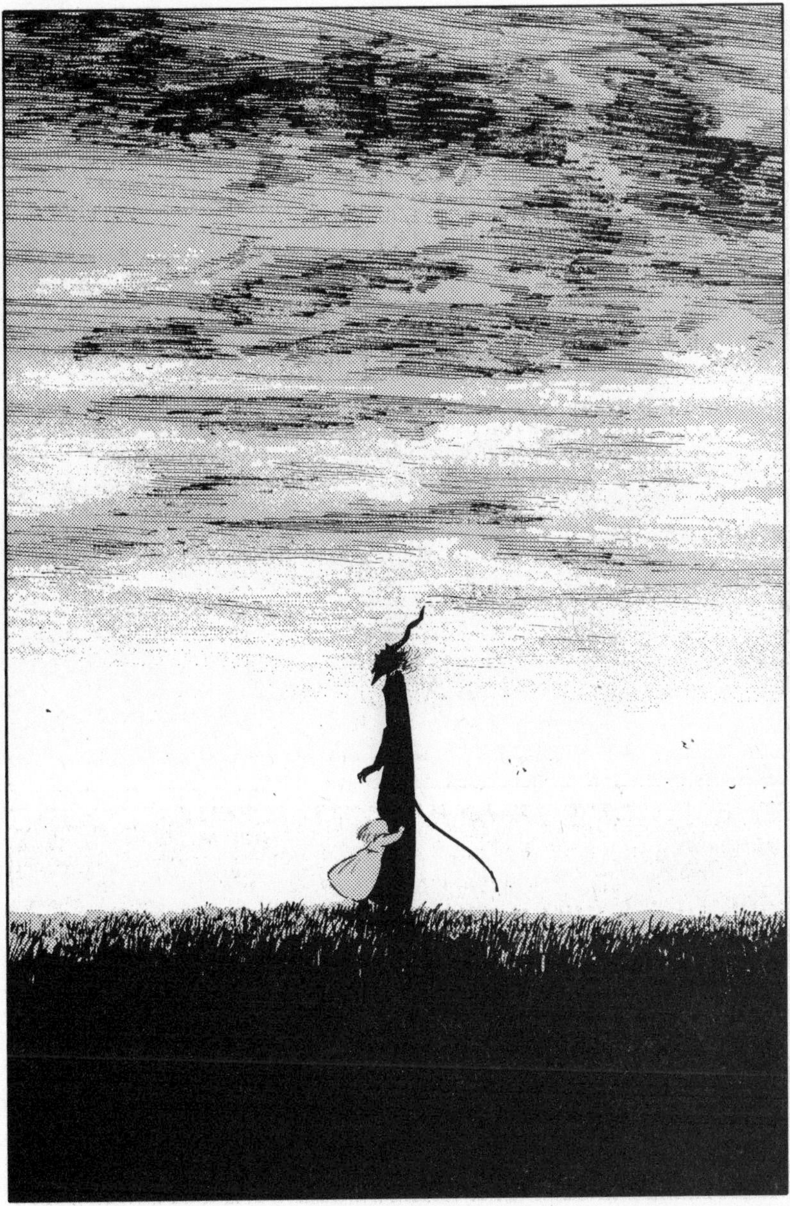

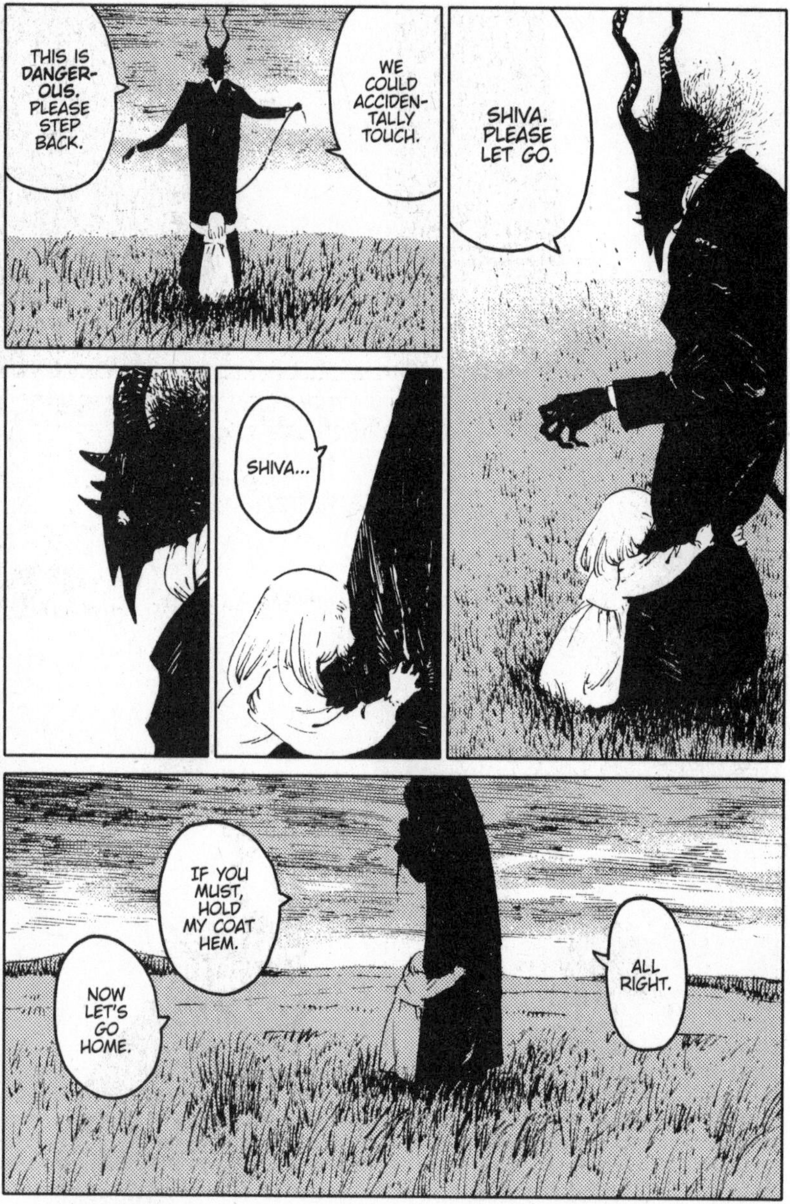
SHIVA. PLEASE LET GO.
WE COULD ACCIDENTALLY TOUCH.
THIS IS DANGEROUS. PLEASE STEP BACK.
SHIVA...
IF YOU MUST, HOLD MY COAT HEM.
NOW LET'S GO HOME.
ALL RIGHT.

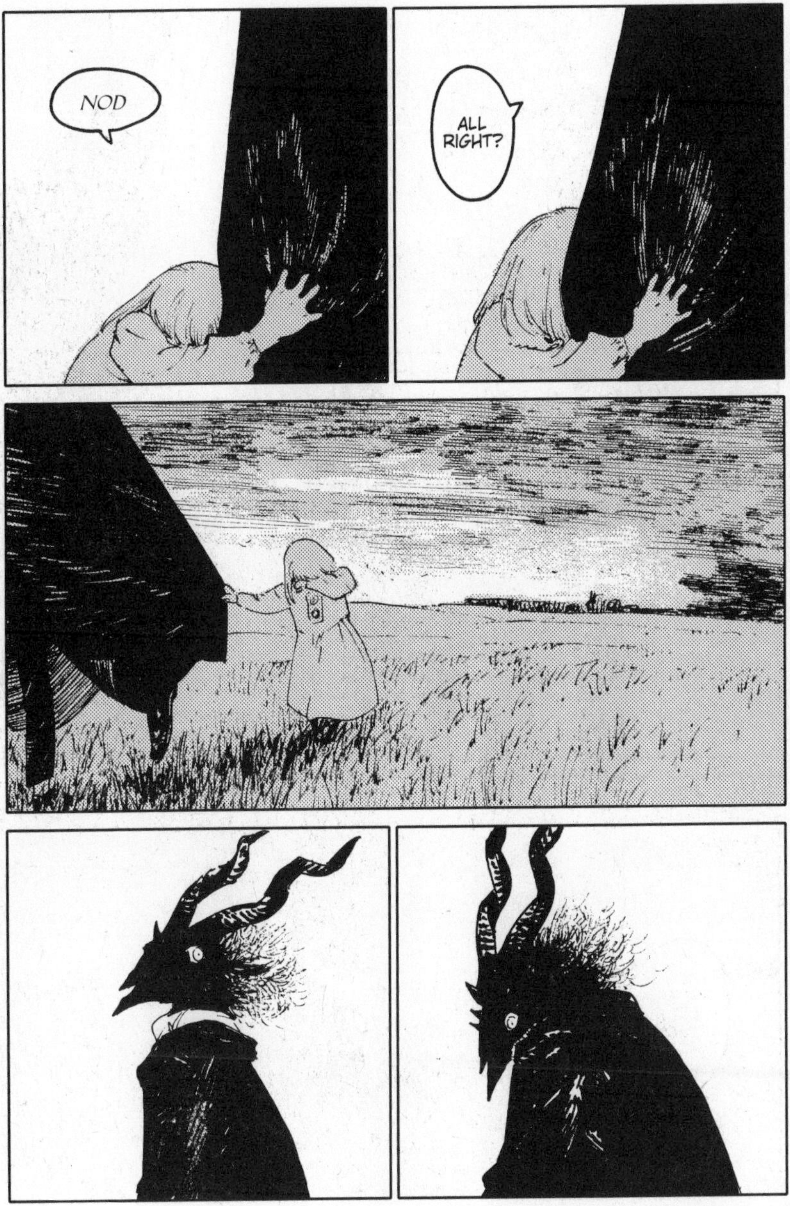
ALL RIGHT?
NOD

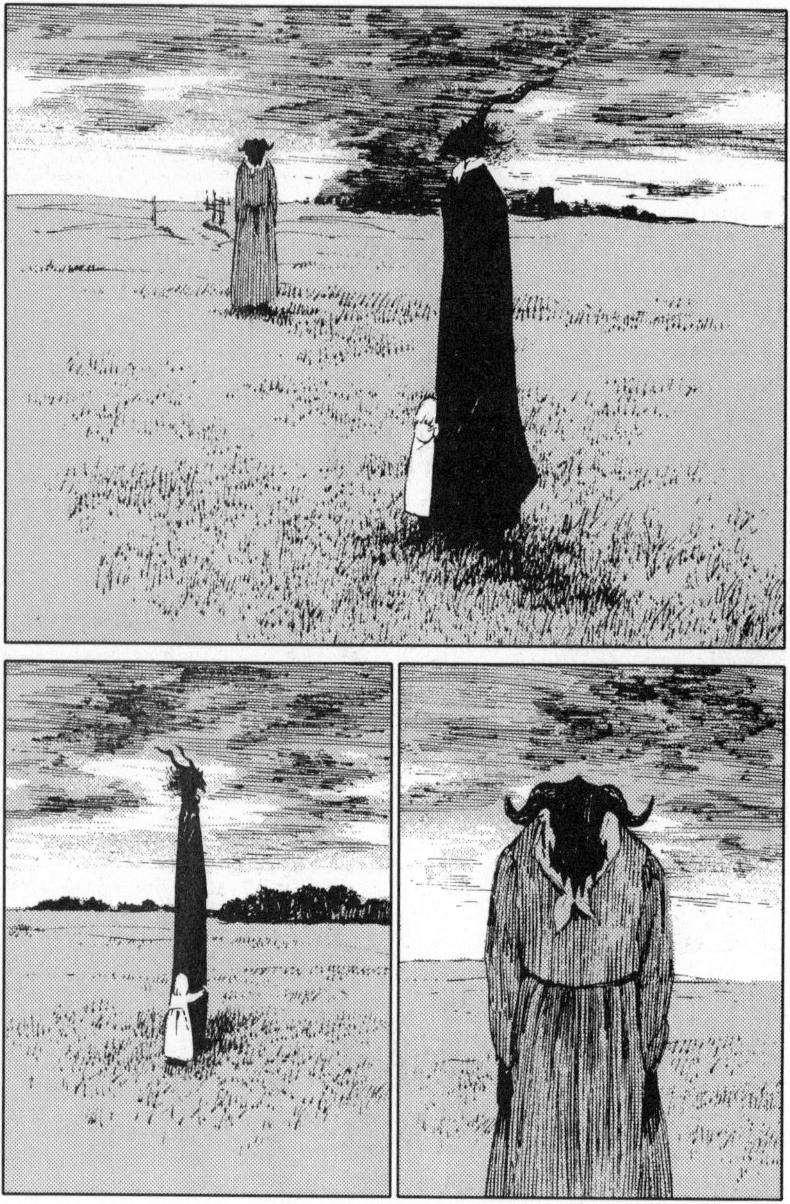

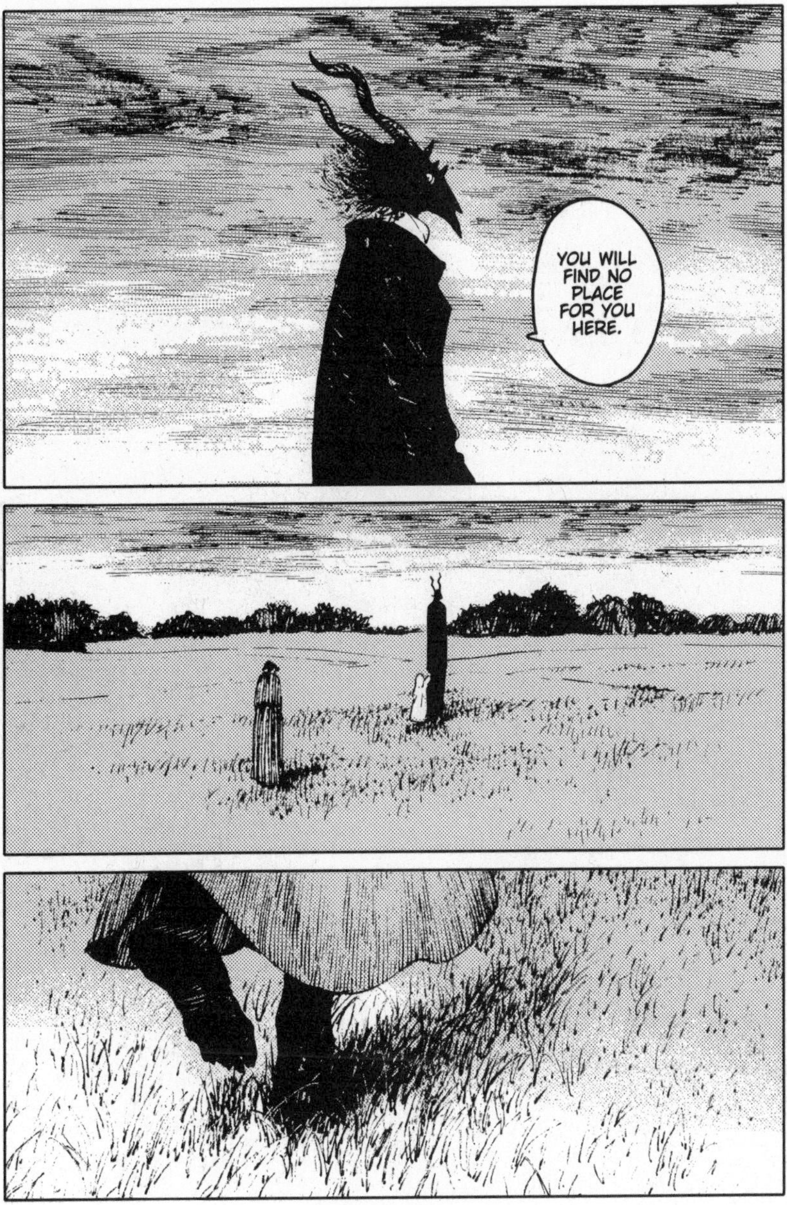
YOU WILL FIND NO PLACE FOR YOU HERE.

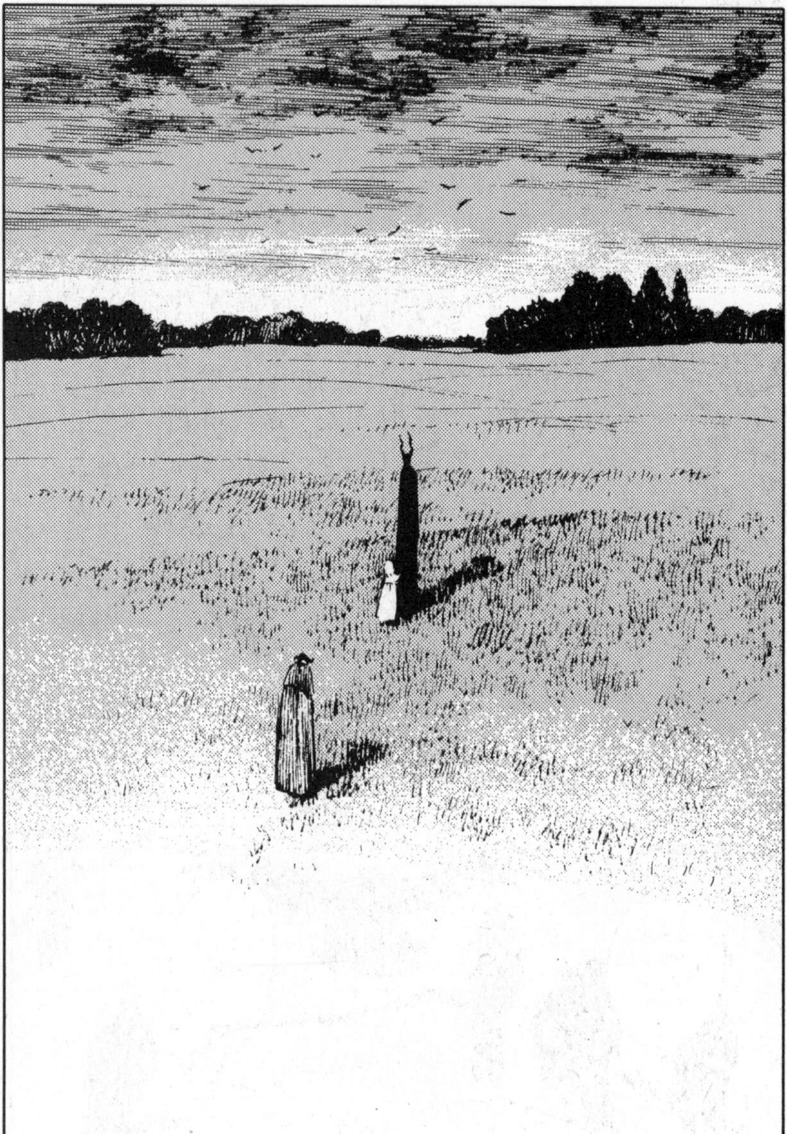

Chapter 15

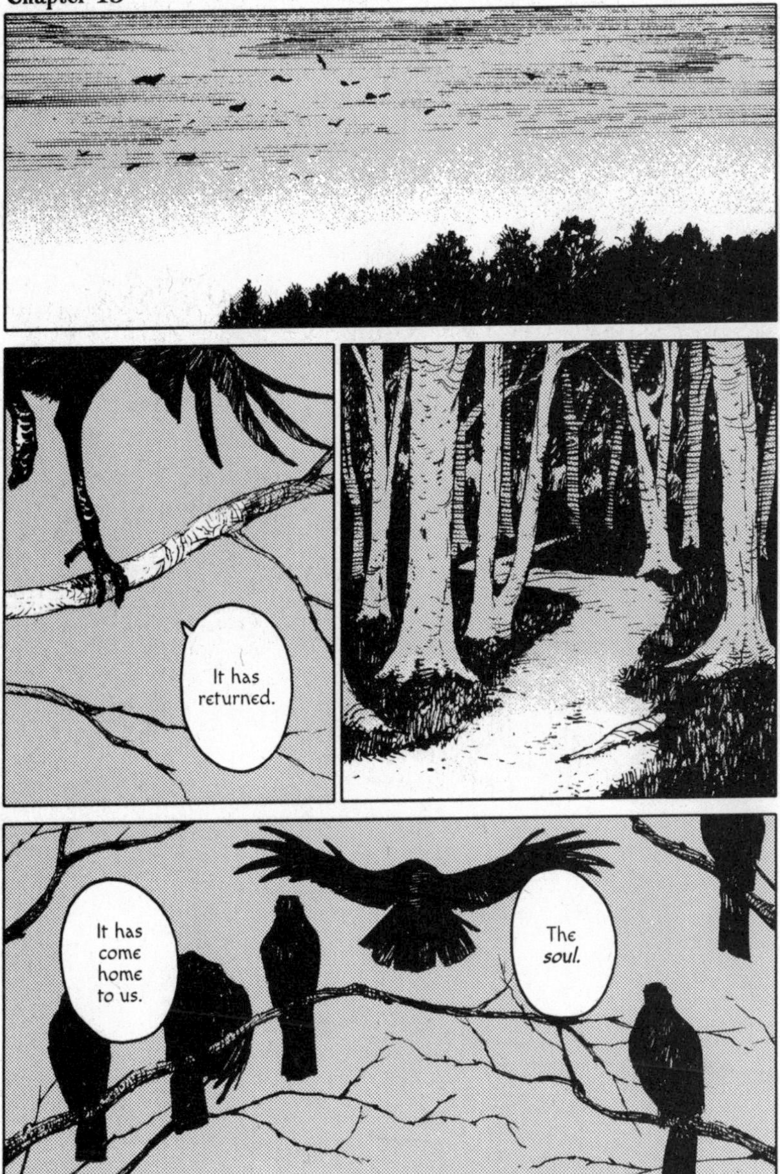
It has returned.
The *soul.*
It has come home to us.

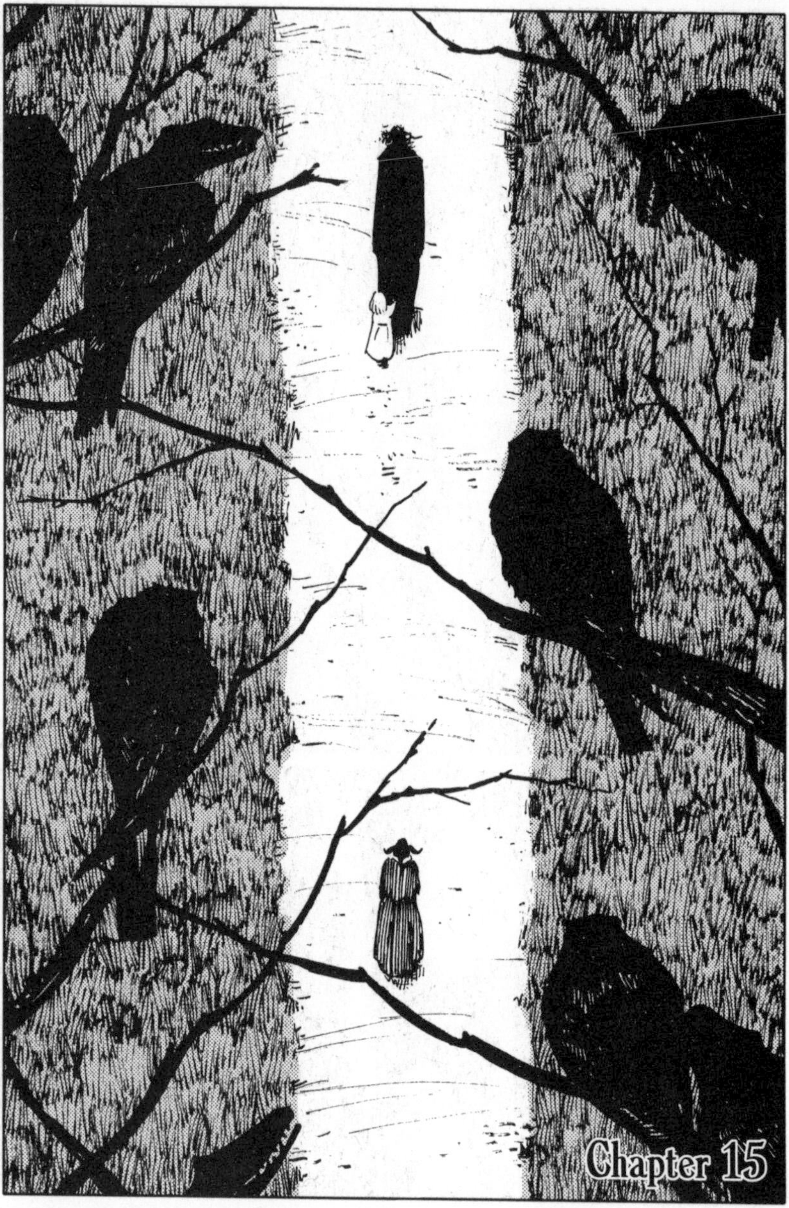
Chapter 15

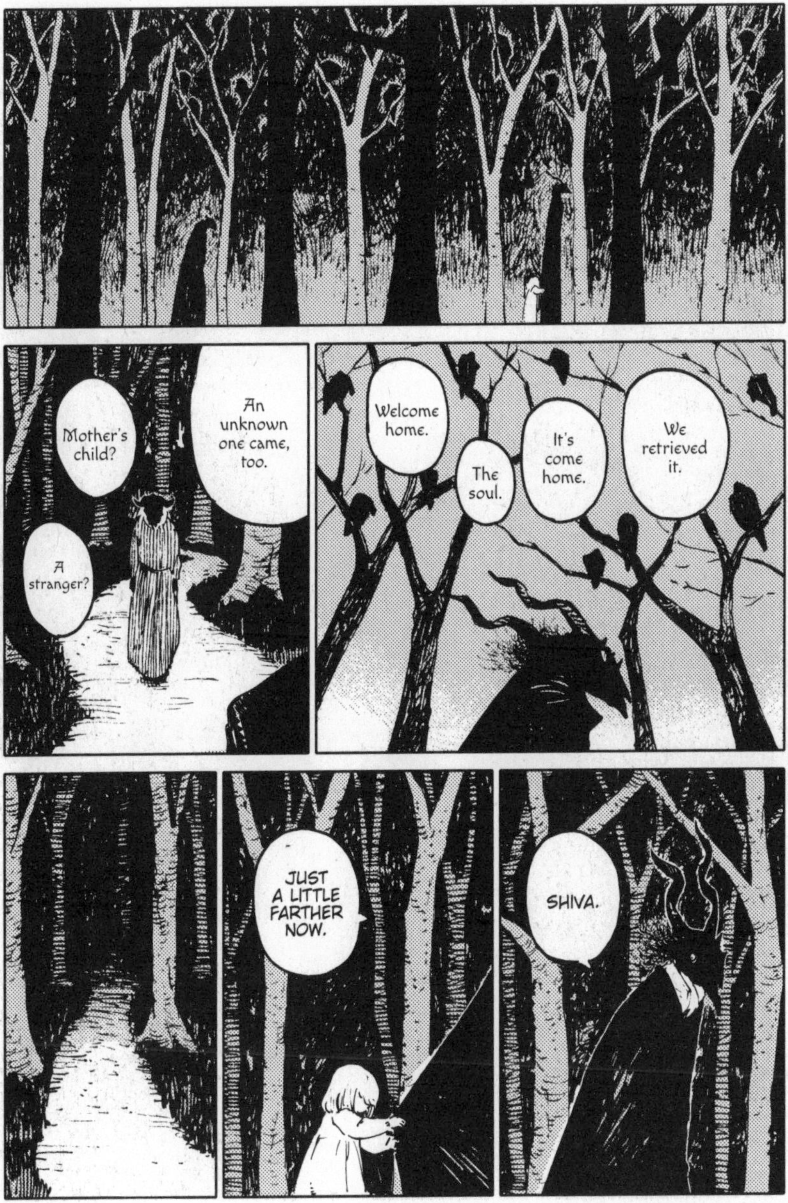
We retrieved it.
It's come home.
The soul.
Welcome home.
An unknown one came, too.
Mother's child?
A stranger?
SHIVA.
JUST A LITTLE FARTHER NOW.

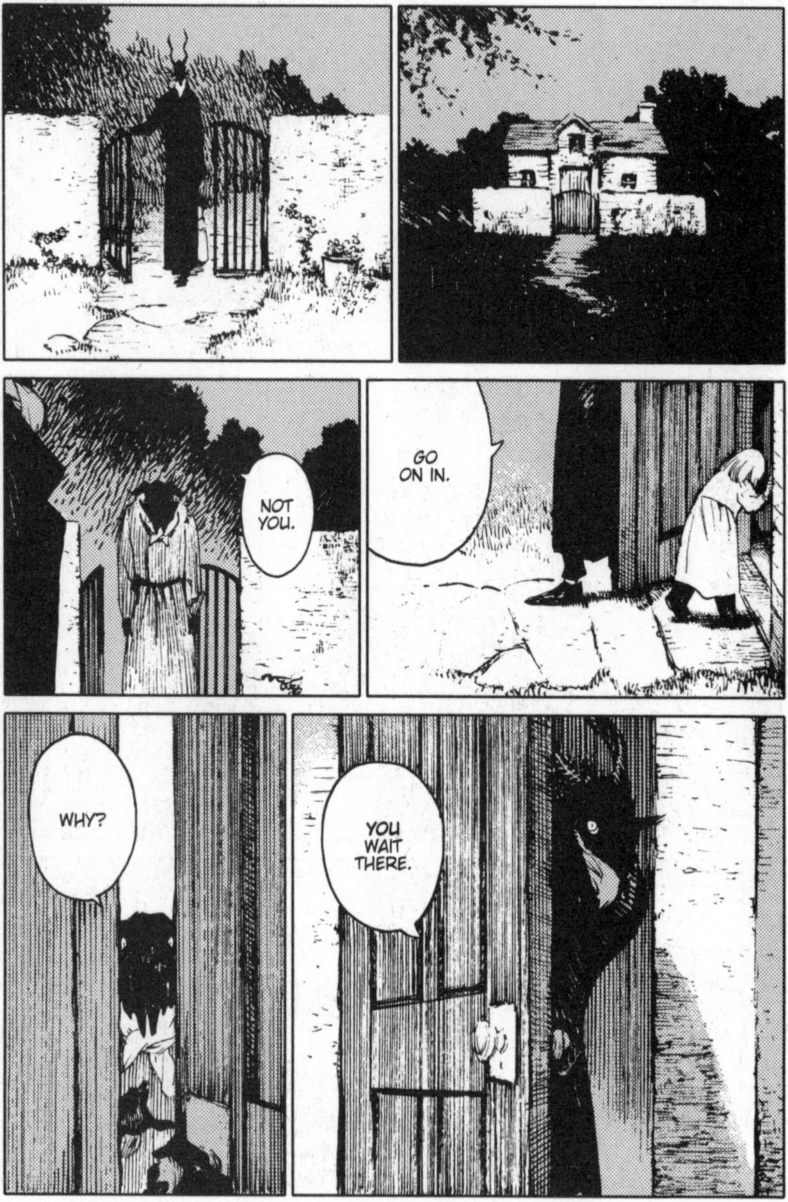
GO ON IN.
NOT YOU.
YOU WAIT THERE.
WHY?

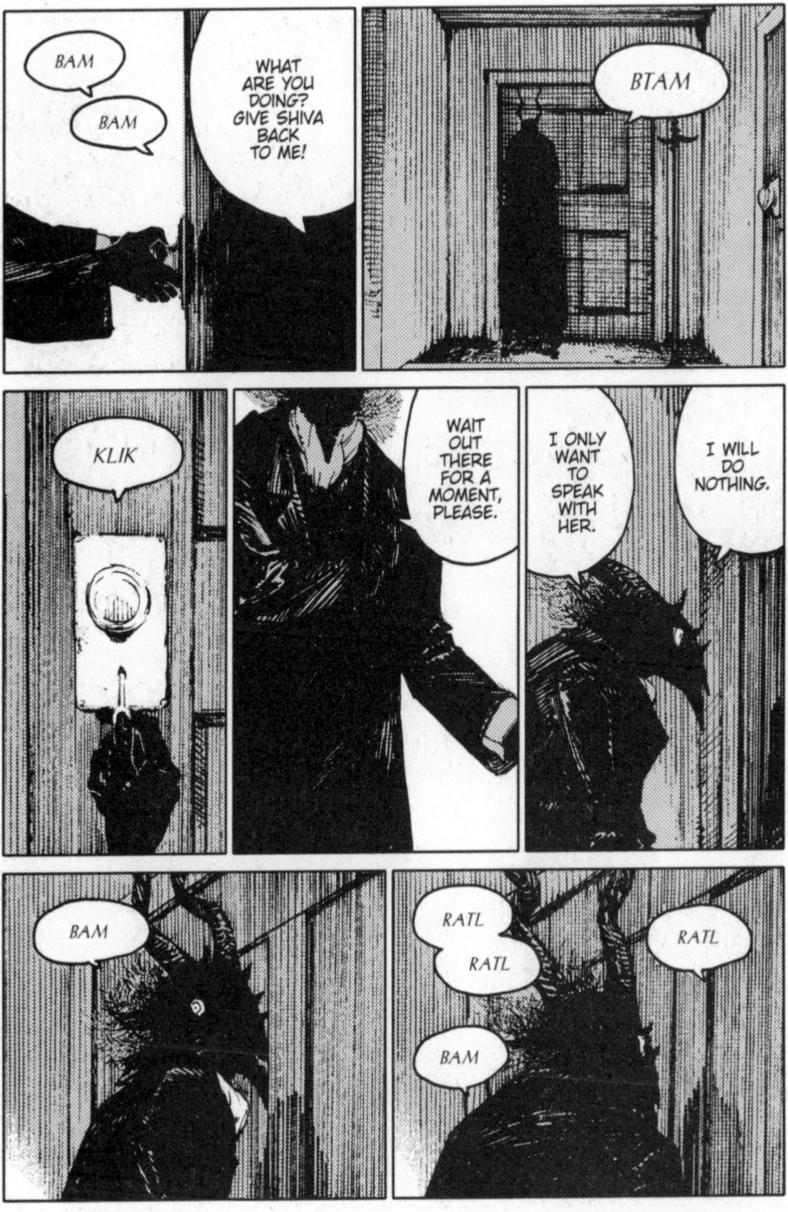
BTAM
WHAT ARE YOU DOING? GIVE SHIVA BACK TO ME!
BAM
BAM
I WILL DO NOTHING.
I ONLY WANT TO SPEAK WITH HER.
WAIT OUT THERE FOR A MOMENT, PLEASE.
KLIK
RATL
RATL
RATL
BAM
BAM

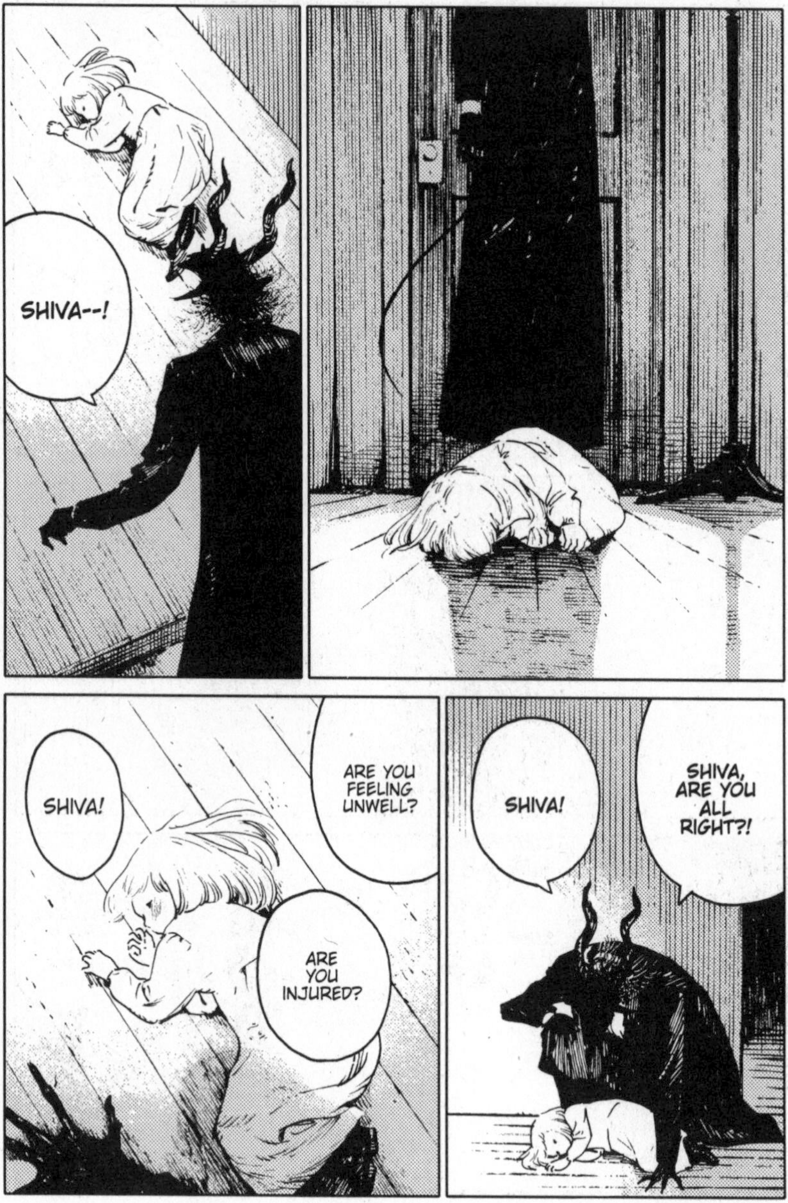
SHIVA--!
SHIVA, ARE YOU ALL RIGHT?!
SHIVA!
ARE YOU FEELING UNWELL?
SHIVA!
ARE YOU INJURED?

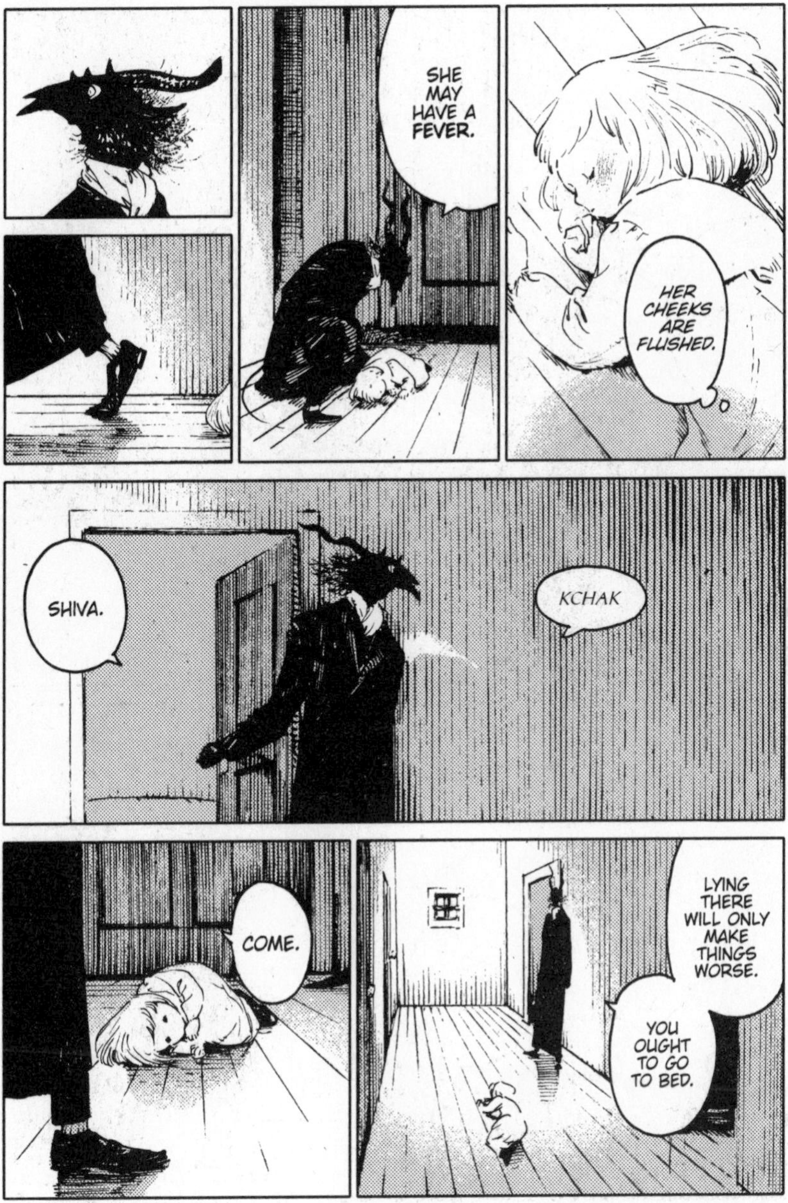
HER CHEEKS ARE FLUSHED.
SHE MAY HAVE A FEVER.
KCHAK
SHIVA.
LYING THERE WILL ONLY MAKE THINGS WORSE.
YOU OUGHT TO GO TO BED.
COME.

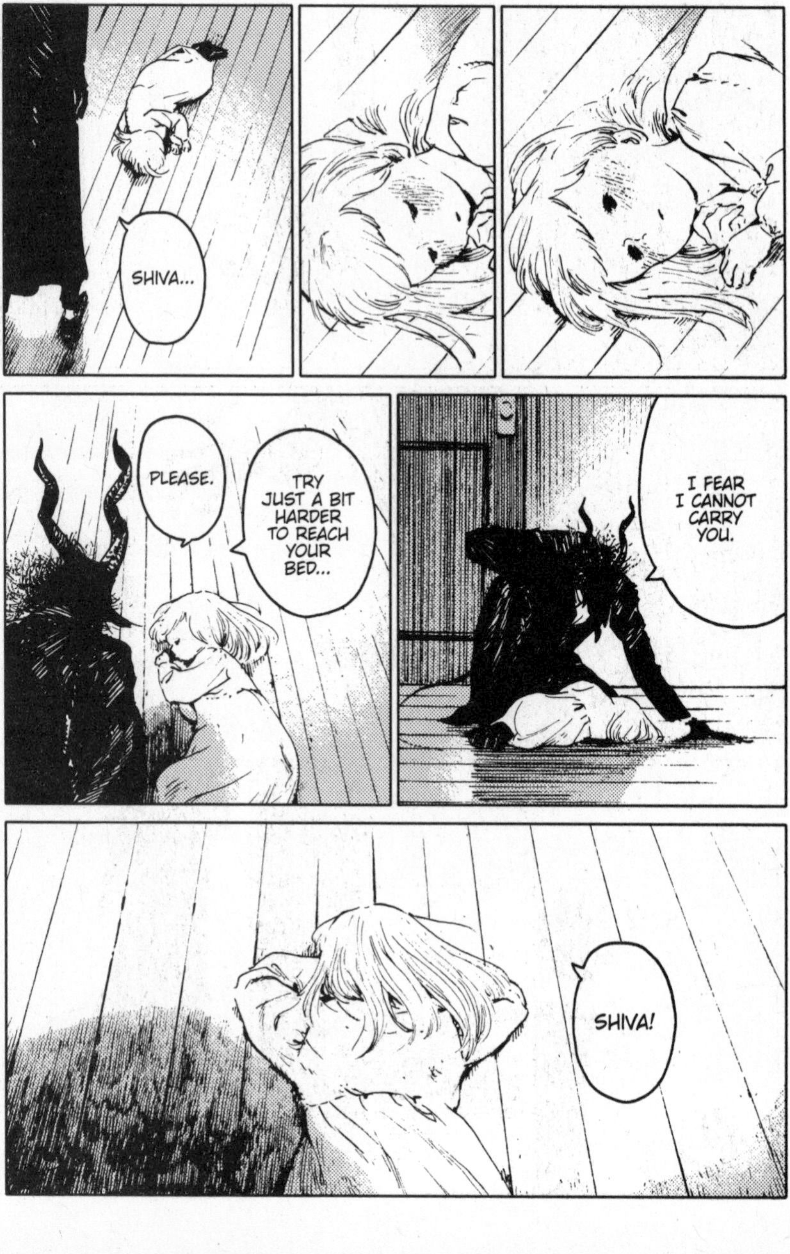
SHIVA...
I FEAR I CANNOT CARRY YOU.
TRY JUST A BIT HARDER TO REACH YOUR BED...
PLEASE.
SHIVA!

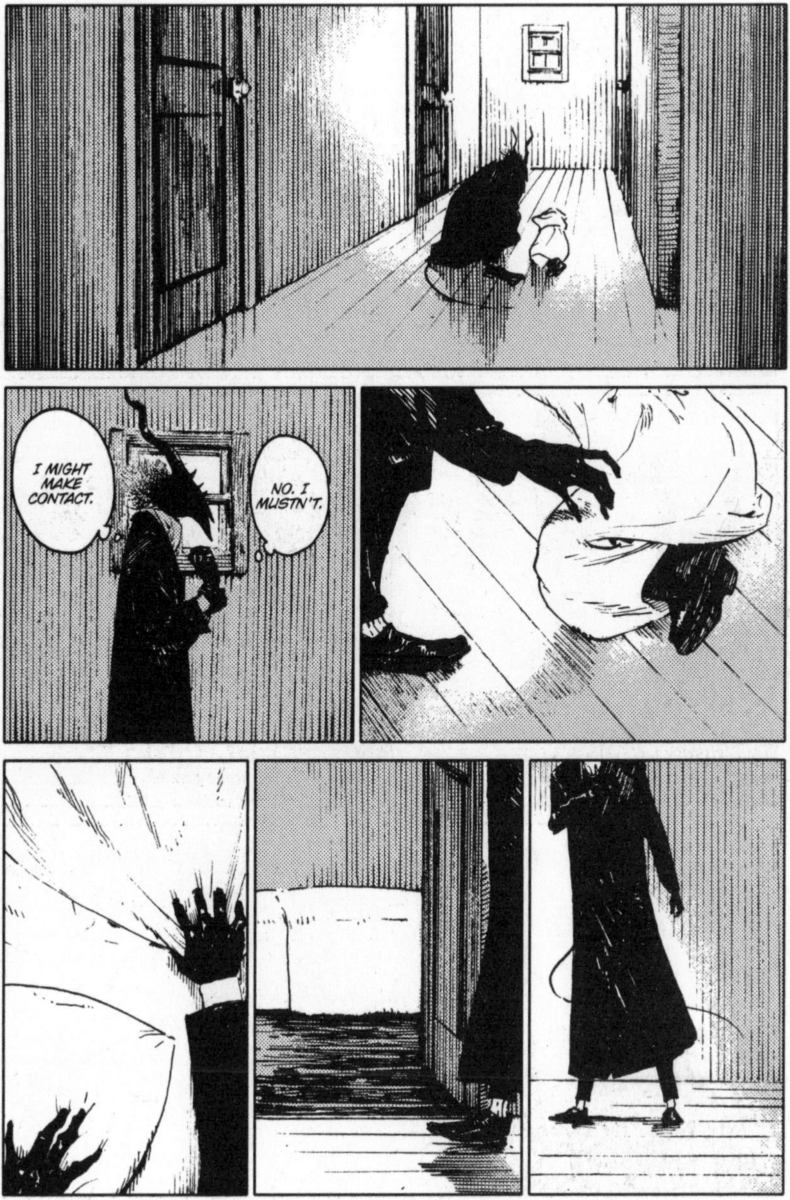
I MIGHT MAKE CONTACT.
NO. I MUSTN'T.

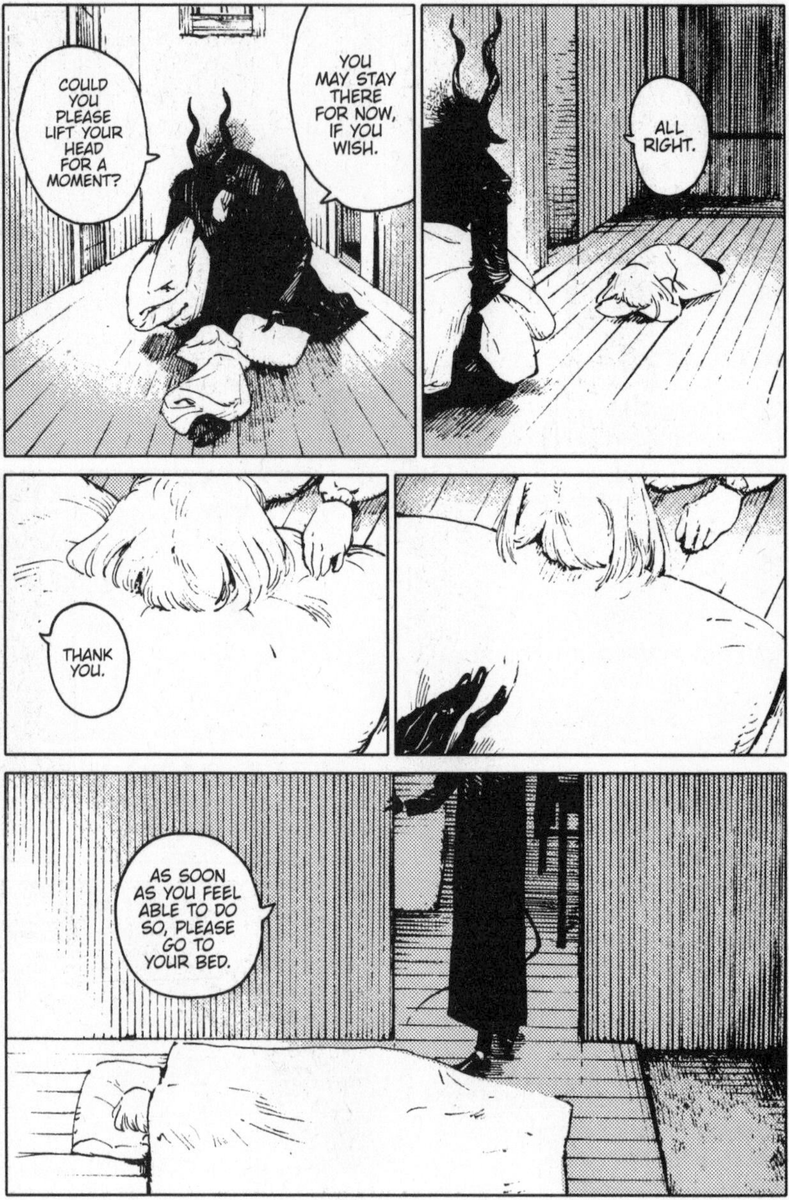
ALL RIGHT.
YOU MAY STAY THERE FOR NOW, IF YOU WISH.
COULD YOU PLEASE LIFT YOUR HEAD FOR A MOMENT?
THANK YOU.
AS SOON AS YOU FEEL ABLE TO DO SO, PLEASE GO TO YOUR BED.

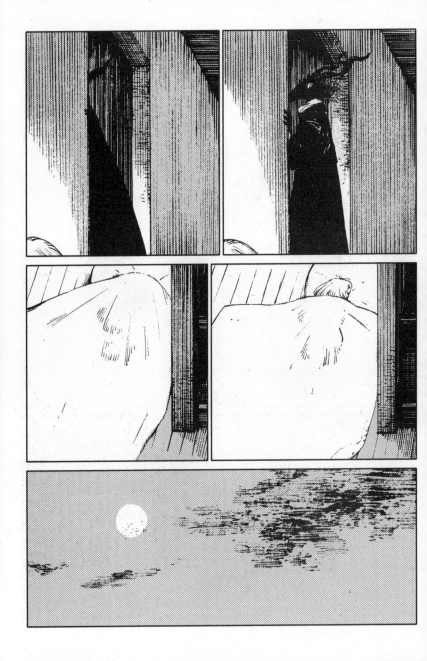

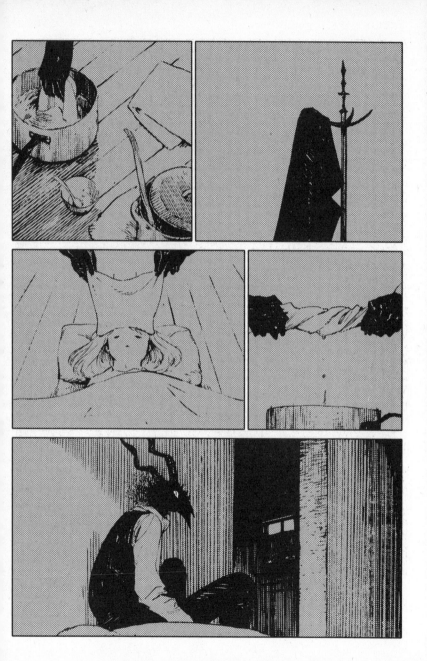

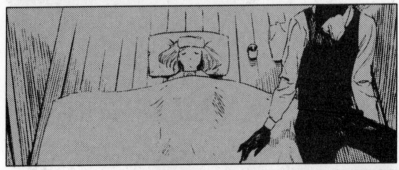

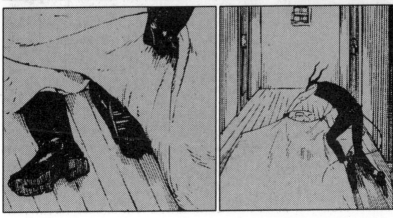

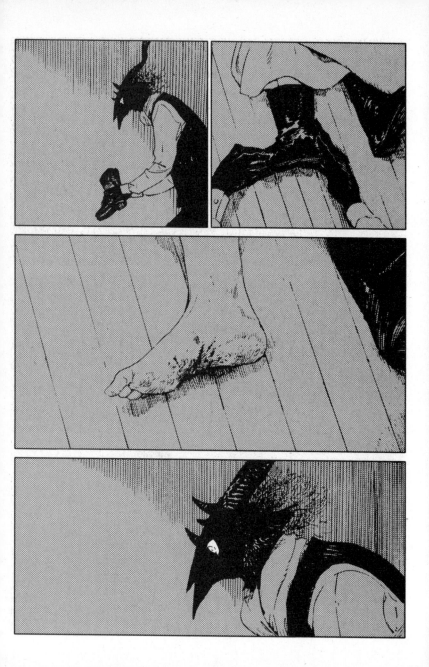

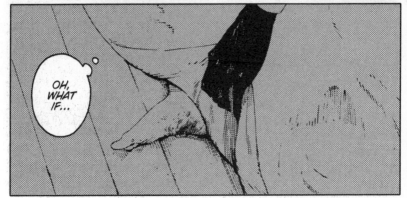

OH, WHAT IF...

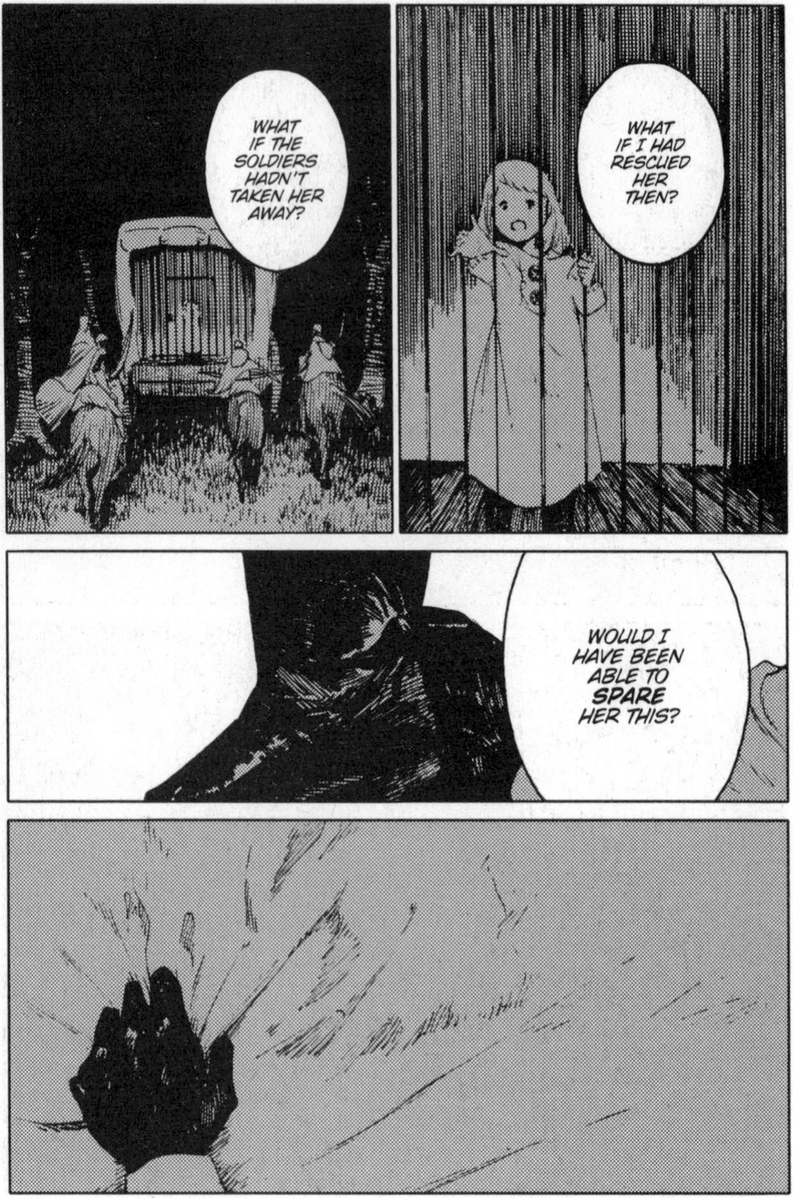
WHAT IF I HAD RESCUED HER THEN?
WHAT IF THE SOLDIERS HADN'T TAKEN HER AWAY?
WOULD I HAVE BEEN ABLE TO SPARE HER THIS?

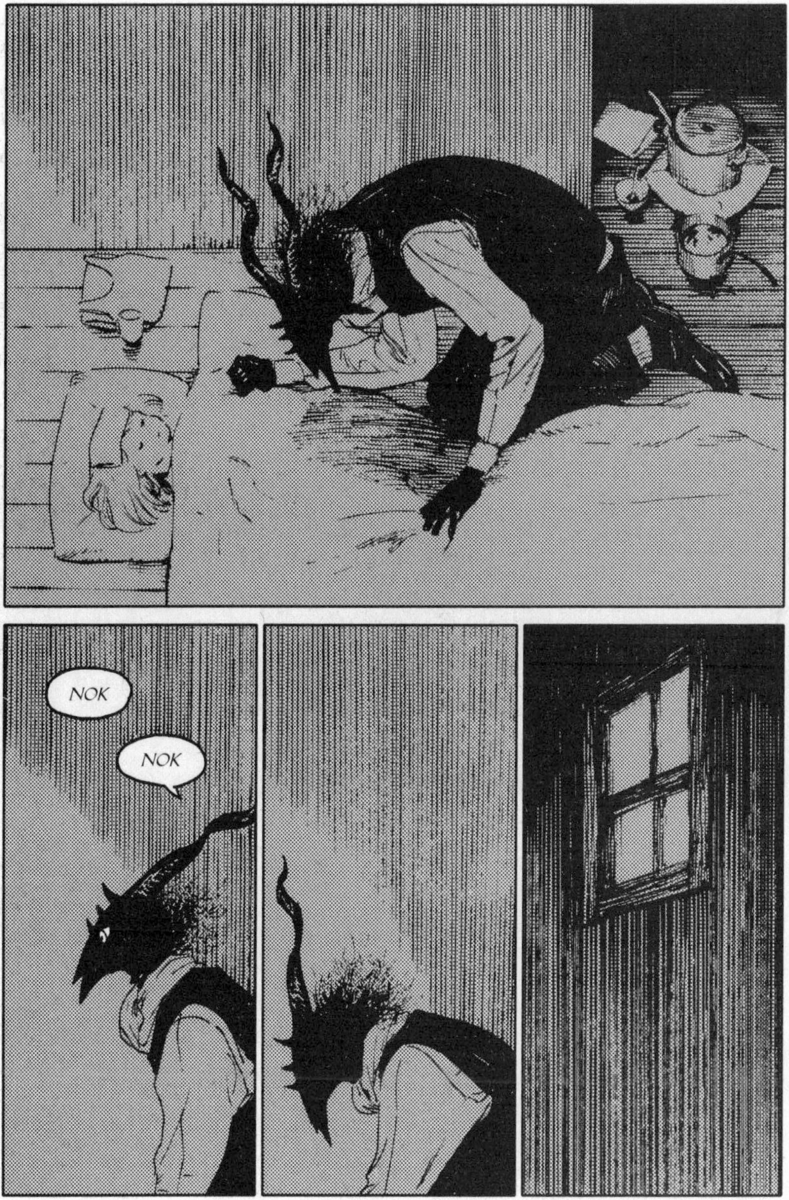
NOK
NOK

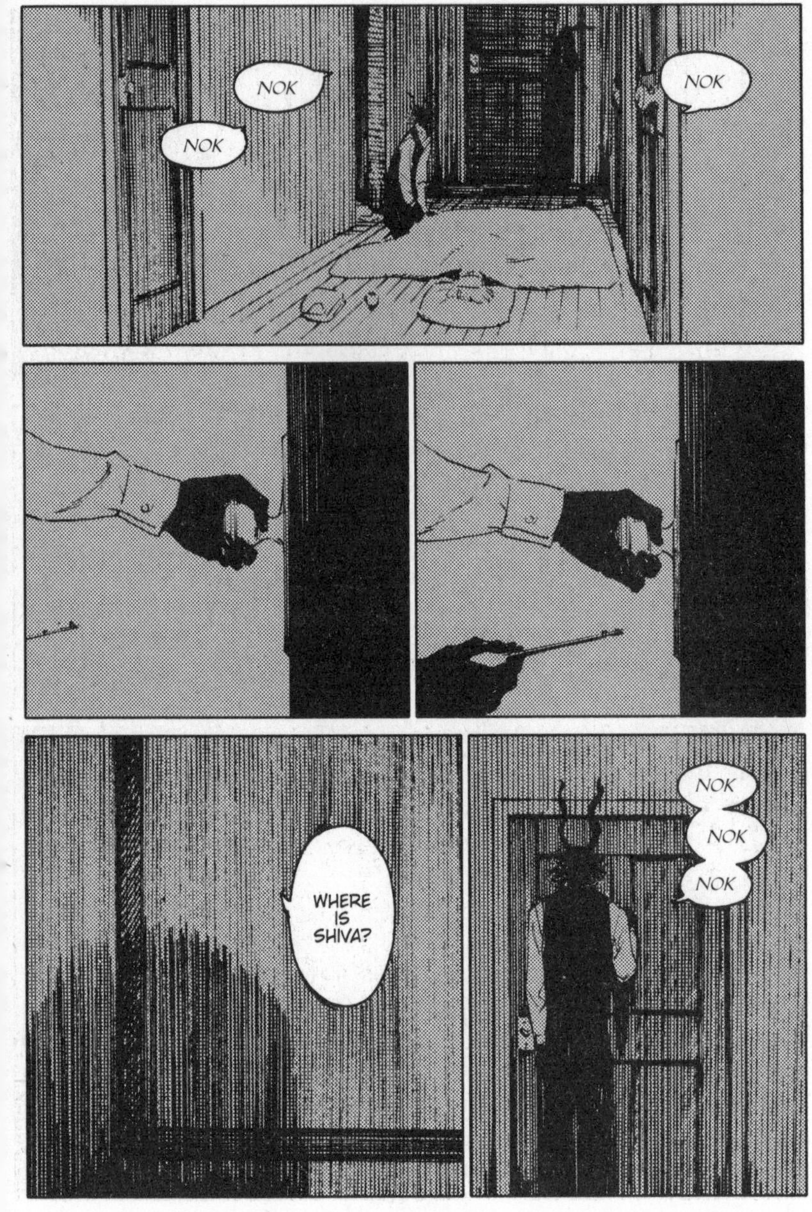
NOK
NOK
NOK
NOK
NOK
NOK
WHERE IS SHIVA?

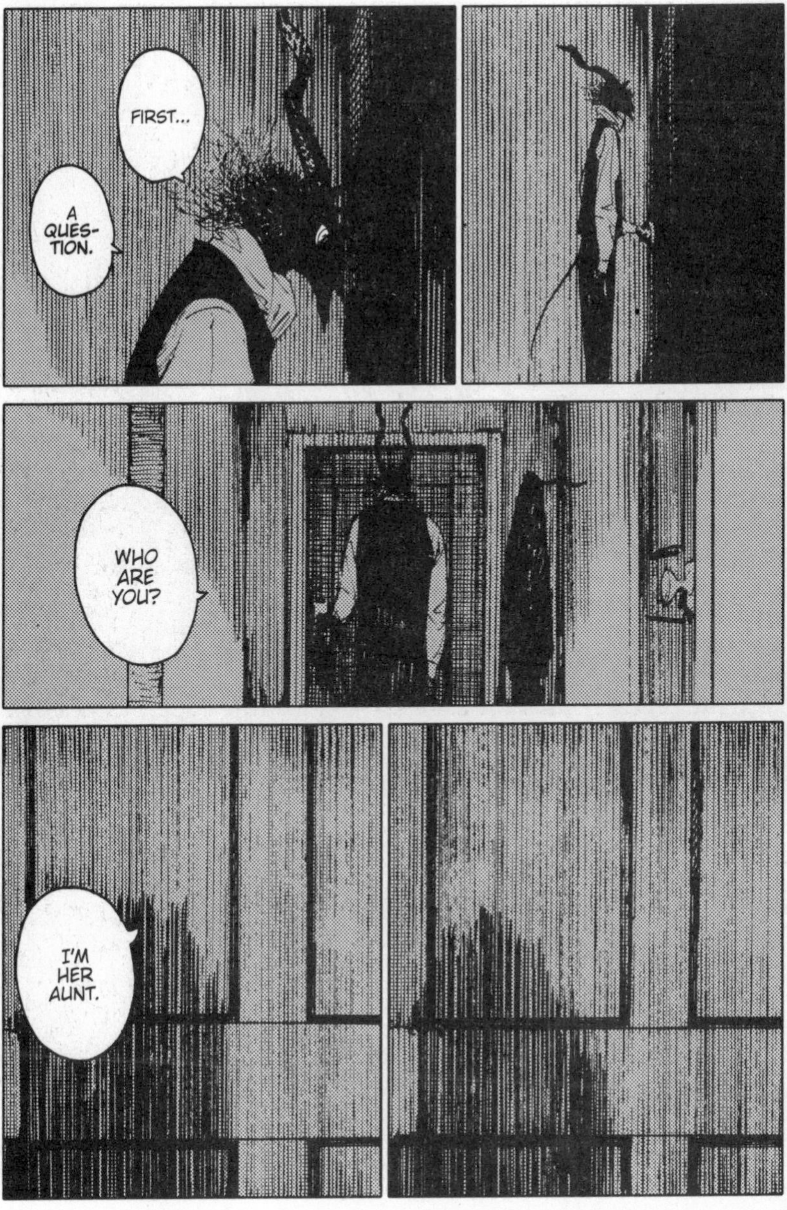
FIRST...
A QUES-TION.
WHO ARE YOU?
I'M HER AUNT.

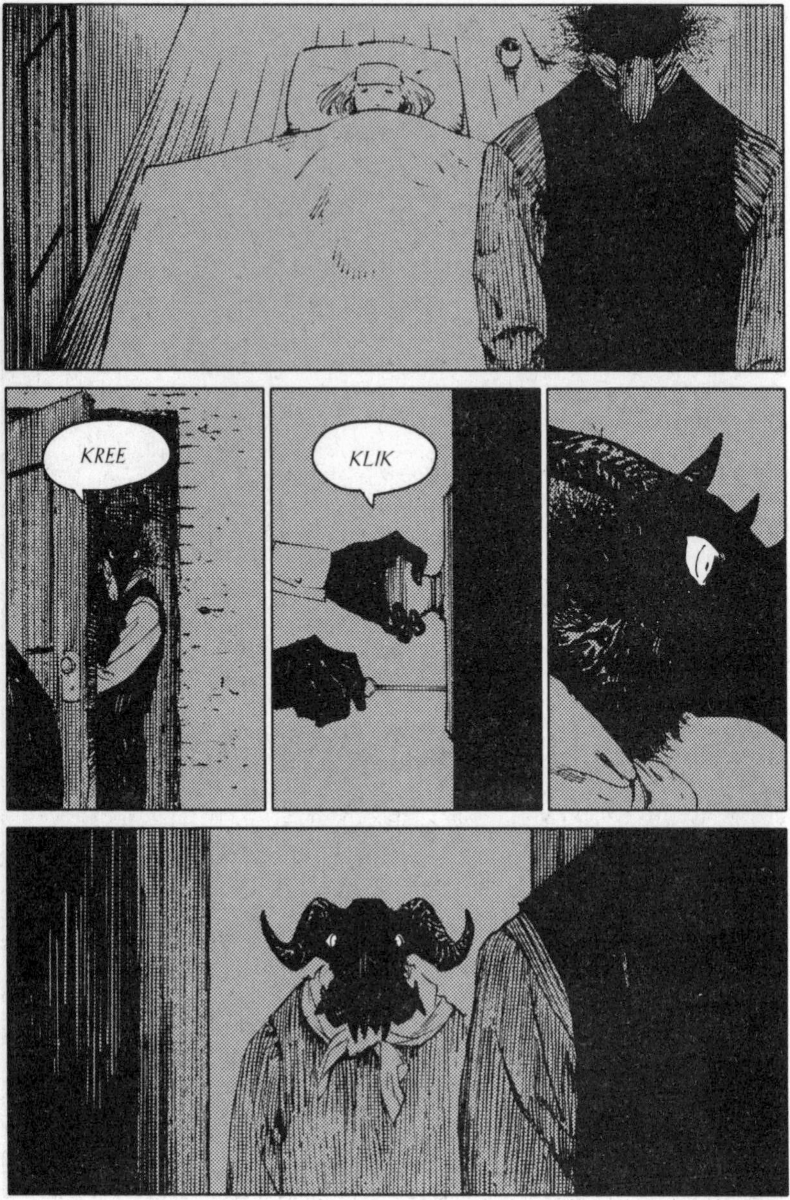
KLIK
KREE

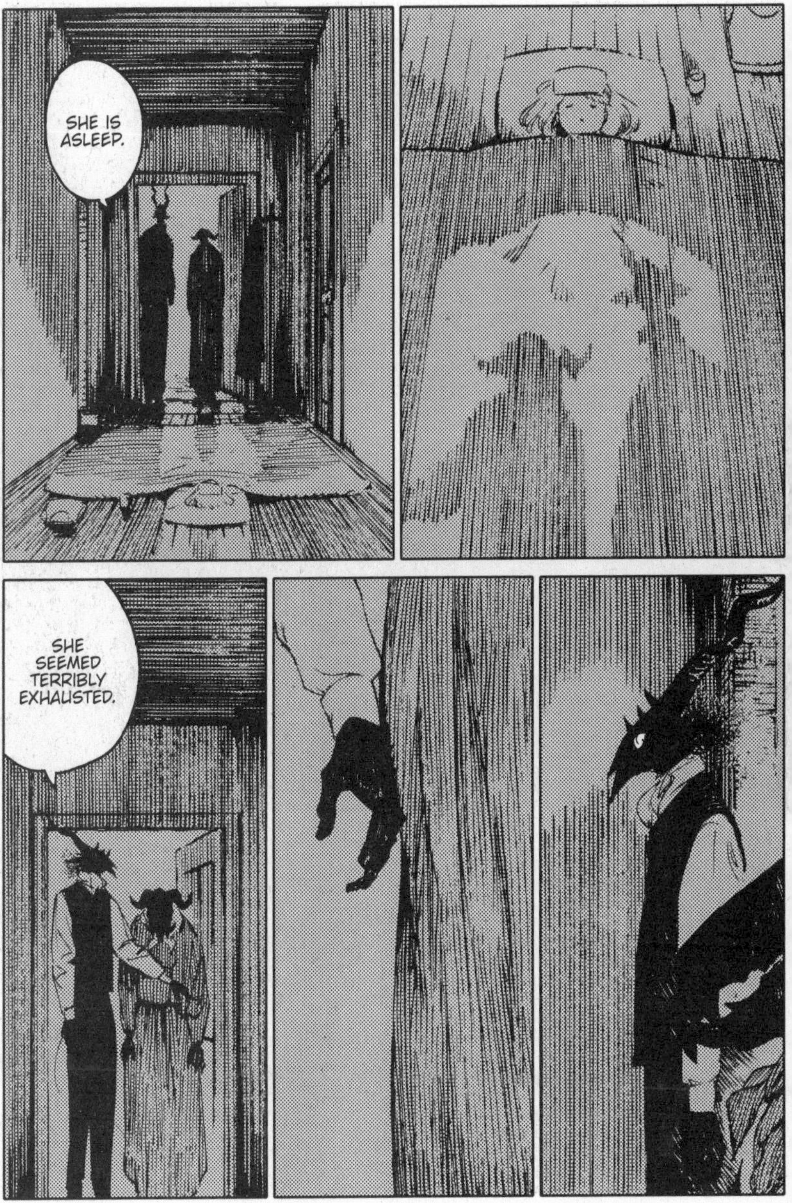
SHE IS ASLEEP.
SHE SEEMED TERRIBLY EXHAUSTED.

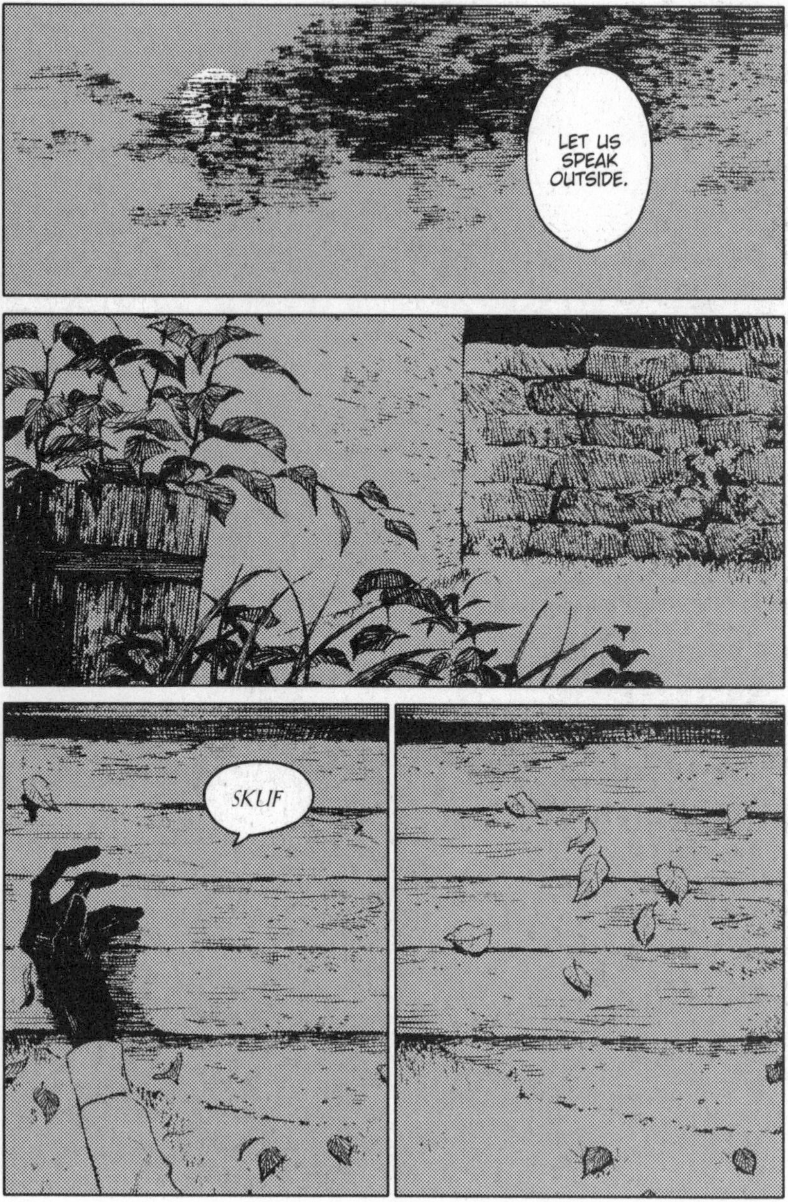
LET US SPEAK OUTSIDE.
SKUF

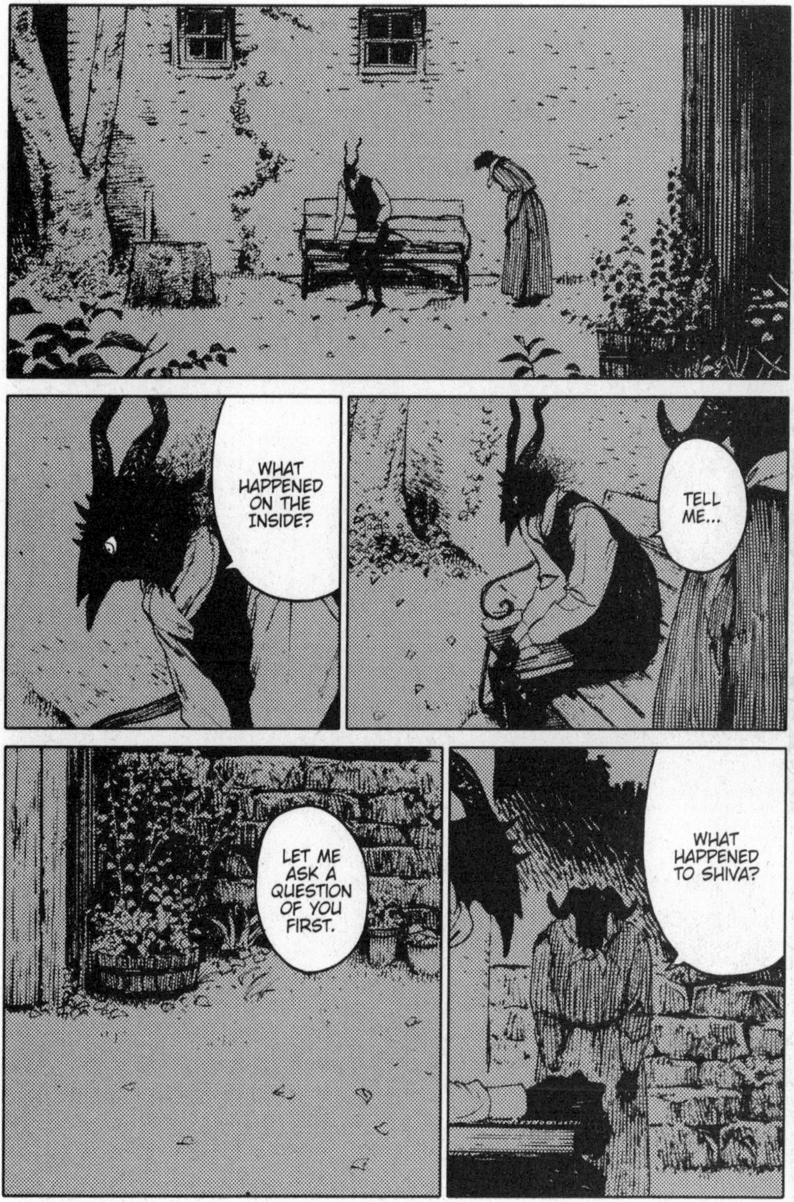
TELL ME...
WHAT HAPPENED ON THE INSIDE?
WHAT HAPPENED TO SHIVA?
LET ME ASK A QUESTION OF YOU FIRST.

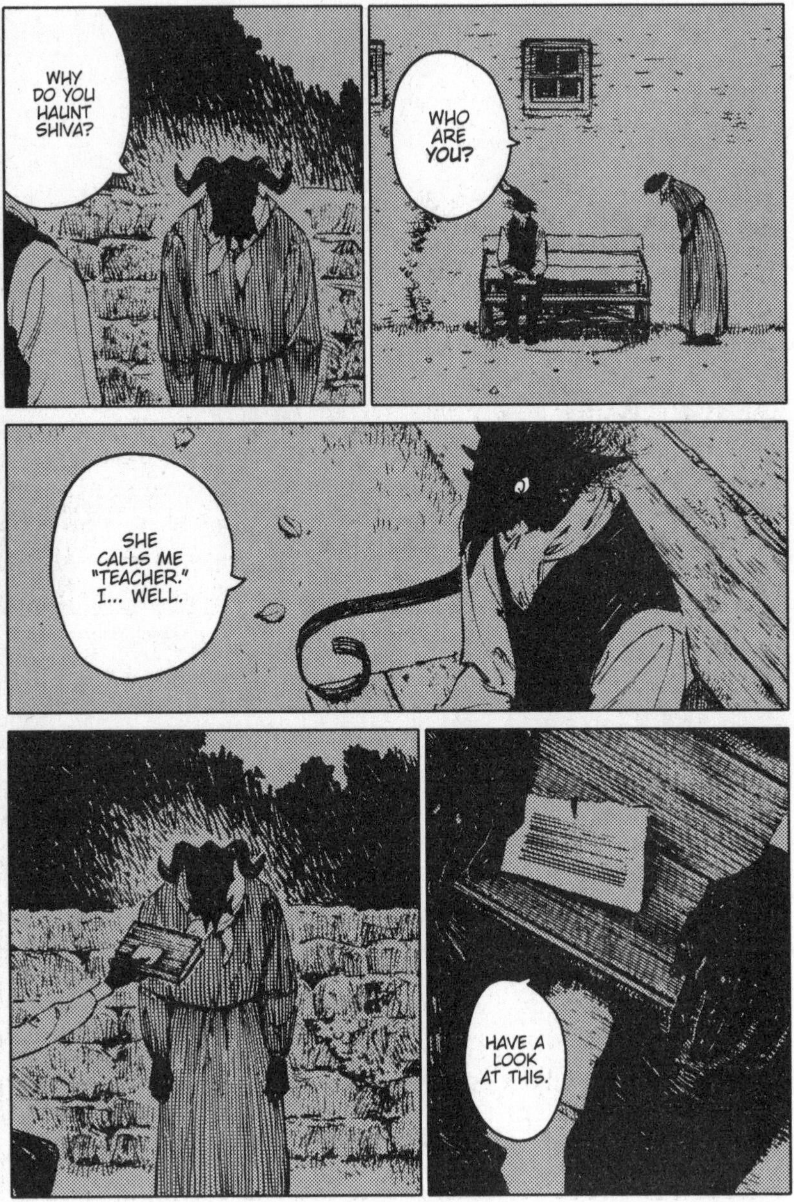
WHO ARE YOU?
WHY DO YOU HAUNT SHIVA?
SHE CALLS ME "TEACHER." I... WELL.
HAVE A LOOK AT THIS.

THAT
IS
WHY.

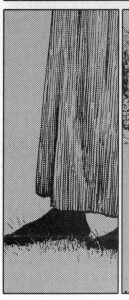

YOU
WERE
THE
ONE.

I
SEE.

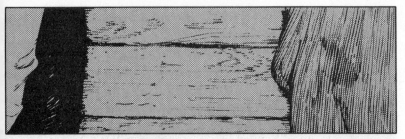

I DON'T
YET
TRUST
YOU.

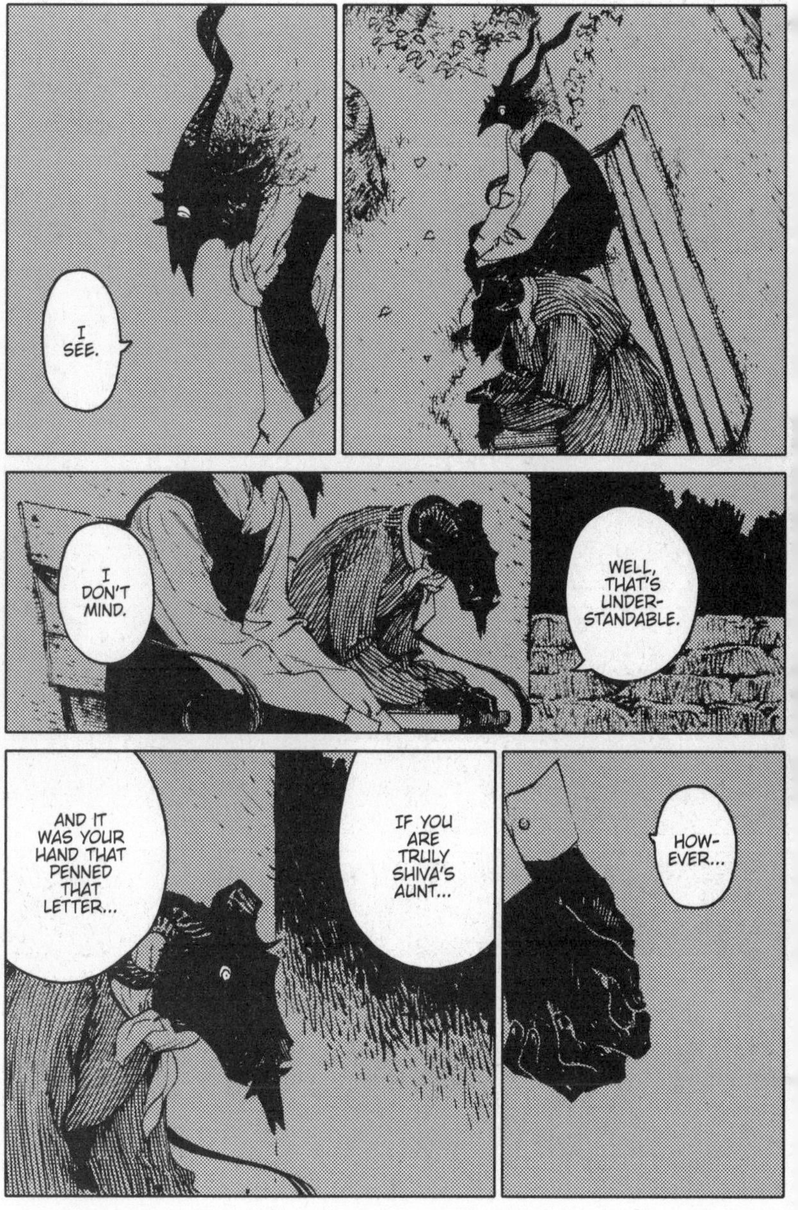
I SEE.
WELL, THAT'S UNDER-STANDABLE.
I DON'T MIND.
HOW-EVER...
IF YOU ARE TRULY SHIVA'S AUNT...
AND IT WAS YOUR HAND THAT PENNED THAT LETTER...

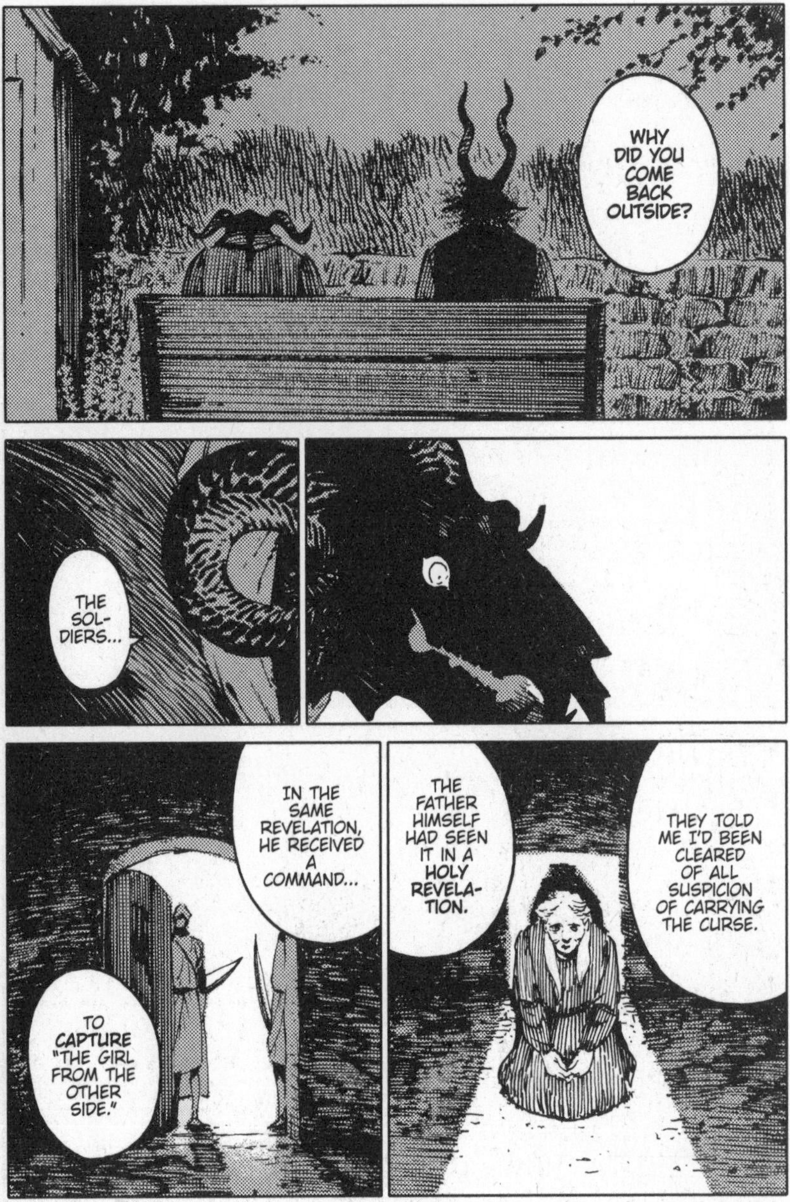
WHY DID YOU COME BACK OUTSIDE?
THE SOLDIERS...
THEY TOLD ME I'D BEEN CLEARED OF ALL SUSPICION OF CARRYING THE CURSE.
THE FATHER HIMSELF HAD SEEN IT IN A **HOLY REVELATION.**
IN THE SAME REVELATION, HE RECEIVED A COMMAND...
TO **CAPTURE** "THE GIRL FROM THE OTHER SIDE."

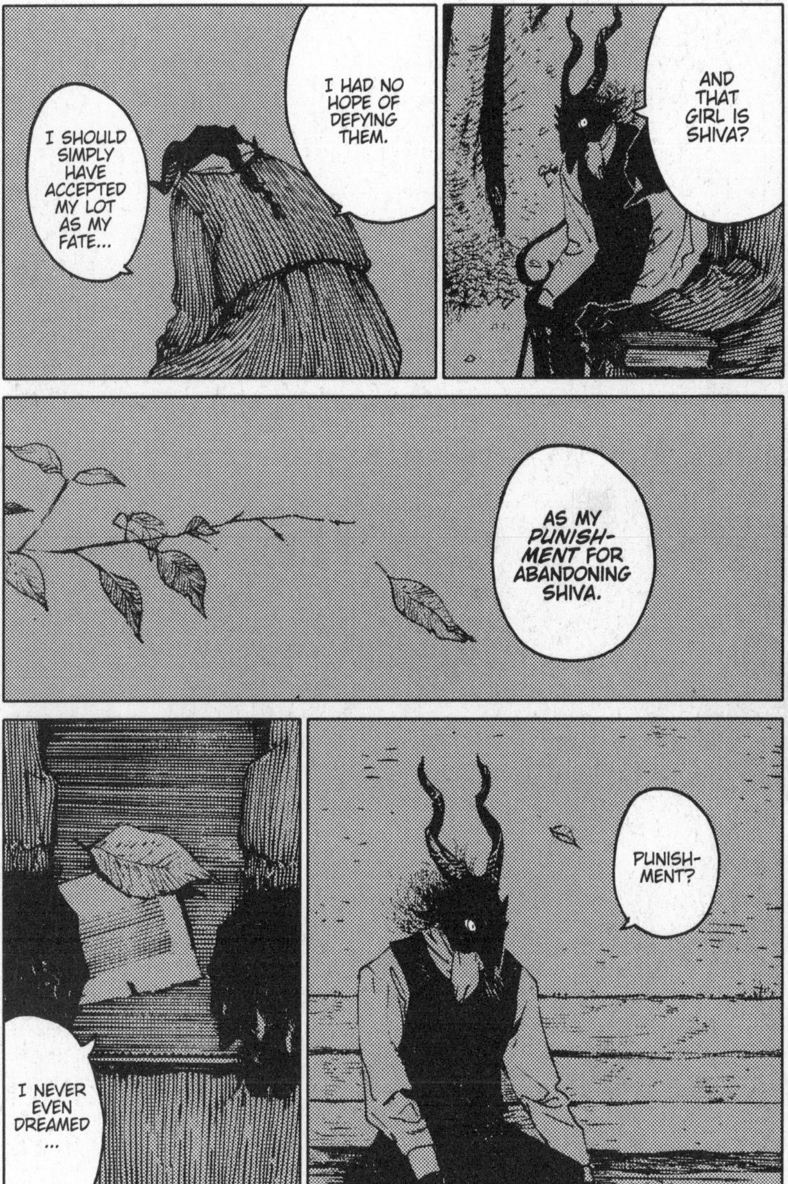
AND THAT GIRL IS SHIVA?
I HAD NO HOPE OF DEFYING THEM.
I SHOULD SIMPLY HAVE ACCEPTED MY LOT AS MY FATE...
AS MY *PUNISHMENT* FOR ABANDONING SHIVA.
PUNISHMENT?
I NEVER EVEN DREAMED ...

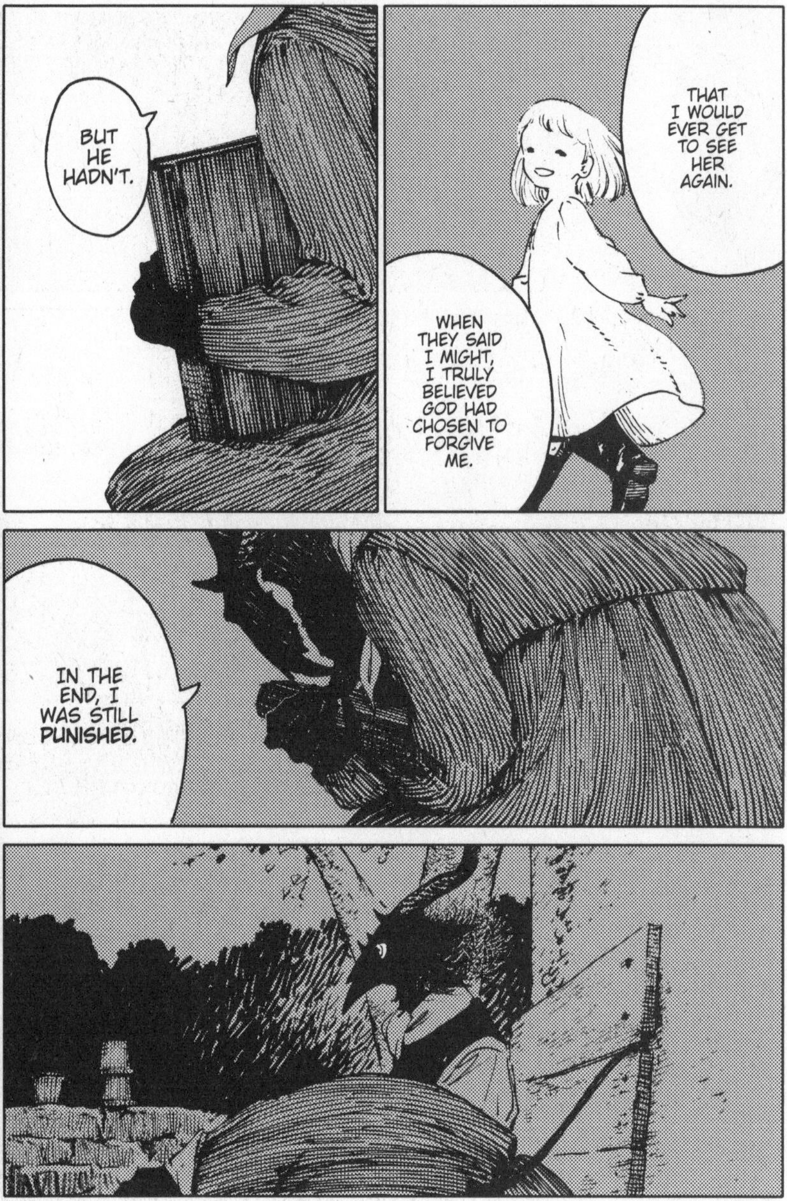
THAT I WOULD EVER GET TO SEE HER AGAIN.
WHEN THEY SAID I MIGHT, I TRULY BELIEVED GOD HAD CHOSEN TO FORGIVE ME.
BUT HE HADN'T.
IN THE END, I WAS STILL PUNISHED.

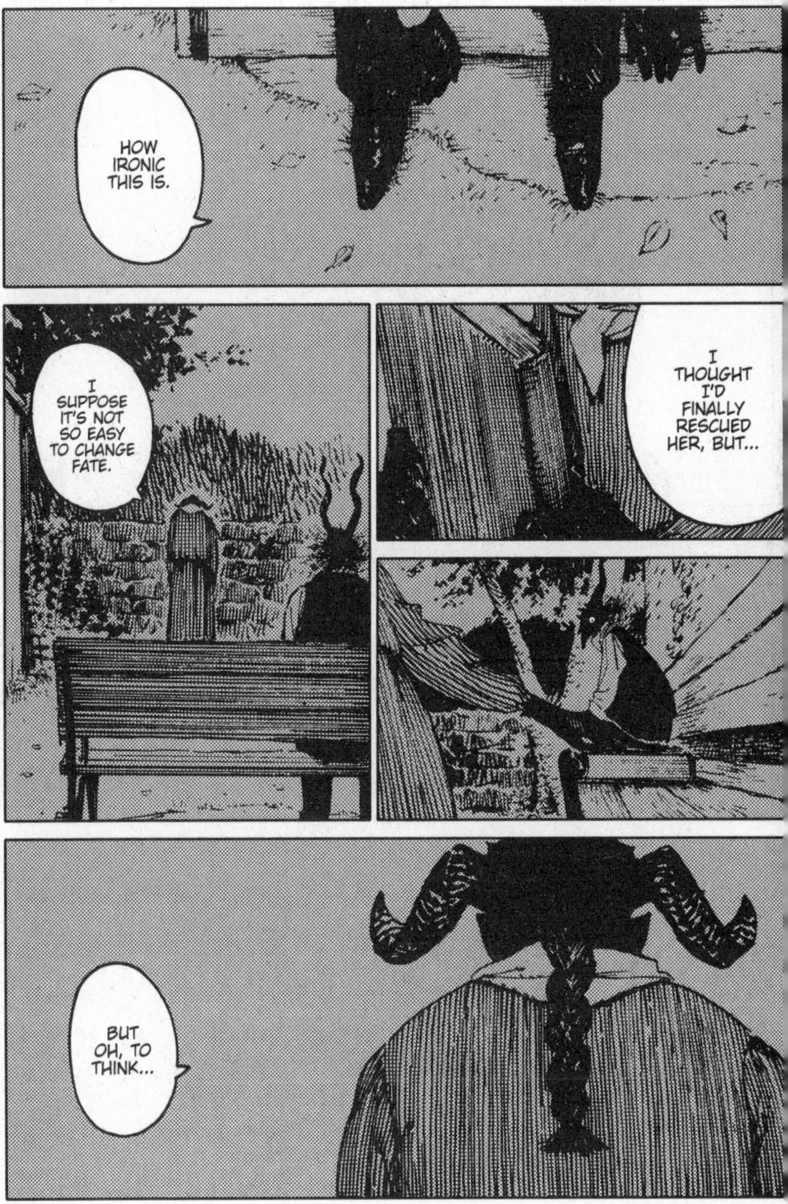
HOW IRONIC THIS IS.
I THOUGHT I'D FINALLY RESCUED HER, BUT...
I SUPPOSE IT'S NOT SO EASY TO CHANGE FATE.
BUT OH, TO THINK...

THAT SHE WOULD BE ABANDONED YET AGAIN.

ABANDONED *"AGAIN"* ...?

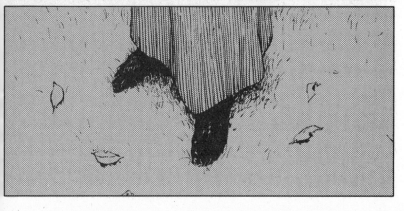

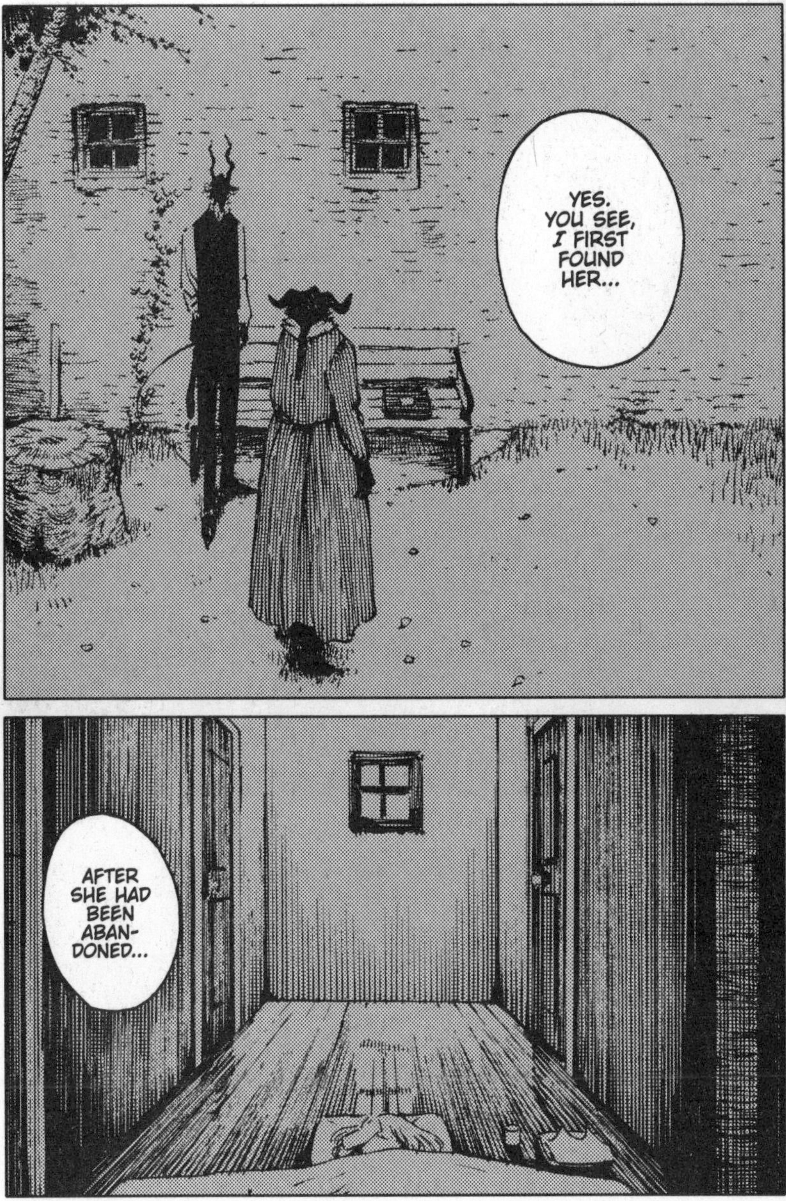
YES. YOU SEE, I FIRST FOUND HER...
AFTER SHE HAD BEEN ABAN-DONED...

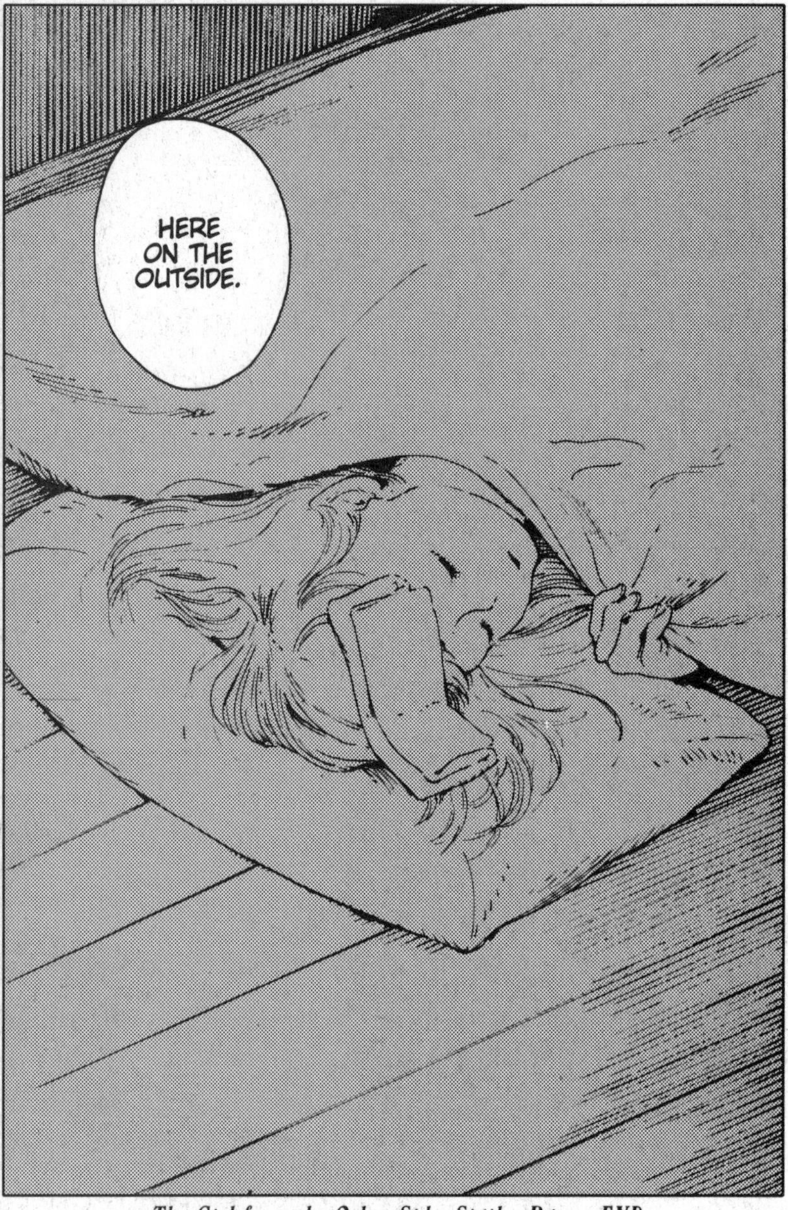
HERE ON THE OUTSIDE.

The Girl from the Other Side: Siúil a Rún – END

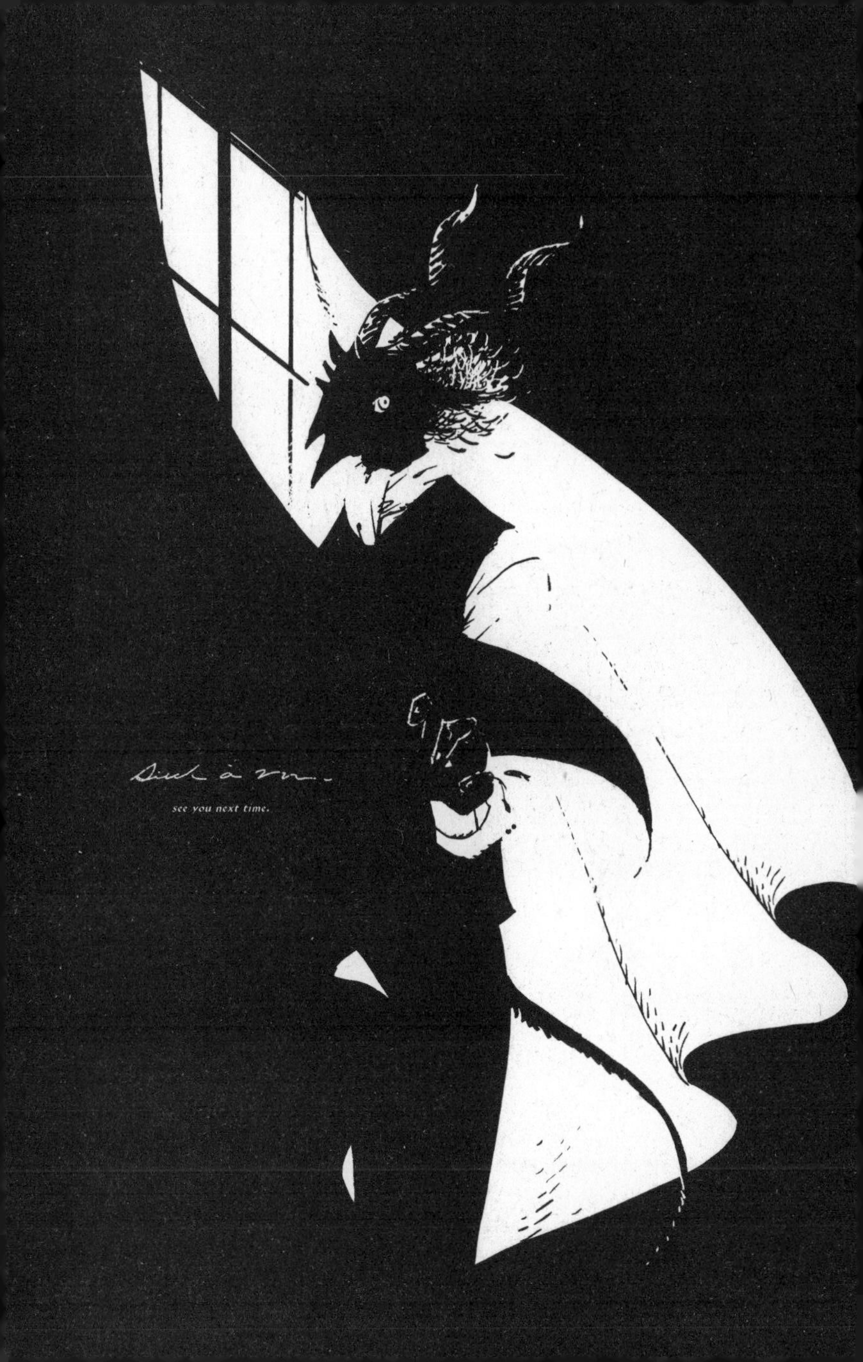
see you next time.

A Bonus from the Other Side

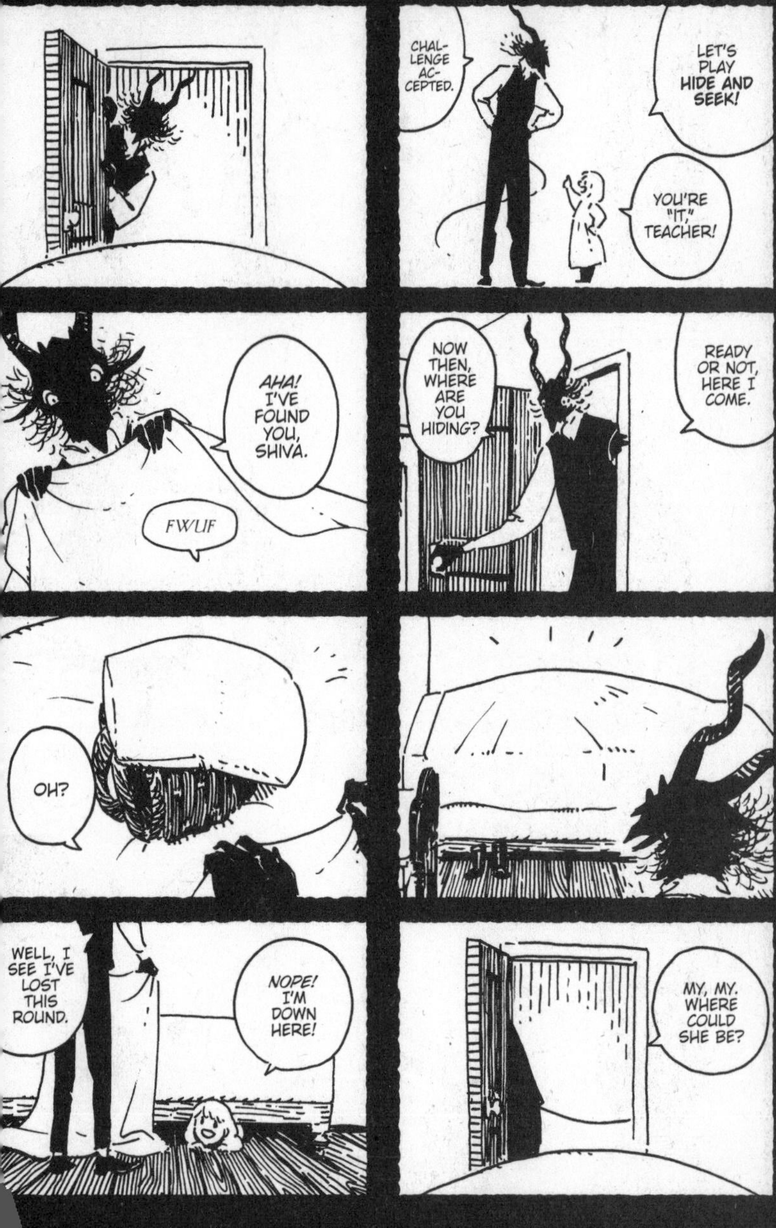
LET'S PLAY HIDE AND SEEK!
YOU'RE "IT," TEACHER!
CHAL-LENGE AC-CEPTED.
READY OR NOT, HERE I COME.
NOW THEN, WHERE ARE YOU HIDING?
AHA! I'VE FOUND YOU, SHIVA.
FWUF
OH?
MY, MY. WHERE COULD SHE BE?
WELL, I SEE I'VE LOST THIS ROUND.
NOPE! I'M DOWN HERE!

A Bonus from the Outside

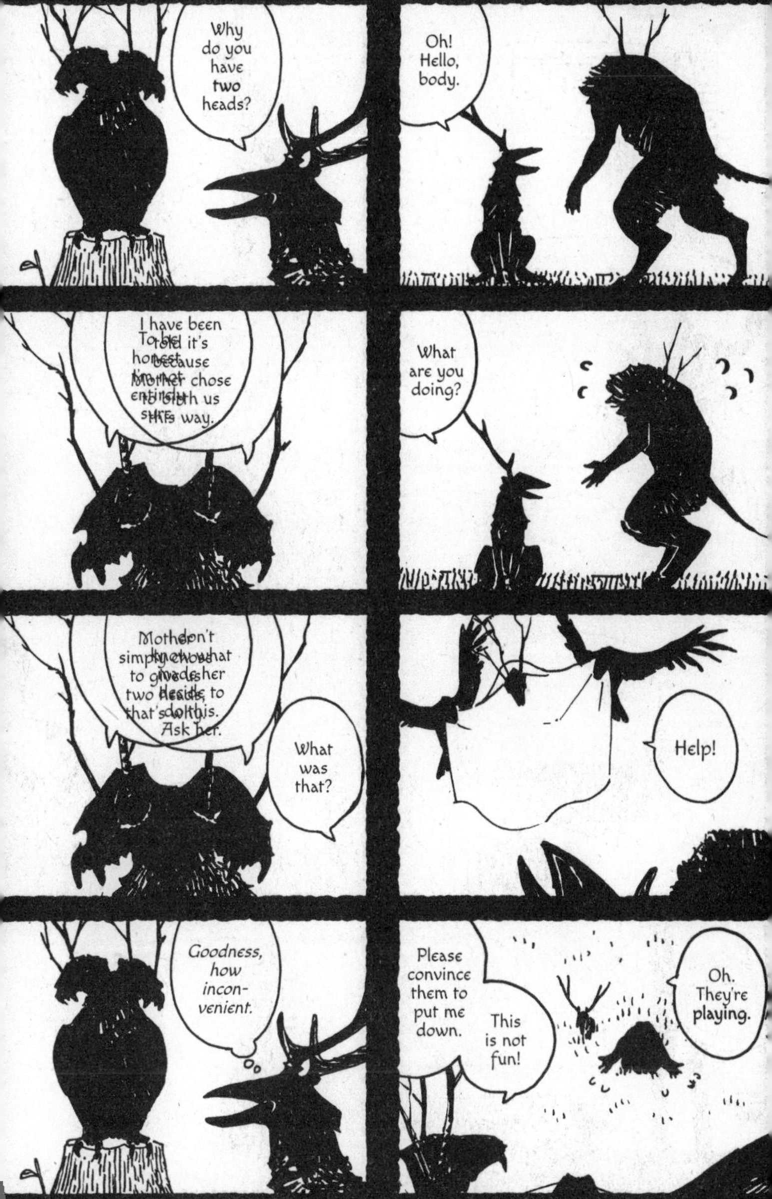
Oh! Hello, body.
Why do you have **two** heads?
What are you doing?
I have been told it's because Mother chose to birth us this way.
To be honest, I'm not entirely sure.
Help!
I don't know what made her decide to do this. Ask her.
Mother simply chose to give us two heads, that's all.
What was that?
Oh. They're **playing.**
This is not fun!
Please convince them to put me down.
Goodness, how incon-venient.

The mystery surrounding the strange girl deepens...

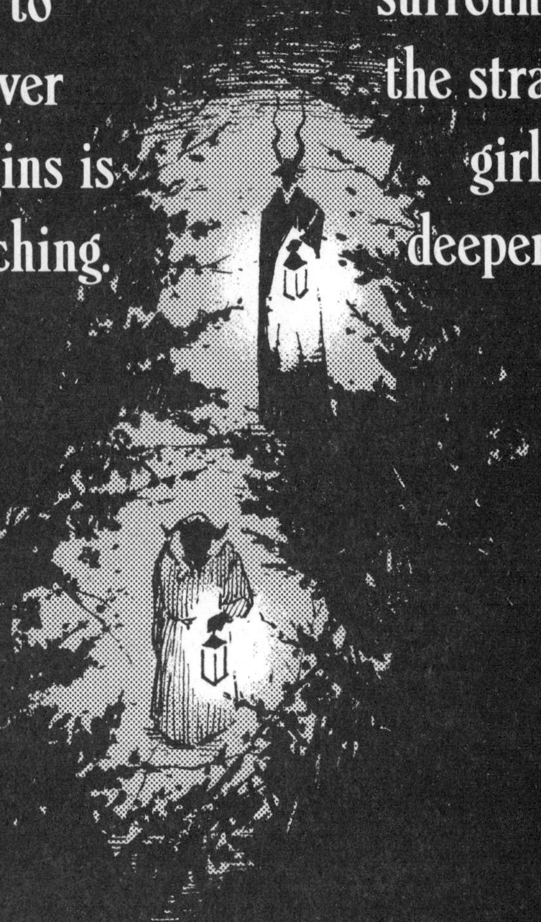

The time to discover her origins is approaching.

Shiva lies on the cottage floor in shock over the carnage caused by her innocent lie, while Teacher sits outside in the darkness, listening in astonishment to the tale told by the monster who was Shiva's aunt.

The dark fate bearing down on the child weighs even more heavily on Teacher's mind, as he desperately seeks the right course of action. And meanwhile, the Outsider who was Shiva's aunt undergoes even further change...

A tranquil fairy tale about those human and inhuman.

VOLUME 4 COMING SOON!

SEVEN SEAS ENTERTAINMENT PRESENTS

Siúil, a Rún
The Girl from the Other Side

story and art by **NAGABE** vol. 3

TRANSLATION
Adrienne Beck

ADAPTATION
Ysabet MacFarlane

LETTERING AND RETOUCH
Lys Blakeslee

LOGO DESIGN
Karis Page

COVER DESIGN
Nicky Lim

PROOFREADER
Shanti Whitesides
Jocelyne Allen

ASSISTANT EDITOR
Jenn Grunigen

PRODUCTION ASSISTANT
CK Russell

PRODUCTION MANAGER
Lissa Pattillo

EDITOR-IN-CHIEF
Adam Arnold

PUBLISHER
Jason DeAngelis

THE GIRL FROM THE OTHER SIDE: SIUIL, A RUN VOL. 3

Originally published in Japan in 2017 by MAG Garden Corporation, Tokyo.
English translation rights arranged through TOHAN CORPORATION, Tokyo.

ISBN: 978-1-626925-58-8

Printed in Canada

First Printing: October 2017

10 9 8 7 6 5 4 3 2 1

FOLLOW US ONLINE: ***www.gomanga.com***

READING DIRECTIONS

This book reads from ***right to left***, Japanese style. If this is your first time reading manga, you start reading from the top right panel on each page and take it from there. If you get lost, just follow the numbered diagram here. It may seem backwards at first, but you'll get the hang of it! Have fun!!

1
2
3
4
5
6
7
8
9

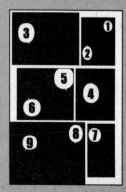